PEACEABLE KINGDOMS

New England Towns in the
Eighteenth Century

Peaceable Kingdoms

NEW ENGLAND TOWNS
IN THE EIGHTEENTH
CENTURY

Michael Zuckerman

VINTAGE BOOKS
A Division of Random House
New York

Library of Congress Cataloging in Publication Data

Zuckerman, Michael, 1939-
  Peacable kingdoms.

    Includes bibliographical references.
    1. Local government—Massachusetts. 2. Local government
—New England. I. Title.
[JS451.M44Z82 1972]   352.09744   72-679
ISBN 0-394-71796-1

Manufactured in the United States of America

First Vintage Books Edition, August 1972

To the memory of
my father
and to my mother

❧ Preface ❧

THIS BOOK GREW OUT OF, and then nourished, my notion that other-oriented communalism is central to a comprehension of the American experience, that sociability and its attendant constraints have always governed the American character more than the individualism we vaunt. The book breaks, therefore, with one of the most widely held conventions of our colonial history, which posits the diminution or disappearance of the original settlers' sharp sense of community as the forces of the frontier or the winds of destiny imposed more individualistic modes. Instead it argues that the consciousness of community, in Massachusetts, continued at least three quarters of the way through the eighteenth century as a prime value of public life, an abiding core of provincial culture. If the argument makes little of development and change, it is because I found little. Themes of concord and consensus seem to me to have been as strong in 1770, or 1750, as in 1700, in values and in behavior.

The book is an attempt to comprehend the culture of provincial Massachusetts whole, to get at its values *and its behavior*. If, for all that, the final result is ultimately more a study of values than of behavior, the values examined are at least the values of ordinary, otherwise nameless men speaking the language and the assumptions of their everyday affairs. They are the operative arguments and axioms which ordered the daily lives of the many for more than three quarters of a century before the Revolution, not the sounding sentiments and rarefied philosophies which were set out for publication by a few towering figures, to be studied more seriously, perhaps, by subsequent historians than by their own contemporaries.

Nonetheless, such subsequent historians have created a lively conversation about the community in colonial New England, and I have presumed a great deal of the scholarship in which I disclaim confidence. History is a cumulative discipline despite itself, and any man who writes a book is indebted beyond any possibility of repayment or even acknowledgment to the many students of men and societies who have gone before him.

The acknowledgments that are possible, though, are a pleasure to tender. George Haskins, George Homans, Benjamin Labaree, and John W. M. Whiting answered my inquiries graciously and helpfully. Leo Flaherty, Curator of the Massachusetts Archives, made my extended research in the bowels of the State House as profitable as any man could have, and his delightful wife made it bearable besides. Dick Brown, Jere Daniell, Ken Lockridge, Peter Parker, and Bob Zemsky were generous enough to let me read and ransack unpublished material they were preparing. Dick Brown, Tom Cochran, Dick Dunn, Oscar Handlin, and Ken Lockridge did me the kindness of their variously devastating criticisms of my doctoral dissertation; and my editor, Jane Garrett, has done the same good service for the book itself.

The Woodrow Wilson Foundation provided financial support for much of my work under its Dissertation Fellowship program. The University of Pennsylvania took care of the costs of typing the manuscript under a faculty research fellowship, and Edith Steene and Dottie Knowles took fine care of the typing itself.

Portions of the book appeared as "The Social Context

of Democracy in Massachusetts" in the *William and Mary Quarterly*, and they appear here by permission of its editor, Thad Tate, who made some valuable suggestions.

Bernard Bailyn, my dissertation director, has suffered through so many drafts of this study that by now he must think it his albatross almost as much as I have often thought it mine. He has been skeptical of my argument at every step, and I do believe he is skeptical still; but he has always made the effort to meet my work on my own terms, and the book is surely a far better one for the challenge of his misgivings. His criticism has been acute, while his encouragement and support have been warming indeed.

Murray Murphey, my undergraduate mentor at the University of Pennsylvania, has influenced me far beyond my ability to convey to him through his impenetrable modesty. By the brilliance of his example he showed me that the study of American civilization might be fit work for a man, and by the inspiration of his integrity he has blessed me with that canker of discontent by which I know this effort for a failure.

My wife, Diane, contributed almost nothing to this book, but she and I know there are more important things than books.

MICHAEL ZUCKERMAN

Philadelphia, July 1969

❧ Contents ❧

PEACEABLE KINGDOMS

New England Towns in the Eighteenth Century

NOTES

Superior numbers in the text refer to bibliographical notes likely to be of interest to scholars. These are placed at the back of the book and may be safely ignored by the general reader.

❧ Introduction ❧

THERE IS SOMETHING about the New England town that still stirs archetypal echoes in the American memory. The quiet of the countryside, the handsome frame houses, the sure proportions of a neat green common, and the simple white spire of a meetinghouse breaking clean above the elms all evoke the springtime promise of a nation that would still think itself new. Radiant images of embattled farmers and town-meeting democracy rise to the mind, recalling, perhaps, Tocqueville's declaration that "the township seems to come directly from the hand of God." [1]

Ever since the time of Tocqueville, that vision of village green and tall white spire has been a part of the imaginative landscape of America. It answered to the aspirations and anxieties of a great many Americans then, and it seems to do so still. Though the assurance of divine derivation has receded, the vision survives, an enduring token of something precious in the ancestral style of life. Almost ineluctably the visitor who discovers Williamstown early on an autumn morning, or comes upon Lexington Common at dusk, senses there an American inheritance and too an irrecoverable American loss.

Yet, like any artifact of the imagination, the archetypal New England town has been tied only tenuously to the actual one. Its inhabitants have been reduced to caricatures of stolid virtue, folkloric figures impossible to conceive sniffling through the dismal winters or fornicating out back in the barn. Its public assemblies have been so steadily extolled for such extraordinary constitutional virtuosity that it is difficult to envision them ever deigning to decide where to build the new milldam or whether to allow the bounty on blackbirds. To the local historians of New England, the town and its town meeting have always been more nearly objects of reverence than of research.

This study is, if nothing else, an effort to move beyond that attitude of adoration. Ultimately it is an attempt to indicate the actual—and altogether mottled—significance of the New England town in American social history, a significance not to be found in its democracy, and assuredly not in its regard for the individual, but rather in the emergence there of a broadly diffused desire for consensual communalism as the operative premise of group life in America. But such suggestions of significance cannot command credibility unless they proceed upon an adequate account of the town in its own time and its own context; and so the largest part by far of this study is an attempt at historical recovery of the conditions of community in the eighteenth century in one province, Massachusetts, the most powerful and populous in New England. Its immediate subject is the social life the townsmen sought for themselves and, as much as most men are able, secured.

Such historical recovery is necessary because New England's own historians have rarely if ever approached the townsmen on such terms. Rather, these historians have celebrated with a fine filiopietism a New England town their fathers would hardly have recognized. They have praised their native hamlets for sustaining the ancestral faith, for maintaining the virtuous simplicity of a golden age, and, above all, for affording an unsurpassed exercise in democracy; but they have praised with the voices of the nineteenth and twentieth centuries. Their fathers, on the contrary, cried out in the voice of Jeremiah, obsessively lamenting their declension in faith and simplicity, and to the founding fathers of New England democracy itself was detestable.

In 1630 a band of true believers entered upon the northern wilderness, possessed of a conviction of absolute and invincible righteousness. Their leaders in that first generation proudly proclaimed that they "abhorred democracy," and, as Perry Miller maintained, "theirs was not an idle boast." The Massachusetts Code of 1648 openly announced that all who settled in the colony were "totally to submit to this government," and Nathaniel Ward explained as well as anyone ever would the one liberty allowed the early settlers in the new world when he declared that dissidents from Puritan orthodoxy "shall have free liberty to keep away from us." [2]

Moreover, the Puritans had the power to enforce such sentiments. At a time when opposition to orthodoxy was proscribed almost everywhere in western Europe, and when uniformity was the universal aspiration of authority in the Atlantic world, the magistrates of Massachusetts almost alone were in a position to act in earnest upon their precepts. In Europe a limited latitudinarianism prevailed despite all official desires to the contrary, because deep-rooted differences in principles and in polities precluded the total translation of aspirations into actuality. The nations of Europe were, in the nature of the case, inclusive communities. They counted as subjects all who inhabited the sovereign's soil, regardless of origins or attitudes.

The Puritans, on the other hand, had organized themselves from the outset as an exclusive society, and the migration to America had only heightened their sense of separateness. In the new world the uniformity that had been visionary in England—the right of every church to keep out the unworthy, which was precisely the point of the Congregationalists' difference with the Established Church—seemed suddenly within their reach. At the Bay they were but a slender fragment of English society; they could begin at the beginning. Unencumbered by the institutional complexities of accumulated centuries, they could convert their English dream into American reality. They could insist not only upon outward conformity but also upon inner assent. As Emil Oberholzer has drawn the distinction, "if Anglican intolerance was expressed in its insistence on uniformity of worship, Puritanism was noted for its demand of uniformity of belief." [3]

The result was, in a very real sense, a totalitarianism of true believers. A man could remain comfortably in colonial Massachusetts only as long as his actions and his ideas coincided with those of his neighbors. Difference inevitably implied deviation, and deviation in a community of saints was indefensible. The Puritans of the seventeenth century could conceive of the good society in no other terms than complete conformity based on common convictions.*

In the century and a half after settlement, the rigor of those terms was moderated by events in Europe and by the necessities of the new environment as well as by the society's own inner dynamic. A colony that forcibly repelled the religious enthusiasm of antinomians and Quakers became a province that declined to do the same in the religious enthusiasm of the Great Awakening; a company that relied upon a charter granted by the King of England became a commonwealth that composed and ratified a constitution in 1780 which, with a complacency that would have

---

* Such conceptions were, of course, cultural; they pertained to ideals and values, which must not be presumed identical with behavior, and especially not with behavior at the local level. Two recent town studies do, however, suggest a substantial congruence between these cultural ideals and the communal realities of the seventeenth century. See Sumner C. Powell: *Puritan Village* (Middletown, Conn., 1963) and Kenneth Lockridge: "Dedham, 1636–1736: The Anatomy of a Puritan Utopia," unpubl. Ph.D. thesis, Princeton, 1965. One other investigation—Darrett Rutman: *Winthrop's Boston* (Chapel Hill, 1966)—finds a considerable disjunction, but Boston was a case unto itself in ways that there is no obvious reason to think Sudbury or Dedham were.

been quite incomprehensible to John Winthrop, rested public powers upon the consent of the governed.

The men who made that constitution were probably not democrats, and they were certainly not new men utterly unlike their fathers, but they were not what their fathers had been, either. Their fathers had been men of doctrine, men whose religious philosophy had, in Perry Miller's words, "imbued them with a sense of invincible rectitude," a sense altogether incompatible with that "openness, ready acceptance of differences, and willingness to compromise and change" which social psychologists are coming to call the "democratic character." [4] The sons were concerned less with ideological issues than with social affairs, and if agreement was ultimately as important to them as it had been to their fathers, that agreement itself became less absolute and more accommodative. Consensus was still the crucial condition of community; but in provincial Massachusetts it became a consensus based on compromise as much as on conviction.

That Puritan passage from autocracy and intransigence to an almost democratic cast of mind and code of conduct poses perhaps the most perplexing and at the same time the most crucial question in the historical development of American Puritanism. It cannot be derived from the premises of Puritan theology because they are, at best, contradictory in these regards. It cannot be accounted for in terms of the external influences of the colonial environment because they do not, in the end, explain enough. The forces of the frontier and the pressures of imperial policy, the assaults of the Indians and the machinations of neighboring colonies, all did indeed propel the province in directions it had not chosen entirely of its own volition. But that is not to say that the men of Massachusetts were creatures of circumstance any more than other men. The townsmen of the eighteenth century were not completely captains of their own fates, yet neither were they blown haplessly about by every wind from afar; external pressures were almost certainly less important than indigenous institutions and inclinations in determining the direction of the society.

Chief among such indigenous institutions was the town. In the provincial period, for specific reasons, the New England town became truly what Carl Bridenbaugh has called it, "a way of life," [5] and town life came to shape men's inclinations just as it had been shaped by them. Men in the Massachusetts town of 1750 saw their society and their place in it rather differently than men in the Massachusetts town a century before had done, and the differences were compatible with, if not caused by, the demands and opportunities of group life in the towns of the eighteenth century. The passage from coercive to accommodative consensus occurred at the intersection of environment and social values, in the hamlets and villages of provincial Massachusetts.

That shift, and the structure of that community life, are the story of this study. The inquiry proceeds from a broad prospect of the towns and their place in provincial life through a series of etchings of the inner workings of the consensual community itself to a concluding view of that community in the wider perspective of provincial politics and the American Revolution. The first chapter seeks a context for the eighteenth-century town and its emergence as the locus of effective authority in the province. The next five chapters take the township as their focus. Chapter Two tests the sources of public values in the provincial villages and finds them all converging to a common concern for harmony and homogeneity. Chapter Three traces this premium upon peace to the towns' incapacity for coercion without widespread consent, and it finds the function of the town meeting in the consolidation of such consensus. Chapter Four turns from principles to practices and discovers not only a prevalence of peaceful communion but also a system for the disposition of the society's occasional conflicts which still more strikingly displayed the commitment to concord. Chapter Five indicates the ways in which the internal mechanics of the town meeting itself were bent to the minimization of contention and the eliciting of agreement. Chapter Six examines the electorate and its leaders and the relation of each to consensual democracy. And then, in Chapter Seven, some of the significance of the townsmen's code and conduct is considered, in their bearing on provincial politics, the Revolution, and the social life of the new nation born in that Revolution.

❧ I ❧

The Context of Community: The Towns and the Province

THE PRE-EMINENCE of the local community in provincial Massachusetts was, curiously, a new thing under the New England sun. The first Puritans who settled at the Bay had been congregationalists in ecclesiastical polity. They had set sail across the ocean only after decades of denunciation of bishops and synods as dead historical husks of Christianity to be peeled away before the churches could regain their primitive vitality, only after decades of disagreement with the Established Church, and the Presbyterian dissenters, over the scope of central surveillance of the churches of the realm. As the *Arbella* headed out from England, its passengers could hardly have conceived that they would flee the control of Canterbury and of London only to create a comparable one in Boston.

And yet, that was what they did. Under the necessity of governing and the temptation of power, availing themselves of the ambiguities of congregational theory and ignoring inconvenient aspects of its clarities, the magistrates and ministers established a degree of direction from the center that would have been unthinkable a hundred years later. It was only with the passage of decades that power passed to the communities; in the colonial era the assemblies and the synods exercised a close care over all that occurred in the communities and congregations.

Throughout the first generation, and in the very teeth of the principles of congregational autonomy which had guided the conception of the colony, the government at Boston practiced an ecclesiastical authority which spanned the settlement. Its control ranged from trifles, such as determination of closing times for services in a single church, to matters of real moment, such as the General Court's 1635 ruling that churches could not be organized at all unless they did "first acquainte the magistrates . . . & have their approbačon herein." [1] Moreover, the ratification of the magistrates was required for all elected church officers, in new churches and in the established ones as well, which amounted to an overt invasion of congregational prerogatives since the minister was among the elected officers of the church. According to congregational theory, a minister was to be called by the communicants, his simple election establishing him in his station; but theory notwithstanding, the colonial magistrates successfully maintained for many years their claim "to approve the appointment of ministers and to suppress offending ones." [2]

Even more revealing than its arrogation of authority over the local ministers was the general government's recognition of responsibility toward them. In the era of initial settlement it was the colonial assembly which first ordered public taxes for the support of the clergy, and colonial authorities rather than local congregations built houses for a pair of pastors at the public charge. A generation later ministerial maintenance was still a subject of central solicitude. In 1657, "when it was reported that several of the ministers were not well provided for, that Court ordered speediest arrangements made for their relief," and in 1654, 1657, and 1660 the legislators launched sweeping investigations into town payments of their pastors' salaries. [3]

In secular affairs the central government exercised an

equally extensive authority. In the very first years of the
colony, when the General Court "legislated on all local as
well as general affairs," the magistrates actually continued
to think of Massachusetts as a single community despite its
geographic dispersion.[4] In 1636 an act of the assembly did
recognize the towns and empower them to manage their
own business; yet even after this admission that the colony
was no longer the single city on a hill which Winthrop had
originally envisioned, the magistrates maintained their
oversight of local affairs. Osgood referred as much to the
period after 1636 as before when he insisted that "the legislation of Massachusetts affected the towns not only at the
time of their organization, but continuously and in reference to their most important internal affairs." [5]

Thus it was the Court, not the communities, which first
made education a public obligation; and it did not do so
until the 1640's. Thus, as late as 1647, more than a decade
after their grant of local self-government, the legislators
were still passing "minute provisions" for such minute
matters as the ringing of swine and the fencing of common
cornfields in particular communities, and before that their
economic regulation had been even more extensive, touching trades, standards, and prices, and calling out the citizens to work on public projects such as roads and fortifica-
tions. In 1655 the Court chose one town's selectmen and
installed them for double terms. In 1661 the magistrates
went so far as to order an Ipswich man's land sold "because
the distance of his home from the meetinghouse had caused
him to absent himself from its service, 'in order that living
nearer the meeting house he might more conveniently attend public worship.'" [6] Such actions were apparently accepted in the seventeenth century. In the eighteenth, they
were not even attempted.

Similarly in the matter of settlement policy, the Court
often asserted an authority which unmistakably subordinated community to colony even in the years after the

colony ceased to be thought of *as* a community. The affirmation of that authority began as early as 1630, when the Court ordered that "no person should plant in any place within the limits of the patent, without leave from the Governor and assistants, or the major part of them." [7] In the midst of the antinomian excitement six years later the colony provided heavy fines for any town which even entertained a stranger longer than three weeks or allotted him any land without central consent, provisions which were made permanent the following year. And in 1639 the magistrates enunciated a still more sweeping form of interference with local settlement policy, declaring that they could "dispose of all onsettled p'sons into such towns as they shall iudge to bee most fitt for the maintenance of such p'sons and families." [8]

In subsequent years, General Court control of settlement swept beyond population policy into the establishment of the plantations themselves and even into their allotments of land and resources. Sometimes the Court itself fixed the manner in which the land was to be distributed or the way it was to be used, and sometimes the Court appointed a committee to do the work; but either way the work was extensive—a committee named in 1667 for a tract near Quaboag Ponds was "to admit inhabitants, grant lands, and manage local affairs until the plantation had become sufficiently strong to be made a town"—and either way the work was done as easily in the 1660's as in the 1630's. Indeed, as late as 1679, considerations of defense and Indian policy were sufficient to persuade the Court to provide that "localities which had been abandoned during the late war should not be resettled, or new plantations formed, except under the direction of committees appointed by the governor and council or by the courts of the county where the settlement was to be located." [9] But by the eighteenth century, though the central government still recognized the close connection between settlement policy, defense, and the Indians, it declined to do anything from Boston. The deputies saw quite clearly that uncontrolled expansion was the most prolific source of provocation to the Indians, yet they defeated measures to prohibit settlement beyond definite frontier lines "until the General Court should be satisfied" whenever such measures were proposed.* [10]

* The Court's incompetence to control settlement stood most starkly revealed in its survey of the new plantations in 1750. By then the assemblymen were well aware of the erosion of their old authority—see, e.g., Thomas Wertenbaker: *The Puritan Oligarchy* (New York, 1957), pp. 184–92—but they did persist in certain vestigial remnants of the ancient responsibility, such as requiring that township grants be settled and cultivated by a specified number of people within a specified time or be forfeited. The survey was designed to measure compliance with those minimal conditions.

According to the terms of the Court's order, the clerks of all the plantations established over the previous thirty years were charged to send an accounting to Boston of the grantees who had and had not fulfilled the settlement standards. In itself, therefore, the order offered the grandest concession of inattention over three decades, since the term set for fulfillment of the requirements never exceeded seven years. The province was, in most cases, asking for reports of grants which were to have been completed five, ten, twenty or more years before.

The reports that were received could hardly have been encouraging, either. One "new township granted at the head of the town of Berwick" informed the province that it had fourteen families settled—sixty was the customary requirement—but that the proprietors were doing the best they were able. Mass. Arch. 115, p. 752. The "new township on Millar's River called Poquoiag"—still "new" in 1752 though begun in 1734—admitted that about two thirds of the grants had not been completed within the five year term initially allowed and only five further grants had been fulfilled in the succeeding years. At the time of the accounting, well over half of the original grants were still uncompleted, and there were "now residing in the township of Poquoiag 18 settlers, that is, 15 families and three single men on their land; no more." Ibid. 116, pp. 234, 239–42.

Moreover, there was not even any sharp alteration of course *after* such returns came in. A law was enacted in 1753 which provided for forfeiture of settlements not completed within eighteen months of the passage of the act—ibid., p. 355 (and see ibid., pp. 13, 356)—but the arousal of the assembly was merely momentary, and the old norm of neglect was soon restored. It was, for example, a full eight years later before any action was taken against the dilatory grantees of townships such as Road Town,

Other important elements of central coordination and control also waned with the waning of the seventeenth century, and especially with the loss of the original charter. In the years before its revocation, for example, there was a residence requirement for representatives to the General Court which was a simple colonial one; after 1693 a delegate had to dwell in the particular town for which he sat. In the half century, after the arrival of the *Arbella* there were four colonial synods, in 1637, 1646–8, 1662 and 1679–80, and Edward Johnson was indiscreet but not incorrect when he alluded openly to the practical Presbyterianism of the Bay congregations. After 1691 there was never another synod to call the local churches to account or provide presbyterian direction.[11]

In all these matters and in others less important, then, authority was not diffused at the outset. Its later localiza-

---

and the action finally taken seemed to ignore the very existence of the legislation of 1753. The Court began from the beginning all over again, enacting a bill "causing the delinquent settlers to fulfill the conditions of their grants" and threatening the reversion of their lands to the province if they did not do so. Twenty-six years after the original grant and seven years after their claims should have reverted by the order of 1753, the delinquents were allowed another three years of grace before any penalty could be imposed. Ibid. 117, pp. 710, 711–12; see also ibid., pp. 376, 401–2.

Similarly, in 1759, six years after the enforcing legislation, nine years after the provincial inventory, and twenty-seven years after its original grant, the "new plantation called and known by the name of Narragansett township #2" asked to be made a town or district, since it had finally gained "near to" the required number of sixty families enjoined by the Court in 1732. In all the intervening time it had met with no disciplinary action whatsoever, though it had never had the requisite cohort of settlers nor—another condition of the original grant—a minister. Indeed, the plantation was at great pains to display before the Court its inadequate fulfillment of the original terms when it also applied for a supplementary tax on the non-residents' lands. The inhabitants denied indignantly a deposition of the non-residents that the plantation had had nearly seventy families as early as 1751; they insisted upon their still-humble status with a certain perverse righteousness, declaring that nearly seventy families "is more than is now in the place or ever was, and at that time there was not above forty families settled." Ibid., pp. 510–11, 516–17.

tion was the essential institutional development of the era between settlement and the American Revolution. And it was supremely symptomatic of the shift that, as the importance of the central government declined, so too did the obligations that attached to its early rights disappear with decentralization. In the first generation the officers of the colony were commonly the leading participants in local projects, such as a 1636 subscription for the maintenance of a Boston schoolmaster which was "headed by the Governor, the Deputy Governor, the ex-deputy Governor, the colonial treasurer, and the selectmen"; later such cooperation became incomparably less common.[12] Provincial governors came to consider themselves servants of the Crown, as indeed they were, and they were seldom able to work so easily with local selectmen. Nor did they ever truly desire to do so, or at least never so wholeheartedly. Winthrop, Dudley, and the others shared something of the same cause and something of the same dream with selectmen all around the Bay; men like Belcher and Bernard and the other eighteenth-century governors listened to different drummers.

The localization of authority was not an impulse altogether peculiar to the provincial era, of course. The process began with the very beginnings of settlement, as the American wilderness imposed its own imperatives, and a little later the dispersion of settlement added others. But deliberate effort and the traditional shape of thought held the tendency to decentralization in some degree of control so long as the colony continued under its original charter.

For almost sixty years from its establishment, the Massachusetts Bay Colony acknowledged no more than the merest shadow of colonial dependence on the mother country. Until the 1660's writs did not even run in the name of the King, and even after the restoration the men of Massachusetts were not inclined to move much closer to the Crown. Royal agents did attempt, repeatedly, to secure some more substantial submission to English authority, but they were repulsed as repeatedly by Puritan ingenuity or intransigence. The result was an unprecedented era of independence for the infant colony, and where the synods and the central government were the inhabitants' own, men saw little reason to license change. In the Bay colony of the 1630's, or the 1650's or 1670's, the salutary application of coordinated guidance to a congregational polity often played an important part in the preservation of the New England Way.

But when the clouds of the Glorious Revolution cleared, William and Mary moved to reassert the authority of England. Massachusetts' original charter was repealed and a new one issued, reducing the almost autonomous colony to a royal province. Under the new instrument of government the settlers at the Bay were permitted to retain full control only over the lower house of their General Court. The Council was now merely nominated by the lower house, subject to the approval of the governor, and the governor himself was now to be appointed by the Crown rather than chosen by the colonists. By that considerable alteration the upper reaches of sovereignty in the province, the control of the executive, were removed from Massachusetts to the mother country. And lest the message of the new subordination be missed by any at the Bay, the new charter also afforded another unmistakable demonstration of change. Before 1691 the colonial franchise had been largely limited to church members; the limitation had been an integral part of the founders' designs for a Bible Commonwealth, and it had also and not incidentally prevented most Anglicans from voting in colonial elections. The charter of 1691 proscribed this religious test. Providing only for a moderate property qualification, it leveled what was left of Winthrop's city on a hill.

As long as the largest purposes of the central government had coincided with those of the communities and congregations around the colony, and as long as the colonial governors had been committed to the Puritan mission, the wide powers of the central government had posed no insoluble problems. But the case was not the same after the arrival of the provincial charter. No similar reliance could be placed in the new government which that charter had installed in Boston, crucially tied as it was to the mother country and her divergent interests and aspirations. For sixty years, against the forces of dispersion and ambition and the very continent itself, the dominance of the central government in Massachusetts had been maintained; with the issuance of the charter, the motives for its maintenance were removed. Central authority, growing gradually more distant in any case as settlement spread increasingly beyond the possibility of close surveillance from the center, grew very remote indeed when the separation between governors and governed became psychological as well as geographical. And as it did, an underlying tendency to the local communities as repositories of effective authority became manifest.

Thus, what was reluctantly admitted in the seventeenth century came to be openly acknowledged in the eighteenth: the public peace could not be entrusted to Boston, but would have to be separately secured in each town in the province. With the arrival of the new charter, a long-running drift toward devolution was licensed and legitimized. From that time forward to the era of the American Revolution, the locus of power and influence over the lives of the people lay primarily in the towns, not in the province. Provincial control contracted to an absorption in such matters as the management of imperial affairs and the very limited patronage that was dispensed from the center. The provincial government touched the daily life of the townspeople principally as a repository of favors and privileges,

enacting into law what the townsmen wished to have enacted and granting what the townsmen wished granted.
Local institutions, interposed between Boston and the
people, became the prime political institutions of the new
provincial society, and as the stakes of political play declined in the capital after 1691, they rose rapidly in the
communities themselves.[13]

One element of the new relationship between town and
province was established at once and almost automatically.
The removal of the executive from the election of the
people eliminated the only elections which had ever called
out the entire colony, those for the governor, deputy-
governor, and assistants. With the governor appointed in
England and the councillors chosen by the governor from
the nominees of the lower legislative house, there remained
not a single occasion which was shared by the whole political citizenry. No office could claim a provincial constituency, and no political pretext existed for mobilization, or
even communication, that cut across all the communities of
the colony. From the arrival of the new charter to the time
of the Revolution, and with the exception only of a couple
of insignificant county officials, no town chose any but its
own officers or its own deputy to the General Court.

The confinement of the towns to the election of their
own inhabitants, which was indeliberate with regard to the
executive and his council, was quite conscious in the case of
the legislative power, and the altered relationship of local
to central authority that it presaged was even more profound. The early legislation which settled the structure of
the new House of Representatives—the one branch of the
legislature left unequivocally to the colonists—continued
that body largely as it had been before, but it provided for
one fundamental amendment which was a dramatic response to the imperatives of the new balance of power: a

residence requirement was instituted for the representatives.

That requirement transformed the very character of
the lower house. The meaning and the magnitude of the
change were enunciated quite clearly in a protest signed by
twenty-one representatives in 1693. The dissidents denounced the new requirement as

> contrary to the liberty granted in their Majesties'
> gracious and royal charter and to the usage and cus-
> toms of their Majesties' kingdom of England and all
> his dominions and plantations and to the particular
> usage of this their province and that which will prove
> destructive to the same[14]

and on almost every count their indictment was a true bill,
even if the prophecy they drew from it was a false one. In
the political theory and practice the colonists had carried
across the Atlantic, a representative did not need to reside
among the constituents of his own electoral district—and
often had not done so—because his true constituency was
considered to be the whole society. He was to speak for the
general welfare.[15]

The denial of that premise—a denial implicit in the
residential qualification—appeared revolutionary to the
twenty-one dissenters, and it was. Eighty years later it was
still sufficiently revolutionary to constitute a prime point
of contention between England and her rebellious colonies, which makes it all the more significant that the substitution of actual for virtual representation in Massachusetts
was not an accident but a deliberate creation of policy, instituted over articulate opposition. The new residence requirement curtailed the tendency of the general assembly
toward autonomy, reducing the House of Representatives
to a virtual congress of communities, a body much more
likely than its predecessor to be a creature of the towns to
which its members thereby became bound. By the middle

of the eighteenth century the principle of actual representation was so well established that a town could insist upon its "unalienable right" to a deputy chosen from among its own inhabitants. As a fundamental matter of political propriety, the petitioners insisted, no town ought to be represented by "a stranger to their interests and circumstances and whose interest is in no wise united with theirs." [16]

The most striking institutional expression of the conviction that the representative must be bound in to his own local constituents was the town mandate. The mandate was an instruction or a set of instructions to the representative, drawn up by a committee of the town and then debated and voted upon in town meeting. There was little of the later *vox populi vox dei* about the mandate—New England Puritans did not conceive man's relation to God as the Jacksonians one day would—but within its sphere the mandate was authoritative. Under its injunction the deputy became a mere agent of the town, an embodiment of the conception of the attorneyship of representation.

Attorneyship of representation was thus an assertion of town sovereignty against invasion by the assembly. The Sunderland petitioners of 1754 said as much:

> Each town having naturally an equal right, so they might enjoy equal advantages to defend, secure, and promote their respective interests and privileges and not have it left to the pleasure of the general assembly to direct and appoint otherwise, for hereby an effectual door would be open for the great part of the province by degrees to be deprived of this privilege and consequently become liable to be stripped of all other privileges and to be loaded with all manner of oppressions and burdens.

The assertion of *legislative* supremacy in the eighteenth century thus became, at least in Massachusetts, fundamentally an expression of *local* supremacy. As Samuel Eliot

Morison has explained, "it was only natural to wish to entrust power to a body, every member of which was elected in town meeting and subject to its instructions." [17]

Direct instruction was by no means the only manner in which towns sought to secure the subordination of their representatives to the wishes of the community. Mandates were merely a small part of a much larger pattern. Throughout the early eighteenth century, representatives were customarily required to render an account of the session's proceedings to the town meeting. Later in the provincial period some towns maintained an active correspondence with their agents while the assembly was in session. At least one town even sent a guardian to accompany its deputies to the General Court to be certain that they observed the town's wishes.[18] And in the excise controversy of 1754 the theory of the attorneyship of representation was elaborated quite consciously in a number of pamphlets such as Daniel Fowle's *Appendix to the Late Total Eclipse of Liberty*, which he subtitled "Being some thoughts on the end and design of civil government; also the inherent power of the people maintained; that it is not given up to their representatives." Fowle called it "slavery" wherever "the representatives have an independent power," a note which was echoed elsewhere, while yet another pamphlet, *The Review*, simply professed amazement, as if unable to conceive of the deputies as independent. "No one suspected," its author declared, "that the representatives of a free people would dare to act contrary to the declared sense of their constituents." [19]

Several other structural devices also curbed the autonomy of the delegates and helped assure their subjection to their own local communities. One of them was the printing and public distribution of the journals of the House of Representatives, a practice which began in Massachusetts in 1715, half a century before any other colony. Such publication was no mere quirk of Puritan intellectuality. A hardheaded determination to secure the fidelity of the deputies sustained it, just as the necessity of the deputies to prove their fidelity had initiated it. The first publication of the records of the assembly occurred in the aftermath of a controversy between the governor and the House, when the deputies decided to release their journals in order to vindicate themselves before their constituents. Thereafter, two copies of the journal were printed for each representative each year—one for himself, one for his town—a pattern which clearly emphasized the attachment of the representative to his community since distribution was wholly confined to those towns with representatives actually in attendance rather than to the full complement of towns in the province. No wider publication was provided because no wider audience was intended; the printed journal was simply an instrument of surveillance, by which the towns might see that their representatives were faithful.[20]

Another instrument in the same strategy of subordination was the annual election of representatives. As *The Review* explained the principle during the excise controversy, "the month of May, which gladdens the face of nature, brings with it also the happy privilege of electing a new assembly." For in the uncommon case of a delegate's disregard of his community's wishes, a remedy was thereby rendered simple: reprisal at the polls. From the perspective of the prerogative that remedy, or at least the threat of its employment, was much more powerful and pervasive than the constraint of an occasional mandate: throughout his long tenure Governor Shirley attempted to prevent the representatives from currying the favor of their constituents by urging upon his English superiors the substitution of triennial elections for the annual ones to which the men of Massachusetts were accustomed. But Shirley never did convince Whitehall, and by 1776 the importance of annual elections was so well established that John Adams could claim that there was not "in the whole circle of the sciences a maxim more infallible than this, 'where annual elections end, there slavery begins.' " [21]

Yet another instrument for the prevention of such "slavery" emerged late in the provincial period. In 1766, upon the urging of a deputy from Cambridge who was himself acting under instruction from his fellow townsmen, the House of Representatives erected a public gallery for visitors. In so doing, the House still further publicized that "special relationship that had always been understood to exist between the representative and his constituents." Displaying its proceedings thus to the public, the lower house gave tangible expression to its situation as an agent of public opinion; and where public opinion in the mother country was something discovered in Parliament, in Massachusetts that public opinion was something out in the country.[22]

All the ties that bound representatives to their constituencies were significant, but it was equally significant that their constituencies were towns. In every colony outside New England the county was the unit of representation; east of the Hudson that unit was the town.* Of course the

---

* Towns were also the units of taxation at the Bay, though elsewhere in the colonies and in England itself taxes were levied on the counties. Actually, the county in Massachusetts existed almost solely as a judicial entity, and even in the relations which a town did have with the judicial system there were inevitable structural supports for a local autonomy unknown in England. See, e.g., Powell: *Puritan Village*, pp. 11–12, 13, 40. In general the negligible importance of the county in New England can hardly be better indicated than by the trifling proportion of the publicly committed resources of the province which were spent to support county institutions. In Wareham in 1757, for example, the total tax bill for province, county, town, and ministerial charges amounted to £215–10–1, of which £2–2–5, or a bit less than one per cent, was for the county tax. Mass. Arch. 50, p. 19. In the seven assessments listed in the town records of Dudley in which the county tax was identified separately, the median proportion of the total tax which it represented was two per cent. *Town Records of Dudley, Massachusetts* (Pawtucket, R.I., 1893–4), I, pp. 113–14, 126, 136,

Bay colonists had always conceived of representation in terms of towns, but through the three quarters of a century before independence, in legislation and in the assumptions implicit in their rhetoric, the preference for that aberrant pattern grew steadily firmer than it had ever been before.

The original legislation which established the House of Representatives under the new charter, in 1692, provided representation for every town with forty qualified inhabitants, but it also permitted any town with less than thirty qualified inhabitants to join another town in sending a representative. That permission obviously impaired the strict identity of the individual community and its deputy, however, and it was eliminated in the amendments of 1731, which declared towns with less than the requisite number of qualified voters "at liberty to send a representative, if they think fit," regardless of their size. Thereafter no demand was ever again made that one incorporated town join another in sending a delegate.[23]

The one failure of strict identity which then remained was an exception which revealed the rule. This was the district, a category of community created at British behest, a town in all respects other than its attachment to an established town in sending a representative. But districts were never in fact numerous, their existence was only a temporary one in the evolution of full-fledged towns, and the few that did exist offended fundamental notions of provincial political propriety. "To elect and send a representative, independent of and without joining any other place whatsoever," was, for the Sunderland petitioners, an "unalienable

---

189; ibid., II, pp. 9, 23, 86. In Weston the county proportion never exceeded three per cent in the ten years for which tabulations can be made, and the average was 1.7 per cent. *Town of Weston: The Tax Lists 1757–1827* (Boston, 1897), pp. 19, 23, 30, 33, 40, 45, 60, 72, 77, 82. And in no case located did the county rate exceed the portion of the total public charges which obtained in Plymouth in 1728, a mere five per cent. *Records of Plymouth*, II, p. 259.

right" or at very least "a just right." They complained that being compelled to join the district of New Salem in an election would "singularize said town, by abridging them of a privilege allowed all other towns in the province," and if their complaint perhaps lacked empirical accuracy, it certainly did not want for ethical conviction. The district system had developed on imperial urging rather than on local initiative, and it had never amounted to more than a temporary expedient. One of the first acts of the Provincial Congress in 1775 was an order that every district in the province would henceforth be a town "to all intents and purposes whatsoever." [24]

Towns were more than merely the constituent elements in the structure of the House. They were also the foundation of financial support for its members, because the basic legislation of 1692 left responsibility for the payment of representatives almost totally to the towns. It reserved to the Court only the residual power to set the delegates' pay scale, and even that was often ignored in the towns, some of them paying as the province required but others giving more than the amount allotted, or less, or nothing at all. [25] Even when subsequent legislative measures of 1726, 1730, and 1731 provided for payment of representatives out of the public treasury, they did not disturb accustomed modes. Towns could and did continue to add their own allowance or require the representative to refund his fees to the local coffer, and in any case the sums disbursed from the center were then added to the tax bills of the towns represented, so that the towns paid the money to the province, which passed it on to the deputies. The General Court and the province treasurer were simply intermediaries. Payment of representatives was never truly a public charge, because only the towns which sent delegates were ever assessed. When an effort was made, in the 1726–7 session of the legislature, to provide for payment of deputies by an assessment upon *all* the towns, "in proportion to their other Province tax," that effort was beaten back. Indeed, even a modest proposal of 1749—that at least the travel expenses of the delegates might be "at the public charge of the province and not laid on the several towns respectively who send a representative"—was defeated.[26]

Thus the burden of financial support for members of the House rested steadily upon the towns throughout the provincial period. Whether the towns paid more or less than the province required, and whether they paid it directly, as they did before 1726, or indirectly, as they did thereafter, the essential element was the simple fact that they paid their own representatives. Such a situation meant that the assembly was not master even in its own lower house. It meant that representation depended on the situation of the towns, not of the province. Towns that considered themselves in sore circumstances might simply decline to send a delegate rather than bear the expense of his salary. Resources were scarce in the towns of eighteenth-century Massachusetts, and when there was more than one demand upon them, representation was unlikely to be accorded primacy. The issue was partly an issue of priority—the construction of a meetinghouse or the building of a road was, in actual fact, likely to take precedence over the dispatch of a deputy—but primarily it was an issue of protocol—the determination of precedence rested with the towns, whatever they decided. As the townsmen of Upton once testified, quite typically, "they are willing to do according to their abilities in supporting government, but their poverty renders them utterly unable to pay more than their common tax." That is, the town would send a delegate only according to its ability, and of that ability it set itself the judge.[27]

In theory the General Court reserved to itself a superior judgment in the matter—the right to fine towns which failed to send a delegate—but in fact such judgments tended to be mere ratifications of the prior determinations of the towns. As an official commentator on the *Journals of the House* noted, the Court was "more than lenient in accepting explanations from communities which did not care to go to the expense of sending a representative." In the session of which he spoke, only seven of the forty-six towns which had failed to send a representative were fined, and that proportion was not extraordinary in any way.* [28]

The result of such local determination was a widespread absenteeism in the House of Representatives which surely suggests that the communities of Massachusetts did not feel representation in the provincial government to be imperative to the maintenance of their own most vital interests. In 1742 Governor Shirley told the Lords of Trade that most of the 160 towns in the province were qualified to send two representatives—a town was allowed a second representative if it had 120 or more qualified voters—but that few except Boston, Salem, Ipswich, and Newbury ever availed themselves of that right. Two decades later Governor Bernard wrote to the Lords of Trade that many towns did not even send a single representative, let alone two:

---

* Exemption was, if anything, a bit greater even than these figures suggest, since towns not excused at the outset could and did file subsequent petitions for relief. Generally these were submitted—and granted—later in the session in which the fine was levied. Occasionally, as in the case of an appeal from Dunstable for 1770, the delay was greater, yet even Dunstable's application, four years late, was successful. See Mass. Arch. 50, pp. 523–4.

Petitions for remission of fines for non-representation are scattered throughout Mass. Arch. 48–50 and 113–18. A tabulation of volumes 49 and 50 shows at least thirty such repetitions, of which nineteen were granted and two partially granted; in the other nine there is no record of the Court's disposition of the case. In none of them is there evidence of the denial of an appeal for remission.

The reasons urged for remission were generally mundane if not trifling. In order of frequency the smallness of the town, its poverty or poor situation, the expenses of caring for the poor, the installation of a new minister, the building or repairing of roads, and the losses or heavy taxes occasioned by wars were the only reasons offered five times or more in the petitions tabulated from Mass. Arch. 49 and 50.

As the sending of a member is a burthen upon a town, instead of being exerted it is avoided as much as possible, so that it scarce ever happens that a town which has a right to be excused sends a representative; and of those which are obliged by law to send one, a great many make default.[29]

Governors Shirley and Bernard were both right: many towns were not represented at all, and even the towns which were represented were generally under-represented. Every town was entitled to a delegate and, as Governor Shirley acknowledged, most towns were entitled to two; yet for the sixty years for which records are available barely four towns a year sent more than a single delegate, and for the eight years for which the most reliable records are available —the years from 1767 to 1774, a time if ever there was one of high excitement and extraordinary provincial political activity—the percentage of towns with so much as a single representative of their own in the House never once exceeded fifty-three per cent. In four of the eight years less than half the towns had their own deputy. Even on the most favorable accounting—including all communities as fully represented which so much as shared a representative —slightly less than three fifths of the towns were represented during a period when the province mattered as much as it ever did in the eighteenth century. Earlier figures, though necessarily less precise, suggest a similar order of absenteeism through the preceding half century.* [30]

---

* Before 1767 the listing of towns without delegates was rather haphazard: the town rolls themselves disclose discrepancies from year to year, and external evidence sometimes suggests even larger lapses. For example, in 1763 Governor Bernard said there were 168 towns in the province (Brown, *Middle-Class Democracy*, p. 74), but only 157 were on the list of the *Journal of the House* for that year; similarly the list for 1766 named only 163 towns—Governor Shirley had claimed almost that many a quarter of a century before—while the list for 1767 named 220 towns, an inconceivable addition of fifty-seven towns in a single year if the 1766 list is to be accounted accurate. Also, petitions in the Massachusetts Archives con-

A commentator on the *Journals of the House* once declared such evidence of vacancies "adequate testimony to the fact that representation to many an eighteenth century provincial was a vital matter only when it was denied," but not even his disclaimer carried the case quite far enough. As a matter of fact, many eighteenth-century provincials were rather eager to deny themselves representation, and with steady determination they succeeded in doing so. If the price of freedom is eternal vigilance, the Bay colonists purchased their freedom at something less than its list price. The original legislation of 1692, which remained fundamentally in force for more than thirty years, obliged towns with forty or more qualified voters to send one representative; a town with 120 voters could send two delegates, and Boston was permitted four. Then, in 1726, a rebellion against those ratios eventuated in legislative

---

sistently came from places not named in the legislative lists. Sixteen of the 112 communities which communicated with the Court in the span covered by volume 113 (1693–1731) are not among the 130 towns listed in the 1730–1 session of the House; thirty-nine of the 129 places whose petitions are in volume 114 (1730–42) are not among the 161 towns of the 1741–2 session; fifty-three of 124 settlements petitioning in volume 115 (1742–51) are not among the 156 towns of the 1750–1 session; sixty-three of the 138 places appearing in volume 116 (1751–4) are not among the 155 towns of the 1753–4 session; and fifty-six of the 132 communities of volume 117 (1755–62) are not among the 176 towns of the 1761–2 session. (There is no index to volume 118.)

The figures before 1767 must therefore be presumed to indicate an absolute minimum of abdication from representation; yet even they show that in about two thirds of the years from 1723 (the first year in which unrepresented towns were listed at all) to 1766, more than one third of the towns declined to send a deputy. Never were as many as four fifths of the towns represented.

The precise sixty-year average of towns sending more than a single representative was 4.1; that average went up only to 4.6 in the years of imperial crisis. Such persistent refusal to send a second representative by the many towns which were eligible to do so reflected not only their frugality and their unconcern for provincial politics but also, as will become apparent, their sense of an undivided town interest that a single representative sufficed to speak for.

amendment, but not to liberalize the limits of representation. Under pressure from the small towns, the popular assembly more than doubled the number of qualified voters necessary, fixing the new figure at one hundred. Only the opposition of the Council, defending as it did the prerogatives of the central power, forced a compromise at sixty, and even that was still adequate to free many towns from the obligation of representation. Five years later the Court went further, raising the mandatory figure to eighty. And though that act was eventually disallowed in England, the province disregarded the royal pleasure; in practice the minimum remained eighty until the American Revolution.[31]

Contempt of the King's disallowance was no course to be undertaken lightly; in and of itself such disdain suggested the importance of the matter to the men of Massachusetts. Moreover, the revisions were not to be explained as mere upward adjustments commensurate with the general upward movement of population in the province, since no effort was ever made to amend the minimum requisite for two representatives correspondingly. The various proposals all left that figure of 120 unaltered; had the original House bill passed the Council as well, towns required to send one representative for one hundred voters could have had another merely for an additional twenty. But such disparities never mattered. The aim of the amendments was focused solely and specifically on the evasion of as much obligatory representation as possible. In the seventeenth century, towns protested reduced rather than excessive representation[32] in a central government which had been able to affect their destinies; the communities of the eighteenth century felt neither necessity nor advantage in maintaining their presence in Boston, since the central government never touched them closely enough.

*   *   *

Representation was merely the most obvious aspect of the
altered relationship between local and central authority.
The same pattern of local isolation and autonomy prevailed in almost every other sphere of public life. That is
not to say that towns were utterly unaffected by their
neighbors or by ideas and attitudes emanating from the
distant centers of the civilization of which they were a part
—no town would have claimed congregational Protestant-
ism as its own invention, or the common law—but it is to
insist that the agreement they did display among themselves was rooted more in such cultural conceptions than in
corporal coercion. It is not to say that autonomy was ever
absolute in the provincial towns, or that isolation was
ever entire, but it is to claim that the common courses so
often pursued by those communities did not derive from
any direct governmental dominion. The towns of the
eighteenth century were free enough of both Boston and
London to enjoy an autonomy which, if never total, was
always genuine.*

Moreover, their independence was quite conscious. Self-
sufficiency was not simply the nature of their case, the inevitable product of a rural environment and an underdeveloped economy. Massachusetts had been even closer to
the wilderness and even less advanced economically in the
seventeenth century, when the towns had known no such

* The conception of autonomy implied here follows the very useful distinction drawn by Robert Redfield between peasant societies and more truly
isolated primitive or tribal peoples. For Redfield it is the latter alone
which exemplify the polar case of an "autonomous cultural system" which
"as it now is keeps going by itself," whereas a peasant society is still "an
aspect or dimension of the civilization of which it is a part." For all its
relative isolation and autonomy, the peasant society "requires continual
communication to the local community of thought originating outside it"
in order to maintain itself; and the student of such societies "needs also
to know something of what goes on in the minds of remote teachers, priests,
or philosophers whose thinking affects and perhaps is affected by the
peasantry" if he is to comprehend them. See Robert Redfield: *Peasant
Society and Culture* (Chicago, Phoenix Books, 1960), esp. pp. 40–1.

independence, and Massachusetts was still relatively rural and economically underdeveloped when it abandoned such separatism after the Revolution. Local autonomy was a deliberate response to a specific historical situation; it represented the very real choices of thousands of men around the colony upon the advent of the royal charter of 1691.*

In the provincial period, then, the towns of Massachusetts acquired an autonomy they had never really known before. To preserve a portion of the ways to which they had become accustomed, they had to go each their own way. The new charter crystallized changes that had been gathering for decades: with the upper reaches of civil sovereignty removed to England the towns retreated to local leadership; and with the central government stripped of its police function for religion, the congregations realized the autonomy that had been their theoretical birthright. In the first decades the magistrates had not scrupled to discipline an errant congregation or community. In the eighteenth century men perhaps recalled the example of the fathers but they lacked the authority to emulate them. Neither the plenitude of sovereignty that their parents had known nor the institutional density that buttressed the central government in the mother country existed in provincial Massachusetts.[33]

---

* More than Massachusetts' own history may be invoked to suggest that the self-sufficiency of the provincial towns is informative rather than merely inevitable. In many other cultures, rural villages in underdeveloped economies are joined in some considerable complexity to other villages at a considerable distance. In rural India, for example, each local community is tied to many other such communities by the cross-cutting lines of caste, to which individuals feel an essential loyalty and from which they derive mutual aid. There is also a far-flung and regularized marital network of villages from and to which a village traditionally gets and sends wives, and in some cases marriage is not even allowed within the village group. See Redfield: *Peasant Society and Culture,* pp. 33–4, and compare Conrad Arensberg: "American Communities," *American Anthropologist* 57 (1955), p. 1149, on the towns of colonial New England: "Hence, fellows of the town were nearer than kinfolk, and kin moving off to another town soon fell away."

Left to their own devices, the townsmen dwelt largely upon local issues. In Braintree, to take Charles Francis Adams' example, the issue which most agitated the town over the ninety-year span of the provincial era was protection of the passage of alewives—small fish used for food and fertilizer—up into the town ponds;[34] and though not every community was so concerned about fish, there was scarcely a single dimension of daily life in those villages which did extend much beyond their own confines. A tabulation of the total business of seven towns shows not a town among them where as many as one in a dozen items involved provincial affairs or the general government. In one town less than two per cent of the entries related to the central authority, while for all seven towns taken together provincial affairs were the occasion of no more than one in every fifteen or twenty local actions. And relations with other towns were even less common than those with the capital. In some towns such dealings comprised less than one per cent of the total, and in no town did more than one item in thirty involve any other town of the Bay.*

In religion and politics, local autonomy not only prevailed but also bore the imprimatur of the highest authorities. In religion no less a luminary than Cotton Mather spoke for orthodoxy's permissiveness of local variation in several of the most central matters of church polity and practice, such as the setting of occasions for the celebration of communion and the criteria of admission to that sacrament upon which full membership in the ecclesiastical polity depended.[35] In politics the General Court itself sanctioned an almost endless diversity among towns in their conduct of business, and it did not exclude such business as elections for representatives to the General Court. A persistent dearth of prescriptive provincial legislation left only local custom and usage as guides for the management of most facets of the meeting, and when directives did issue

* For a fuller elaboration of these claims, see Appendix I.

from Boston they generally just made that discretionary management more explicit.[36]

Even in affairs which could have been expected to carry the townsmen beyond their own boundaries, parochialism prevailed in the eighteenth century. Considerations of defense, for instance, never did compel the villagers to join each other across local lines, according to such students as Carl Bridenbaugh and Walter Millis, and the same "community feeling," as William Weeden called it, kept most economic activity within the town as well. Practicing an "exclusiveness reaching out in many directions so as to narrow and restrict the privileges of trade," the towns regulated their resources in order "to confine the benefit and privilege . . . to their own townspeople." [37]

In the face of such adamant insularity, the central government soon became, in practice, the creature of its constituents. The business that the deputies brought before the Court was basically the business of their fellow townsmen, and, in the absence of any initiative from the governor beyond his opening address and an occasional proposal, the legislative agenda was substantially set by petitions from the towns and their inhabitants. As J. R. Pole put it, the Court "dutifully attended to huge quantities of information and passed laws, after three readings each, on the pleas of innumerable townships, merchants, farmers, planters, clam-diggers, husbands, or wives." [38]

Moreover, the Court's acquiescence in those local desires was quite regular, and in some of them it was unfailing. Administrative appointments were vested formally in higher authorities but actually left totally to the towns to settle for themselves. Appointments of commissioned officers in the militia, issued from Boston, were based in every case upon nominations made by a town committee of militia. Local judicial officers, placed in their seats of judgment by the higher tribunal agencies of the province, really owed their places to presentment to those authorities by their own towns. And even tavern proprietors were installed as the captains and commissioners were, being licensed by the General Court or the county courts but only upon the prior approbation and recommendation of the town of the town's selectmen.[39]

Local wishes were likewise the province's commands in matters of policy, almost as consistently as in matters of personnel.* Petitioners seeking to be sent off to another town nearly always had their pleas granted if they could show the approval of both their present and prospective communities. So too did applicants for a separate precinct,

* It goes without saying that acquiescence was not absolute, any more than autonomy was; what is claimed is simply that a strong preponderance of the evidence displays it. There is not a single case in the Massachusetts Archives in which a unanimous local request was unequivocally denied by the assembly, and there are only two in which applications even had to be trimmed because one legislative house or the other would not accede to the original appeal. See Mass. Arch. 114, pp. 732, 733a, 736, 739, and ibid. 116, pp. 648, 661-2. On the other hand, though, such divergent decisions by the two houses do indicate that the Court did have options, even in the face of local accord, rather than being utterly bound; and the same implication is sustained almost as well in two other cases in which the intransigent chamber did finally concede the community's request. See ibid. 115, pp. 693-4, and ibid., pp. 700, 701. Indeed, even the occurrence of delays—recommitments to committee, shelving and revival, and the like—in cases of unanimous appeal and eventual approval, suggests that endorsement was not entirely automatic. See, e.g., ibid., p. 487. Court acquiescence did not necessarily come at once even when it came ultimately, and it did not come invariably even if it did come generally.

Another significant testimony to the towns' lack of any iron-clad assurance that their applications would be honored occurs in some petitions from the towns themselves. In them a town sought confirmation of an agreement reached within the community, yet it appeared to consider the Court's response problematic, which is to say that the participants themselves did not always display absolute confidence that their own agreement obviated denial by the assembly. See ibid. 49, pp. 380-3; ibid. 117, pp. 33-4. But in the event these local arrangements *were* ratified, and, in any case, even petitions such as these were uncommon. On balance, effective authority was significantly on the side of the towns.

district, or town who were able to show a favorable vote of the town from which they sought separation.[40]

Inhabitants of the towns were aware of the Court's disposition upon the appearance of local unanimity,[41] and they acted accordingly. Men who spoke the sentiments of their communities steadily sought complete concurrence, in order "that we may carry our petition to the Great and General Court and the more easily get it granted." Men who found themselves in the opposition took pains to convey to the Court their circumstances, lest the legislators be "deceived" by a semblance of general agreement and mistake a majority vote for "the vote of the whole body of the town." As the citizens of Bridgefield, who subscribed a 1738 memorial opposing a petition of the west precinct for separation as a town explained, they feared "that it may be represented to your Excellency and Honors that all who are inhabitants within said boundaries are consenting to and joining with the petitioners." The memorial drew no conclusions at all about the consequences to be feared from such an appearance of consent; it did not seem to be necessary. For through all these appeals ran the unquestioned assumption that a crucial component of any decision of the assembly was the sheer presence or absence of concord in the community. Unless they were shown opposition, the deputies were disposed simply to authorize the local decision.[42]

Concord in the community was indeed the operative condition of effective authority in the province. Court and community alike subordinated provincial considerations to the particularistic demands of local unity. Towns quite commonly set the law aside, without ever a word that went beyond the town boundaries, when the law proved inconvenient for local purposes; and they did so without ever displaying any fundamental animus against the law as such. They simply set their own exigencies above it.

In the area of education the exercise of such local options was so advanced that the General Court itself admitted it. A legislative investigation of 1701 revealed that
provincial school standards were "shamefully neglected"
and that "the penalty thereof [was] not required." Another Court inquiry, seventeen years later, found "by sad
experience" that non-compliance was still common; and,
though those legislators thought the delinquent towns
were at least paying the fines to which they were liable,
more modern study of the subject has shown that evasion
remained easy throughout the provincial era. As Bernard
Bailyn put it, "the broad stream of enforcing legislation
that flows through the statute books of the seventeenth
century thinned out in the eighteenth as isolated rural
communities . . . allowed the level to sink to local requirement." [43]

In other affairs too, the province proposed and the
community disposed; and not infrequently the local disposition was to ignore the edicts of Boston. Thus there were
general laws which regulated the requirements for admission to the franchise, yet communities could decide, as
Needham did decide in its election meeting of 1750, simply
to let all freeholders vote. There was a law which forbade
town meetings to consider any business not previously announced in the warning for the meeting, yet towns could
with equal impunity set that prohibition aside as well.[44] Indeed, though few towns intended to flaunt the central government and fewer still foresaw open confrontation with it
when they did deviate, there was scarcely a law on the
books which a town could not safely have neglected. Virtually all of them were, in practice, affairs of local option, on
the model of the school requirements. Their enforcement
was, as a student of public administration in Massachusetts has said, merely "a matter of local choice." [45]

Such choices were the freer for being so rarely regarded
beyond the confines of the community, but even when vio-

lations were discovered in the capital they were not always corrected. In fact, the more ancient and extensive the town's offense, the less likely was its rebuke, for in such cases the deputies almost invariably extended their retroactive approval to the practice at issue. In 1752, for example, it was called to their attention that the procedure of notifying meetings in the first precinct of Westborough had been illegitimate since the establishment of the precinct eight years before; the response of the representatives was an explicit pronouncement that all the proceedings were "good and valid, any exceptions to the contrary notwithstanding." Other transactions in other places that were contrary to law but not to local customs were also confirmed by the Court, "any illegal actions of the Town . . . notwithstanding." [46]

Accordingly, towns and townsmen brought before the General Court for alleged violations of the law assumed no necessity for abject apology if they could tie themselves to local traditions. In a reply from the town of Sudbury, for instance, the respondent to a charge of illegal closing of the polls could confidently base his defense on unanimous local custom however irregular: "in answer to it I say, it is not the custom of the town and never was—and I appeal to the town as to the truth . . ." The town itself, challenged upon legality of its election proceedings in 1757, replied without ever recognizing its obligation according to the letter of the law. To one charge the townsmen declared directly their disbelief that "the intent of the law" could be as it literally appeared, thus constraining the town so inconveniently; to another, they answered only that they had not acted "in contempt of the law," despite their transgression of it, and on that account they asked the Court to uphold their election anyway. Moreover, their request stood on solid precedent, for technical irregularities were indeed excused by the Court when they had not been "in willful contempt of the law" and "inasmuch as rendering void [their proceedings] would greatly perplex their affairs." [47]

And as the towns displayed no particular penitence before the Court for violations of the law, so too they seemed
to feel no qualms about openly asking the assembly to authorize abrogation of the law when it clashed with their
own exigencies. For instance, a law enacted at the middle
of the century obliged town officers to swear an oath not to
accept paper money of the neighboring provinces. Pelham,
having ignored the new requirement for five years, finally
asked the legislature for a retroactive validation of its proceedings of the previous half decade; and while the Court
complied within a week of receiving the application, its
compliance was not nearly as revealing as the town's request. For in its petition Pelham conceded that all its officers had "neglected" to take the oath, yet still the town
insisted that the assessments made during that time were
made "justly and truly," that the highway assignments
were "just and equal," and that the few who sought to take
advantage of the failure to swear oaths were occasioning
"injustice" by their insistence on maintaining the law. The
divergence of provincial law and local notions of justice
could hardly have been clearer, but the assembly endorsed
the town's claims.[48]

Actually the assembly did not even require evidence of
such minimal good faith as Pelham or Sudbury had displayed. Local agreement, as such, was the *sine qua non* of
provincial policy, and to protect it, particularly in cases of
previous contention, the province was prepared to accept
new-made illegalities as easily as it accepted the established
ones. Settlements such as that which concluded a Salem dispute over tax assessments, a dispute which had raged for
almost two years and been before the Court itself for almost a year, were ratified by the Court not for any intrinsic
merit they may have possessed but because they had the
adherence of each of the contending factions. In truth,
their merit must have been minimal in the eyes of the as-

semblymen: though a portion of the accommodation simply followed provincial directives on assessments, other important parts quite openly ignored provisions of the law. The legislature did take cognizance of this abridgment of its own authority—the ratifying resolution was divided into two parts, one an injunction to "proceed according to the following rules and directions as agreeable to law, viz. . . ." to cover those provisions in the agreement which were legal, and the other an injunction to proceed "inasmuch as the parties of said town contending about said taxes at a meeting of said town on the fourth instant agreed and desired this Court would enforce their said agreement, viz. . . ." to cover the provisions which were illegal—but the legislature did no more than take cognizance. The resolution passed.[49]

In Princeton too the restoration of peace and good will required a breach of the provincial code. Provincial law was not sacred to the townsmen so long as both parties agreed on its abridgment, and neither was it sacred to the General Court committee which came in to survey the situation:

> Although there might have been a more regular method observed in the management of the meeting in March last, yet the committee are of opinion that as there really was an agreement among themselves to overlook what a number of the inhabitants supposed to be objections to the regularity of their proceedings at that time, upon certain conditions which were complied with, the committee therefore are of opinion that it would be most for the interest and peace of that district that the proceedings in the meeting aforesaid should be accepted valid.* [50]

---

* Many other cases in the Archives also present conflicts in which the values of town peace and/or stability were counterposed to the maintenance of the uniform application of the law. In a substantial majority of them the General Court made whatever adjustments had to be made to

And other resolutions and requests also cleared the Court, even when the Court's own interests were more immediately involved. Towns claimed a prerogative of independent judgment not merely on local matters like elections but also on matters presumably within the provincial sphere of competence and concern, such as taxes. Communities frequently informed the Court that it had made "some mistake" in its levies, or simply that they could not or would not pay; and almost as frequently the Court reduced or suspended the tax as it was asked to do.[51]

One of the most interesting such applications came from the township of Dorchester-Canada in 1764. The settlers' request for relief—an assertion that they were "unable to bear the [tax], they being still in their feeble state of infancy"—was not extraordinary in its own right; it was extraordinary because, at the very same time, the plantation was also petitioning to be made a town, citing in support of that appeal its increased numbers and capacity to assume town obligations. Yet, despite its brazen affront to the intelligence of the representatives in Boston, the plantation's confidence in the priority of local demands was not misplaced. The application for township status was in fact granted, almost at once, while the appeal for tax relief was so far successful that, almost a year later, the General Court had still taken no action at all to collect the tax or even to affirm it.[52]

---

accommodate the letter of the law to local exigencies, but an exact tabulation is difficult since the specific cases varied so widely between the trivial and the weighty. (In general, the more trivial the issue the more certain was provincial allowance of deviation from the law, though the relations of authority thereby revealed were not necessarily trivial. See Mass. Arch. 113, p. 393. Some of the instances not already cited in which the Court abridged the letter of the law when that law contradicted community practices include ibid. 116, pp. 103–4, 160–1, 201, 291–2, 367–8, 465, 578–9, 580–1, 637–8, 646–7, 765–6; ibid. 117, pp. 34–6, 42–3, 462–5, 496, 596–7; ibid. 118, pp. 154–5, 833–4. Instances in which the Court did insist upon an unbending application of the law include ibid. 50, pp. 42–3; ibid. 115, pp. 465–8, 472; ibid. 116, pp. 367–8.

In much the same manner, and despite the assembly's obvious interest both in the revenues themselves and in the discipline they implied, a variety of fines and taxes assessed against towns were written off with revealing consistency. Of the seventy-four petitions for remission of fines or abatement of taxes tabulated in the Massachusetts Archives, there were forty-four which were granted, seven which were partially granted, and twenty-three in which there was no record of the outcome. Never once was there a denial of such a request for relief.*

Sometimes towns went still further in their disregard of the law, displaying their defiance before the Court and also, quite consciously, preparing a plan of defense for it. By 1754 the law gave legal protection to several dissenting Protestant denominations: upon presentation of certificates from their churches, members were to be excused taxation for the support of the Congregational church. Yet in 1754 the town of Dudley met to vote "to se if town will agree that ye constables shall strain upon the separats in our town for the minesters rate and if they do to se whate methode the town will take to defend them." Since to "strain" was to levy distress—that is, to confiscate and sell sufficient of the victim's property to satisfy his supposed obligations—such a vote was possible only for men who paused not at all at the substantive intent of the law but only at the pragmatic problem of defending their infringement of it.[53]

---

* The seventy-four applications represent a compilation of every case from the Massachusetts Archives, Volumes 49, 50, 117, and 118. For some particularly preposterous appeals which were granted, see ibid. 115, pp. 791–2; ibid. 118, p. 191. The seven partial grants provide another indication that the Court did exercise a degree of independent judgment; its strong tendency to enact local desires arose from pressures more subtle than a formal definition of the local-central relationship. For some specific forms the partial grants could take, see, e.g., ibid. 50, pp. 517, 533; ibid. 117, p. 375. Other provisions of the law posed threats even emptier than the assignment of a provincial fine. See, e.g., Shipton: "Locus of Authority," p. 145; Mass. Arch. 117, pp. 494, 496, 498–9.

Twenty years later Dudley did the very same thing. In
September, 1774, the town voted "that our constable Samuel Healy shall not make any Return of Jurymen in obedi-
ance to the New act of parliament and that the Towne
save him harmless." [54] It was the old challenge—flagrant
disobedience of the provincial law and united local determination to resist any provincial efforts to compel conformity—in a somewhat different setting. And this time it
was a challenge which, multiplied a dozen times over, on a
dozen dimensions, sounded throughout all Massachusetts;
on its resolution hinged a portion of an empire. Among the
Intolerable Acts was a prohibition on all town meetings,
except one a year to choose officers, without the consent of
the governor. That act compelled the culminating confrontation of local and central government of the entire
period, and in the showdown the towns flaunted provincial
authority with impunity. As Harry Cushing described it:

> By a technicality the necessity of asking such consent
> was avoided; and soon the protection even of a tech-
> nicality was scorned; soon could Samuel Adams read
> of "many town meetings which will all be called with-
> out asking his excellency's leave." Plainly and uni-
> formly the towns sanctioned the blunt resolve "to pay
> no regard to the late act of Parliament, respecting the
> calling town meetings, but to proceed in the usual
> way" . . .[55]

Revolution was not precisely "the usual way," but town
supremacy was. According to Samuel Eliot Morison, the
towns had become "in fact the several sovereigns of Massachusetts-Bay. Their relation to the General Court closely
approximated that of the states to the Congress of the Con-
federation, with the important difference that there were
not thirteen but almost three hundred of them." [56] This
sovereignty once established visibly to all, the towns went

on about their business as they had come to see that business. They wrought a revolution.

The governor's authority now embraced little more than Boston; the royal treasurer soon failed to receive payments of recognition from the towns; by the towns had been brought about the end of the royal legislature; at their instance the royal courts had been abolished; and it is significant that in this general collapse the town system, and that alone, had maintained an existence and an activity that were practically continuous. By this element the government of the King had been destroyed; by it the reconstruction was to be effected.[57]

❧ II ❧

Principles of
Peace

THE REALITIES OF PUBLIC LIFE in provincial Massachusetts must, then, be sought in two or three hundred towns and villages scattered about the Bay settlement, for it was in those places that the inhabitants gained their sense of the social order. Their operative ideas of appropriate authority and meet relations among men were those they drew from daily conduct in the communities; and if they did not always, or often, articulate those ideas in formal theory, that is simply to say that the men of Massachusetts saw themselves as dimly and as anachronistically as most men do. The ideas grew in men's minds anyway, eroding as they did the experiential basis that gave resonance and even self-evidence to the ancient principles.

As the town became the only governmental agency with more than a sporadic impact on the lives of its residents, and as it came to provide most of them with the only essential experience of public authority they would ever know, it encroached ineluctably upon the traditional prerogatives of the central government. As the Revolution eventually revealed, the very maintenance of order in the province had come to depend, in the eighteenth century, upon the towns. Yet even after the Revolution, Americans would still grope for terms in which to describe this new fact of the dispersal of effective authority. They would speak of "the people" or "individualism" when they meant merely the people or individuals aggregated on different principles than those of the centralized state, when what they really meant was sovereignty in severalty, the sovereignty of local groups and localities.

Such sovereignty was, to be sure, revolutionary. Power had indeed passed from the Crown to the commons, from a king to the community. But for all that, its passage represented something less than an unequivocal advance of freedom. Freedom in such a society would be defined by the options and opportunities presented by its precincts; and in Massachusetts the communities of the eighteenth century were little more than rural villages and hamlets, whose inhabitants suffered all the constraints of such confined country life.

For one thing, very small societies simply cannot support any extensive range of social roles or allow much differentiation of labor, and the provincial communities were very small societies indeed. In 1710 there were barely sixty thousand people in all of Massachusetts—or less than a hundred adult males in the average town. As late as 1765, when the final census of the provincial period was completed, a substantial majority of places still had less than a thousand inhabitants. Only fifteen towns among more than two hundred had populations of twenty-five hundred, the minimal census threshold of urbanism, while Boston itself, with three times as many residents as any other place in the province, counted less than fifteen thousand souls.[1]

Other constrictions beyond those of sheer size were imposed by the nature of provincial society. In England too there were small villages, but in England such villages were settled in their ways and their ways were often more medieval than modern. Immemorial custom and a few families governed such communities, and men did much as their fathers had done before them. In America the sea-passage cut the colonists off from the full force of traditional authority, so that even the maintenance of law and order had to be managed in the absence of any customarily accepted agencies for its establishment or enforcement. Initially order had been obtained at the Bay by the common commitment to the creation of a Bible Commonwealth, but the ideological authority that thus supplanted traditional rule survived only as long as the fervor of the first decades could be sustained. After that, and especially after the original charter was vacated and effective authority devolved upon the towns, which lacked even the traditional institutions and sanctions of the central government, there was no recourse which remained to the men of Massachusetts but the collective authority of the group. As one recent student of the subject stated, "the towns were small and compact, the congregations watchful; every person was tuned to the movements of his neighbor." Residential arrangements, as another investigator found, "made for close living" among others "visible and ever-present," and the deployment of social space was precisely paralleled by the use of time: there was "frequent daily intercourse of neighbors and townsfolk," "continuous contact of the young people," and "enforced frequent sabbatarian communion." Together the utilization of time and the arrangement of space contributed to what Conrad Arensberg called, in a felicitous phrase, "a dense collective experience." [2]

That close communal life, in turn, contributed mightily to the shape of social values in provincial Massachusetts. The very demography of the country predisposed its inhabitants toward peace, for men who live at such close quarters must "get along," at least by an outward show of amity, or imperil even the simplest daily intercourse. Among men who are privy to each other's secret sins, overt hostility becomes unlikely as the basis of enduring relationships; aggressive impulses must be suppressed if not extinguished, because they can rip the community apart. It has been found, for example, that an isolated settlement pattern is often connected with substantial self-reliance, but "closely packed" settlement forms are likelier to be linked to a high evaluation of "responsibility to the group." As one anthropologist has suggested, "you cannot afford to have fighting" under such crowded living conditions.* [3]

The premium on peace and the insistence on the strict control of aggression which demography demanded did, in fact, obtain at the Bay. Accommodation to others *was* ex-

---

* Whiting's work actually concerned crowded living conditions within the household; the propositions advanced here extend a bit beyond his empirical data to suggest that a similar outcome derived from a dense communal experience according to much the same imperative.

As for family structure itself, dependable data simply do not exist on any wide scale for Massachusetts in the eighteenth century. Some students have concluded that there was an extended family norm at least until the middle of the century: See Bailyn: *Education,* pp. 24–5; Alice Ryerson: "Medical Advice on Child-Rearing, 1550–1900," unpubl. Ed. D. dissertation, Harvard Graduate School of Education, 1960. Some figures which sustain inferences supporting such conclusions are in Charles Grant: *Democracy in the Connecticut Frontier Town of Kent* (New York, 1961), p. 34; Peter Parker: "Some Notes on the Suffolk County Probate Records, 1680–1724," unpublished paper, U. of Pennsylvania, 1966; G. D. Scull: "Historical Notes and Letters Relating to Early New England," *New England Historic and Genealogical Register* 38 (1884), p. 379; Mass. Arch. 118, pp. 406–8. Several social practices of provincial Massachusetts also sustained a household that could be considerably larger than the conjugal unit: See, e.g., Allen: *History of Wenham,* p. 55*n.*; Roland Bainton: *Christian Unity and Religion in New England* (Boston, 1964), p. 270; Alice Earle: *Child Life in Colonial Days* (New York, 1899), pp. 81–4; Edmund Morgan: *The Puritan Family* (Boston, 1956), pp. 36–8, 85–6; Weeden: *Economic and Social History,* pp. 230, 273, 293–4. On the other hand, other students have insisted that there was always a nuclear family pattern predominant in the province: See Arensberg: "American Communities," p. 1150; Wendell Bash: "Factors Influencing Family and Community Organization in a New England Town, 1730 to 1940," unpubl. Ph.D. dissertation, Harvard, 1941, p. 188 et seq.; John Demos: "Notes on Life in Plymouth Colony," *William and Mary Quarterly,* 3rd ser., 22 (1965), pp. 264–88. George Homans: *The Human Group* (New York, 1950), also insisted that there was no extended family, but he added that parents often lived with their grown children's families and that "every farm had at least one hired man, who was treated as a member of the family"; see p. 341. Another recent study proposed that, at least in one town, there was a "modified extended family": See Philip Greven, Jr.: "Family Structure in Seventeenth-Century Andover, Massachusetts," *William and Mary Quarterly,* 3rd ser., 23 (1966), pp. 234–56.

pected, and harmony *was* held dear, in the towns of the province; precepts of concord and control were everywhere about the townsmen of the eighteenth century, for they were at the very core of the community's social code. In every sphere a man met the same attitudes and expectations and was urged to abide by the same standards. The strictures against contention which he heard from the pulpit on Sunday were echoed in the quest for consensus which he saw in town meeting a few days later. Out of the past—his own past, his society's past—came still other preachments of the same proprieties. Every significant source of public values converged to the same definitions of decorum and the same insistence upon the illegitimacy of conflict and dissent.

The Puritan everywhere had an unprecedented obligation to think for himself, but the Puritan in provincial Massachusetts had no less an obligation to think as his neighbors thought. Accordingly, the private consciences of the community had to be brought into concert. The minister had to help his hearers think for themselves, and the magistrates had to keep a watchful eye upon the political promptings of the populace; the community had to be correctly informed. And the same shaping of information and attitudes which ministers and magistrates provided for grown men had also to be extended to the young, for they too would one day be full participants in the public life of the town. So the pattern of socialization—that cumulation of tender teachings and subtle suggestions, of rewards and punishments, by which children learn the ways of their society and learn, too, to believe what it is good for them to believe and to want what they are likely to get in any case —sustained the same social values of harmony and homogeneity which were pre-eminent in political and religious life. All public standards were of a piece, and all of them rehearsed the same rule: "You cannot afford to have fighting."

• • •

Such consensual communities had been sought from the first settlement at the Bay, and that in itself was a significant source of values for the townsmen of the eighteenth century. A society's notions of good and evil, success and failure, salvation and damnation, are in no small measure a product of the society's history, since its past is a vital part of its sense of identity and thus of the forces of social propriety that play upon its members. In Massachusetts the dispositions and decisions of the first decades forged the historical tradition of harmony and homogeneity and of the control of some of the truest impulsions of the self for the sake of such concord.

In fact, the concern for concord preceded settlement itself, for, as Perry Miller acknowledged, the Puritans in England "had been heroically striving for an absolute uniformity" since the sixteenth century. Even before its removal to New England the Massachusetts Bay Company instructed the governor of its frontier outpost in Salem to "bee careful to maintaine peace and vnitie" and to "suppress" disputes; and the Company traced such disputes and "different judgment" almost wholly to men "led more by their will then any good warrant out of Gods word." In its eyes, and in the eyes of English Puritans everywhere, the good citizen was not one who sought self-expression rather than repose in the external authority of the Bible, any more than the good society was one that contained differences in judgment. John Winthrop's classic speech, with its central metaphor of unity—"We must be knitt together in this worke as one man"—was delivered while the *Arbella* was still upon the Atlantic.[4]

Of course, few Englishmen in the first third of the seventeenth century would have wished for anything other than Winthrop did. The expectation of orthodoxy was a commonplace of the age. But the Puritans defined it more

stringently than any of their countrymen, and they pursued it more fervently. In their provisions for church polity, for example, "the essence of the Puritan contention"
was that the very "minutiae of ecclesiastical practice had
been prescribed ages ago by Christ himself [and] were to
remain forever unchanged by any man," whereas Whitgift
and the Churchmen flatly denied such divine dictation, insisting instead that God left such practice for men "to
determine for themselves, permitting it to be variable
'according to circumstances of time and place.' " [5] In the
authority to which they allowed appeal, the Puritans were
also less open to experience and less receptive to relativity
than the Establishment; their "harsh bibliolatry" admitted
only the Scriptures as a warrant, while the Anglicans denied that the Bible had "ever been designed to be a complete guide for all activity" and recognized as well "the collective wisdom of Christianity, the interpretations of the
councils and the Fathers, the traditions of the Church . . .
arguments from reason, nature, from the law of nations,
or from the character and origin of public society." [6] The
difference in diversity was important because every basis of
legitimacy endorsed by the Established Church was also, at
least potentially, a source of legitimate opposition, whereas
Puritanism, with its single source of authority, offered a
correspondingly constricted basis for legitimate opposition;
and the importance of that difference was deepened by
Puritan conceptions of the very nature of truth. For Scrip-
ture was more than just the sole source of authority among
the Puritans. It was, in its own right, "self-evident." As
Perry Miller put it, "Every verse admitted of but one interpretation." The Puritans therefore expected that reasonable men would be able to agree on *the* meaning of any
passage, and that expectation compelled them to call dissidents unreasonable men if they persisted in their opinions
after having been shown the light. Thus in England the
Puritans had not been able to conceive that the monarch

had heard them, since they were convinced that their arguments, once considered, were irresistible, and thus in America they could conceive no alternative to the expulsion of men like Roger Williams. The continuation of such men in the colony would have amounted to "an admission that reasonable men might lawfully hold differing views on fundamental issues." The Puritan intellect could not make that admission because it lacked the epistemological equipment. Its axioms were simplistic, even simple-minded: meanings were single, and the Puritans were in exclusive possession of them. Inevitably, then, they "were compelled to pronounce all their foes so many heretics" or even "deliberate minions of Antichrist." [7]

In New England, in the first generation, such pronouncements were legion. Roger Williams was merely the most prominent of dozens of dissidents who were hounded out of the colony in the first decade. Gorton, Child and others followed in the 1640's, the Gortonists being "banished from the patent, upon pain of death," despite their offer to submit their differences with the ministers to arbitration. At a time when England was advancing into an unprecedented toleration, the most colorful spokesman for the New England Way was still raging against "polypiety" and insisting that "he that is willing to tolerate any unsound opinion that his own may also be tolerated hangs God's Bible at the Devil's Girdle." The Puritans may have embraced a position no different from that espoused by other men of their era, but they took that position more solemnly, maintained it more stringently, and clung to it long after others had let it go. [8]

The rigidity and intensity of the Puritan adherence to ideas of uniformity surely constituted one element in the Bay Colony's attachment to intolerance at the very moment England was beginning to break away from them; but since Puritans as well as Churchmen learned toleration in England, that element could hardly have been determinative. Other elements unique to the American settlements must be invoked to account for the parting of Puritan ways and the peculiar precisianism of New England.

One of them was obviously the wilderness. The darkness beyond the clearings, and the Indians who seemed to be lurking everywhere, were not matters dreamed of in English Puritan philosophy, but they were very real incentives for men to remain "knitt together" in a cohesive community which could give them protection against their common enemies.[9] Another, no less patent, was power. The early settlers of Massachusetts were able to go their intolerant way because they held sway in the new land as those who remained behind could not hope to do in the old. Their power permitted them to exclude all who assailed or even threatened to assail their authority, and so it permitted them to maintain uniformity in the community by maintaining homogeneity among its inhabitants. The sharp cleavages of class and religion which divided England against itself were simply not present in the first settlements at the Bay,[10] and the first settlers engaged in a concerted effort to deny them entry. In towns such as Sudbury they enacted resolutions to bar from their company "such whose dispositions do not suit us, whose society will be hurtful to us"; in places like Dedham they agreed at the town's foundation "to keepe of from vs all such as are contrarye minded. And receaue onely such vnto vs as be such as may be probably of one harte." [11]

Distinctive elements and common ones came together in the institution and the idea of the covenant. The covenant was the keystone of the Puritans' intellectual edifice, the conception which Perry Miller considered the master idea of the age for the Congregationalists. Unanimous consent was its form and the pledge of peace an essential part of its substance; by it a divine sanction was secured for the "mutual love and respect" thus sworn by a community "bound up together in a bundle of life." And because such accords were voluntarily subscribed and then morally binding upon their subscribers, they not only constituted a model for other town actions but also conferred a special solidarity upon the social and institutional arrangements of the communities.* [12]

Thus the covenant provided more than just a model and a moral obligation. Its truest significance and its relation to public authority became explicit in John Winthrop's speech on liberty in 1645. There Winthrop went

> beyond the accepted seventeenth century doctrine that men must submit to their rulers because God orders them to submit. He was making the further point that by joining in a covenant men renounce their liberty to do anything but that which has been agreed to, and, further, that the duty to do that which is "good, just, and honest" extends beyond the field of moral law and is the basis of political authority in the state. In other words, none might have the benefit of the law except those who subject themselves to it, and none have the protection of authority except those who obey it.

The covenant, then, committed men to conformity. It stripped away any basis for legitimate opposition to authority and placed any opposition, by definition, outside the law. On such a definition as Winthrop's, the covenant became both an emblem and an engine of monolithic, unassailable authority.[13]

The sense of appropriate authority embodied in the covenant conception was established definitively, in the fateful first decade of settlement, in the purging of the

* The external covenant, with its promise of temporal prosperity for outward obedience to the will of God and the community, provided a religious motive to uniformity and self-suppression which is almost too perfect an instance of Durkheim's theory of the sacred as an embodiment of group norms. See Emile Durkheim: *The Elementary Forms of the Religious Life* (New York, Free Press, 1965).

religious controversialists from the colony. Williams and
Hutchinson and even John Cotton had preserved the
yearning intensity of the initial Puritan impulse, and for
the fathers of the infant colony that was precisely the problem. The ecstasy of that soul-ravishing moment when God
granted a man grace and a new birth was the most in-
tensely anarchic experience a Puritan could ever know,
and it had, therefore, to be dulled and defeated. That the
preachers of New England set out to do. Led by Shepard
and Hooker, an almost united ministry pondered over the
psychology of salvation until they had specified its every
stage and dissected its most subtle degrees. Charting the
minutest motions of the soul in its ripening for regeneration, the pastors developed the doctrine of preparation—a
substitution of good works and gradualism for apocalyptic
fervor—to a length theretofore undreamed of, and then
they ordained that no man could be converted who had not
passed, in the only sequence they authorized, through each
of the set stages. Against Anne Hutchinson's steadfast conviction that the shattering moment of conversion could be
unexpected and inscrutable, that grace might descend
differently on different individuals and that the human
psyche could not be comprehended in a single morphology
of conversion, not even the morphology of such a psycholo-
gist as Hooker, the ministers decreed that every man's experience of grace was to be broken and harnessed to the
same gait. When the Hutchinsonians were exiled for dar-
ing to depart from regular canons of regeneration, and
when John Cotton declined to defend them or depart with
them, bending instead before the massed ministry of the
Bay and surrendering as he did some of his most profound
beliefs about the nature and pursuit of the happiness the
Puritans called grace, orthodoxy in Massachusetts was secured, or perhaps even created.[14]

From the time of Cotton's capitulation on preparation,
there was no legitimate place for varieties of religious ex-

perience in Massachusetts, no allowance for the various voyages of individual souls. Grace was defined then as an orderly, controlled process, and the definition persisted for at least a century afterward. In the middle of the eighteenth century an English observer found that still "everyone's religious experience must be broken in, to the prescribed measure and form. . . . Everyone must believe certain things, and do certain things, and pass through a certain process; or he is lost." [15]

Whatever the weight of the decisions and dispositions of the first decades, though, it was not historical tradition alone which compelled the townsmen to cling to the canon of orthodoxy and sustain it through three quarters of the eighteenth century. Men who continued to seek concord and control probably found support for that course in their sense of historical identity; but other pressures for perseverance also impinged on the provincial citizenry, and some of those pressures were more immediate than the threads of identity that filtered forward from the past. The social values that surrounded the townsmen in their daily affairs also promoted peace, and chief among the sources of such values in provincial Massachusetts were the principles and practices of eighteenth-century religious life.

The primacy of peace was pervasive in the sphere of the sacred, and it began at the fount of all sacred conceptions. Provincial people conceived of God Himself in terms of concord. They expressed that conception in everything from private diaries to pamphlets published for all the English-speaking world to read; they exhibited it in everything from the elevated invocations of the God of peace in the church covenants to the homely thanks that two parishioners gave to Him at the conclusion of a feud.[16]

Heaven too they figured forth in terms of harmony and homogeneity—"there you shall be united in the same in-

terest, and shall be of one mind and one heart and one soul
forever," Jonathan Edwards promised Northampton—and
an image of amity controlled the revivalists' conception of
the heaven on earth of the millennium, which Edwards envisioned as all the world "united in one amiable society
. . . knit together in sweet harmony." And Edwardsean
history also posited a pre-lapsarian age when "all was in
excellent order, peace, and beautiful harmony." * 17

The significance of such conceptions of the millennial
future and the pre-lapsarian past, of heaven and even of
God, is precisely that their objects are beyond the actual
experience of men. Such notions are, for that very reason,
best conceived as vast ambiguous stimuli upon which men
project their cultural ideals; understood that way, they disclose concord and consensus as the ideals of eighteenth-
century Massachusetts. When revivalists such as Edwards
spoke on those subjects, they spoke not simply for themselves or their followers. They and their opponents then
spoke as with a single tongue, and that the mother tongue
of the communities of Massachusetts in every generation
before the Revolution.[18]

Even at the very height of the Awakening, and despite

---

* It is, of course, possible to argue that these glowing evocations of mutual
love and everlasting peace were set in antithesis to the realities of eighteenth-
century Massachusetts, but such an argument by inversion is unsound. Not
only does it depend on a definition of reality which excludes the values
men profess—whereas precisely such values are the subject of inquiry at
this point—but it uses values as an index to behavior in an indefensibly
simplistic manner besides. An inverse relation *might,* indeed, have obtained, but so might many others: affirmation of ideals is at least equally
compatible, in logic, with injunctions to keep up the good work, or with
ritual reaffirmations intended only to reinforce what is already accepted,
or with exhortations to continue straining to avoid overt expression of
what has so far been suppressed. That is, it is clear enough that the maintenance of peace was problematic; in any society the suppression of aggression entails tension. But to argue, merely from statements of aspiration such as those of Edwards, that maintenance of peace failed in fact,
would be an unwarranted inference.

their other disagreements, Calvinists and conservatives shared the same assumptions of harmonious community. The Old Light leader Charles Chauncy appealed to them when he complained that the "law of charity" proscribed the separations agitated in some churches, but so too did an earlier convention, favorable to the revival, which pronounced such separations "unscriptural." Chauncy opposed the exhorters for "spiriting people to Schism and Faction," but a counterconvention of ministers friendly to the Awakening had already cautioned their adherents not to indulge "a Spirit of *Censoriousness, Uncharitableness, and rash judging the state of others.*" Opponents of the movement decried George Whitefield for his violations of the canons of peace and emotional control, but many of Whitefield's most prominent ministerial supporters also denounced emotional extravagance and Whitefield himself issued a similar disavowal.[19] Whatever the ultimate consequences of the Great Awakening, then, leaders on both sides, New Lights no less than Old, initially conceived of the movement in terms of the promotion of unity. Even the slender legacy of institutionally established separatism which the revival did leave in Massachusetts showed its own intellectual origins and the ideological climate of the province unmistakably: the charges to which separatist apologists were most sensitive and the denunciations they were most concerned to deny were those of division, splitting, and contention.[20] Thus the separatists themselves conceded the moral values from which the charges proceeded, the values of peace and unity, as legitimate standards of judgment.

The ecclesiastical premium on peace and unity provided the core of a larger complex of values which might be called a conception of the moral community. A prime function of the conduct of religious life in the towns and churches of provincial Massachusetts was the maintenance of group integration. To obtain that objective, the congregations engaged in a variety of outward observances and supported one very striking institution.

Most broadly based among the observances were the compulsory sabbath services which nearly every local society sustained and which were used quite consciously as measures of community control. Such services were initially designed to bring men to "civill obedience & allegiance unto magistracy" as much as to faith, and they were maintained for the same reasons. Indeed, it was in significant part to their "enforced frequent sabbatarian communion" that Arensberg attributed the dense collective experience of the towns and with it the "chance for internalization of these rigidities of role and habit" and the "readiness to seek consensus." [21]

At the sabbath service itself the message was likely to be even less mistakable. According to one sampling the most common purpose of ministerial sermons was "to promote mutual love and peace among Christians," while the next most common was "to prevent murmurings and promote patience." [22] And in such sermons the minister simply did his acknowledged duty, for he had the obligation of his "solemn ordination pastoral covenant" to promote peace, and he could draw the censure of a church council for failure to "take them by the hand as a pastor ought to do to heal and lead them." [23]

The celebration of communion also stood pre-eminently as a token of the united moral community. Men who took the Lord's Supper together were presumed to be at peace. Those who were not at peace with their fellows were forbidden that supreme sacrament of Massachusetts Congregationalism. And contention which extended beyond a few individuals to embrace factions in the community required the complete elimination of the rite. "While a battle was on, the Lord's Supper could not be celebrated. Brethren were not in peace and harmony with brethren, and until at least a truce could be declared, this precious 'ordinance' had to be postponed." Such prospect of postponement made the sacrament an inducement to peace as well as a symbol of its presence.[24]

But perhaps the most important inducement to peace —and certainly the most illuminating—was the institution of church discipline. Church discipline took its intellectual origin from the Puritan concept of sin, according to which all the sons of Adam were sinners. Since such depravity was a truth beyond doubting, salvation through innocence was altogether impossible. Instead, salvation rested in renunciation and repentance for sins. Discipline was accordingly designed less for punishment than for penitence, and such penitence played a crucial role in promoting community cohesion.

As Cotton Mather described the process, the offender was to be confronted first by the one who knew of the offense. If that failed to bring the culprit to contrition, one or two others might be brought into the affair and, upon further failure, the pastor. All of these first steps toward reformation were informed by a strong preference for circumspection, to minimize disruption of the neighborhood, and at every stage it was "repentance" and "humiliation" which were sought. The errant one would, hopefully, "relent." Only if he continued "obstinate" were further steps taken, and only those further steps involved the initiation of formal church discipline. Discipline was instituted in successive stages from early admonition to ultimate excommunication. Each stage was an increasingly severe symbol of community condemnation, and each was invoked only upon the failure of repentance at the stage before. Repentance took the form of a public confession, which was generally recited at the meetinghouse before the entire congregation. The immediate purpose of a church censure was to secure such a confession and, with the confession, restoration of the offender.[25]

It was this conjunction of censure, confession, and restoration which constituted the crux of the notion of moral community. For when a New Englander was driven to stand before his assembled neighbors and confess his transgression, more than mere punishment was involved. All societies punish the behavior they define as criminal or immoral, because violation of their ordinances is a challenge to the legitimacy of the normative order and so cannot pass unrebuked; but in the punishments meted out by the churches of Massachusetts the offender himself acknowledged his recognition of the morality he had violated. He as well as his pastor and his peers attested to the justice of his humiliation. He was the object of the community's punishment, but simultaneously he was a member of the community which was punishing, so that even in the act of retribution the solidarity of the society was not upset. Only the offender who failed to confess stood outside that social order; only he truly sinned, because he asserted his own inclinations and impulsions, his own will, against the standards of the community. Confession was a curbing of such pride, a denial of the individual will, and an affirmation of the primacy of public values over any possible private ones. The original church censure that brought the culprit to his confession was consciously designed to achieve all of those things, and the offender's acknowledgment and restoration made that plain, representing as it did a symbolic reaffirmation of the community's mores and a reintegration of the moral community.[26]

Precisely because the preservation of peace and the restoration of the moral community were always the objects of discipline, no censure was ever final. Repentance rather than retribution was the rationale even of excommunication, and repentance—"an Exemplary REPENTANCE," as Cotton Mather styled it—was the way to get even that gravest of penalties "taken off." For excommunication was less a separation from the community than an extreme attempt to reunite it: the bond of brotherhood was not broken in the interval. An excommunicate was always potentially penitent; he was therefore "not to be treated as an enemy but as a brother in need of admonition, never as a 'common Sinner' who had always been outside the Church." Men and women who had been excommunicated were not merely permitted but actually required to attend church services, since it was known that sermons were the most effective means to bring men to a conviction of their sins, and if an excommunicate did come to such a conviction he was "restored to church fellowship, rather than admitted *de novo*, for he had never ceased to be a member, although he had temporarily forfeited the privileges of membership." [27]

Aware of that offer of readmission, men did repent. Excommunication, and more often the mere threat of its employment, were extraordinarily effective in bringing the strayed sheep back to the paths of peace and propriety,[28] and their efficacy was all the more impressive because the force they represented was ultimately only the symbolic moral condemnation of the congregation. "The united sense of the Church" was necessary to institute excommunication, but it was little more than that sense which constituted the punishment provided by the penalty; the church could mount no material sanctions. Excommunicates incurred shame, perhaps, and condemnation and the withdrawal of community support, but they suffered no civil penalties at all on account of their obstinacy. Any persuasion that was achieved was achieved only by making the offender a moral isolate. Effective power was communal rather than coercive in any obvious physical sense.[29]

Nevertheless, the success of church censures under such conditions is not really surprising, for the power of the community was not negligible even in the absence of direct sanctions, and moral isolation was no minor matter in a community of a hundred families. Moreover, the confessions which were demanded by the towns in their desire to get men to make a public commitment to unanimity and consensus were probably more powerful agents of agreement than most men suspected, for there is now a large body of modern experimental evidence which "convincingly demonstrates the power of role-playing to change deeply held attitudes, values, and even conceptions of the self." That is to say, outward acknowledgment of a position tends to pass into inner acceptance of it. Men making public confessions —thereby admitting the legitimacy of the morality they had violated—would have had a tendency to internalize the legitimacy of that morality; and as they thus increasingly accepted the authority of communal morality of their own volition, their acceptance helped to render gross coercive measures less necessary.[30]

The substance of that morality whose transgression men were required to unbosom was as revealing as the confessional requirement itself, for the transgressions were far less often private failings than they were threats to the peace of the congregation. Maintenance of the moral community was not only the form of church discipline but also a major part of its subject matter. The sanctions of censure were directed primarily to the end of subduing interpersonal antagonism, whether it made itself manifest in a passing acrimony among members, a slander or defamation, a discordance within a family, or feuding and fighting among men. Discipline was designed to restore amity in all these affairs, and a brief display of "unwarrantable anger" necessitated public confession no less than an actual assault. In their concern to suppress aggression, churches presumed to search the souls of men even in the absence of overt hostility, demanding acknowledgment of "a contentious and quarrelsome disposition" or "ill-temperedness" quite as much as of actual bad behavior. Contention simply had no legitimate place in the covenanted communities of eighteenth-century Massachusetts, least of all in a man's heart.[31]

Peace was the pre-eminent value of the secular sphere no less than of the religious. In a variety of times and places, styles and situations, the townsmen of provincial Massachusetts acknowledged the primacy of peace and unity in the conduct of the community. Over and over again they were granted to be goals of public life which were good intrinsically rather than instrumentally. They did not have to be justified as ends of action; rather, other ends were justified in terms of them.

Sometimes the testimony was abstract, explicit, and all-embracing. In Springfield the citizens said that "harmony and unanimity" were what they "most heartily wish to enjoy in all their public concerns." In Dunstable men made a compact among themselves "To the intent y^t we may live in love and peace together." Upton, plagued by a division over the location of a new meetinghouse, reported that "much time and money, by committees, by town meetings, and other ways, has been expended in order to unite the people and bring the unhappy disputes to an end," while earlier the town had asked that the General Court decide the dispute, which "would reconcile all parties and the town be at peace," which was "so desirable an end." And in an election sermon of 1754 Jonathan Mayhew spoke the sentiments of most of Massachusetts when he concluded that "union is the source of public happiness." * [32]

---

* It should be unnecessary to explain that peace and harmony were not the *sole* consummatory values ever invoked in provincial Massachusetts, only the most customary ones. Sometimes other values (material convenience, "God's glory and the good of man") were accorded a higher authority—Mass. Arch. 115, pp. 393–6; ibid., pp. 412–13; ibid., pp. 729–30; ibid. 117, p. 561—and sometimes such values guided petitions in which peace was

More often, though, the primacy of peace in the protocol
of public values was expressed less explicitly and less precisely. Not many men ever had the obligation or the occasion of an election sermon to stimulate such wide-ranging
examination or schematic formulation of the hierarchy of
social virtues; most of them confined themselves instead to
the cut and thrust of immediate issues, and so their assertions were less abstract and sweeping. Peace would not be
declared the highest value in the culture but merely held
higher than any others in the issue immediately at hand.
Provincial law, as has already been pointed out, was quite
consistently subordinated to the necessities of local agreement,[33] and so too, on more than one occasion, were even
the most material considerations of a man's livelihood.
Ministers were particularly solicitous for the solidarity of
their congregations. Some, such as the Reverend Green-
wood of Rehoboth, seemed moved by little else. Green-
wood had served as the town's minister for thirty-six years
when, in 1757, he was asked to resign his pastoral charge
due to "bodily infirmity." He was under no compulsion to
do so—indeed, he had certain contractual claims upon the
town, including a claim to his annual salary, which he
could have maintained at law—and he could have had no
ulterior advantage in relinquishing those claims. Nonetheless, he did relinquish them, "for peace's sake, and that the
gospel might not be hindered." [34]

If few assertions of the primacy of peace were as pointed
as Mayhew's, many of them were even more sweeping than

never mentioned at all—ibid. 49, pp. 380–3; ibid. 115, p. 410; ibid. 116, pp.
644–5; ibid., pp. 702–5; ibid., pp. 736–8. Perhaps the most dramatic declaration of this sort was the contention of a (Connecticut) Separatist in the
Great Awakening that "the real question is, is it right or wrong? If it is
wrong according to the Word of God, it ought to be rejected, 'let the consequence be what it will.'" Goen: *Revivalism*, pp. 135–6. But such an insistence that peace and order were only pragmatic considerations, subordinate if necessary to righteousness in God's word, was well-nigh unique
in the towns of provincial Massachusetts.

his for being less schematic. For Mayhew the formulation
was explicit: peace was primary. For others the formulation was implicit: peace was a premise. "Union is the
source of public happiness," Mayhew proclaimed; "unity
must subside and then it's plain what will follow," the selectmen of Worcester announced, describing the consequences of a Court failure to follow their recommendations. The description was without a single detail, because
what would follow was so "plain" that the spokesmen of
the town felt no need for further specification. Unity was
so much the *sine qua non* of successful town operation that
no explanation was necessary, and the lack of any such necessity was explicit testimony to the implicit fundamental-
ity of peace and unity in public values.[35]

Similarly a Springfield petition spoke of "the absolute
necessity they were under of receding from that spirit of
contention and discord." The petition cited the earlier recommendation of a town committee that it was "absolutely
necessary for the peace and happiness of the whole" that a
division be sought to separate the contending elements "as
the only expedient to restore peace or to prevent the
various increasing mischiefs of discord and contention
among them"; and in endorsing that advice, the petitioners
explained that such division was indeed "absolutely necessary for the peace and happiness" of the town. Enveloping
those various "absolute necessities" were seven pages of argument. There was a narrative account of the town and its
recent difficulties, there was a description of the tactics attempted to resolve those difficulties, and there were reasons
offered for the appeals then made. Seven pages were required because all of those points had to be argued. The
"necessities," on the other hand, had merely to be mentioned. It was *assumed* that peace was intrinsically valuable; it was axiomatic that, in case of contention, restoration of the peace was essential.[36]

Contention was discountenanced as strongly as peace

was enjoined in the eighteenth century, being almost invariably characterized by the townsmen as "unhappy."
"Our long unhappy differences" were lamented in Framingham; Weston feared that if some of the town were set
off it would "lay an unhappy foundation for strife"; and
many other towns and the General Court expressed an assortment of similar sentiments.[37] Indeed, the condemnation
of conflict was quite capable of standing alone, as it did in a
Rutland memorial which simply stated that a proposed incorporation of a corner of the town would "bring the remaining part of said town into a division and so into a contention as to the place where the meetinghouse shall
stand." No elaboration of the objection was offered, and
none was deemed necessary. Similarly, citizens of Concord
who warned against the annexation of a community with
"different sentiments subsisting among us with respect to
religious concerns" went no further in explaining their opposition than to declare that "strife and contention will
unavoidably ensue." And these were no extraordinary arguments, for the General Court itself acknowledged the
self-evidence of the danger of differences.[38]

Moreover, men were willing to accept a number of
other undesirable consummations rather than risk disharmony in the community. In the plantations of New Braintree and the west wing of Rutland such men preferred to
forego the material advantages of formal town status in
order to avoid the greater disadvantage that such a town
would incorporate "different opinions" and "greatly tend
to breed confusion and discord."[39] In Dunstable a council
approved the dismissal of a minister because of "the unhappy prospect before him" in a parish broken by "unhappy contentions." And in Rehoboth a minister was
driven from the community, though there were no legal
grounds for his dismissal and though a council recommended that he remain, because, as the committee put it,
"there appeared an unhappy alienation of affection in his

people to him and incurable, which was the true cause of
our advising to his separation." [40]

The organized embodiment of conflict was the party or
faction, and the strictures against such schism were strong
on every side. "Contention and party spirit" were denounced in the pulpit thunderings of the Calvinist Jonathan Edwards as "iniquity" which left men's souls "desti-
tute," and equally in the election sermon of the rationalist
Jonathan Mayhew, who insisted that a true public spirit
"would never produce 'parties and contentions,' for factions arose only from 'the pursuit of separate, distinct interests, and a want of public spirit.' " [41] Identical sentiments reverberated in villages throughout the province.
Townsmen everywhere sought identification solely with
the entire community; anything less was faction, and the
brand of faction was the brand of infamy. To speak the
expression "party" was to utter an epithet, as in a contested
election in Haverhill where depositions were sworn to discredit an opponent simply by declaring him "a party
man." * [42]

When contentions did erupt, communities undertook
to end them as speedily as possible, acting "in order to prevent those difficulties for the future and cultivate a good
understanding and harmony amongst ourselves." [43] And
once a dispute was brought to an end, that was to be truly
the conclusion of the matter. Not only religious but also
civil sanctions stood against its renewal. In Fitchburg a
contest over a meetinghouse pew was resolved in the local
assembly and "both partys . . . Each of them agred and
actualy sined the towns Vote both of them never to make

* In fact, a number of petitions were attacked as contentious when contentiousness had nothing visibly to do with the issues involved. Such resort
to incantation and irrelevance was very revealing of social values, since
only values which are very central to the culture can be dragged in on
almost any occasion to damage almost anything distressing or undesirable
to those invoking them. See Mass. Arch. 49, pp. 361–2; ibid. 50, pp. 30–1;
ibid. 115, pp. 626–7; ibid. 116, 91–4; ibid., pp. 256–7.

aney un Easiness further about s^d pue if the money be paid by s^d scott in one Weke from this Day." In other towns it was common procedure to enter private agreements on the public record, to signal the resolution of a conflict and prevent its recurrence.[44]

Pursuit of private ends never was approved in provincial Massachusetts. Subordination of the individual to the group began with the very first Puritans, and it remained constant to the very eve of the Revolution. Assertion of the self against the community was considered conducive to contention; selfish interests were assumed to be opposed to the public interest, and the public interest was primary. The values of the settling generation—transplanted Englishmen adapting English customs and preserving English values from an England rather more medieval than modern—persisted through the succeeding century and a half in Massachusetts. While Enlightened intimations of individualism appeared in Philadelphia and Virginia, not even the New England rationalists could embrace that aspect of the Age of Reason. For a man such as Jonathan Mayhew, the "public good" still took precedence over any prerogatives of individual interest.

> Partisans, he explained, "have always something else in view than, what they would be tho't to have, the public good," and "at the bottom" of their every venture may be found "private pique, or private interest; or a general temper and turn to wrangling." A public spirit, Mayhew propounded, embodies a spirit of liberty, but it is, far more importantly, "a spirit of union . . ."[45]

If even the rationalists could not condone self-seeking, then of course the far greater numbers in the province who clung to more traditional values could hardly be expected to abandon their old antipathy to combinations or interest groups within the community. To the very end of the provincial period most men of Massachusetts saw such groups solely in terms of "sinister ends and a selfish temper," [46] and more than once the indictment came so easily to mind that it lost all but its most elemental meaning. In such cases *both* parties to a controversy contrasted their own devotion to the general weal with their opponents' presumed private purposes, and *both* bent to denying the other side's accusation that mere malice and selfishness motivated their own position. In these disputes the contending parties agreed on almost nothing except what was most important: the public good of the town as their accepted standard of judgment.[47]

The priority of public welfare to private interest was asserted equally in distant parishes and in the capitals of culture, on ceremonial occasions and in daily decisions. In Springfield men were told that they might be forced to continue in the town against their will if it should "appear best for the whole." In Ipswich a man who was absent too often from public worship actually had his farm sold by the selectmen, "so that he may be compelled to live nearer the sanctuary." In Dorchester parents were compelled by the town to give up two of their children because of insufficient "outward estate." And in Stockbridge it was found "inconsistent with the rules of the Word of God" for an eligible widow of the town to wed a recently arrived schoolteacher who had offended some of the townsfolk.[48]

If motherly love and marital desire could be set aside when they came in conflict with considerations of community, there was no question that public interests had precedence over private ones in the political sphere. A petition which spoke solely for its author while purporting to address a public issue could be discredited on just that account, and even the men who were authorized to speak for their communities spoke a particular language, the language of the undivided community and the suppression of internal differences. Thus when the town of Brookfield

met one morning in 1750 there was "a considerable debate" before its citizens voted to reject the request of some
townsmen to set off as a separate district or town; but by
that afternoon, when the town drafted its memorial to the
General Court, no slightest trace of the debate remained, or
at least none appeared in that petition. By then it simply
"was and is the sense of the town in general" that granting
the petition would be "greatly detrimental to the town in
general." [49]

Prerogatives of personality would not always be set so
starkly subordinate to the requirements of society. In the
new world of the nineteenth century, Americans would
begin to dedicate themselves to the liberation as well as the
suppression of individual difference. Seeing dimly that self-
serving might be harnessed to the service of society, they
would move to legitimize competition in the political
arena, the marketplace, and the marketplace of ideas, trust-
ing to the will of the people, the law of supply and demand, and the ineluctable power of truth to impose benefi-
cent order. But order was obtained otherwise in provincial
Massachusetts, and accordingly the world of the eighteenth-
century towns was a starkly different world than the one of,
say, Ralph Waldo Emerson. The men and women who inhabited that world were different too. They located themselves differently in history. They lived by different values
of public life. And they taught their children that location
and those values, so that their children would one day sustain the system as well. Children who grew up in provincial
Massachusetts grew up in a society which insisted on concord and consensus; as they grew they became, subtly, almost irresistibly, people who could live in such a society.

   In this, of course, there was nothing singular. Every society attempts to impress its values upon the young, so that
they may assume the postures and positions of their parents

and perpetuate the social order that seems only right and decent to all around them. But for that very reason the education of children is an extremely useful index to the values of the society of adults. Such values must be transmitted in terms so simple that even a child can understand them, and so they stand out even more plainly, quite often, than the attitudes and assumptions of the elders in addressing each other.

Yet they do not stand out as starkly as they might, for in eighteenth-century Massachusetts there was no clear distinction between child and adult. Portraits of Puritan children show only scaled-down adults, not children as the romantic nineteenth century would have recognized them. Age is evident in the wigs on their heads, in the "premature sadness" of their faces, and in the very clothes that they wore, the same clothes that their parents wore, simply smaller. If clothes do not make the man, they do mark social differentiations; a distinctive mode of dress for children never developed before the Revolution. As Monica Kiefer explained, since children "were expected to behave like adults, they quite logically wore clothes appropriate for the role." [50]

The limners of provincial Massachusetts painted as they saw, and they saw as their society saw. Which is to say that they scarcely saw the child at all. Indeed, by subsequent standards, there were no children in eighteenth-century New England. The culture had no conception of the child as a being with distinctive needs and desires, and it accorded the child no distinctive places or roles. Massachusetts children two centuries ago did not live separated from the society in a protected preserve of carefree innocence; they were part of a single undifferentiated community. Even very small boys and girls were brought to church services and compelled to stay there for the duration, well before they were capable of comprehension or proper conduct. And on the child's small shoulders rested

the same momentous responsibility for his own everlasting
fate which his parents assumed for theirs. "Wilt thou tarry
any longer, my dear Child," asked one book for the young,
"before thou run into thy Chamber, and beg of God to
give thee a Christ for thy Soul, that thou mayest not be
undone forever?" Massachusetts children appeared in their
portraits as, to their elders and so to themselves, they appeared in life: responsible people wrestling with the de-
fects of their nature.[51]

Original sin was the heart of the matter, because it was
believed to be "bound up in the heart of a child." "You are
all of you naturally the children of God's wrath," Jonathan
Edwards denounced the children of Northampton in a sermon to them in 1740. "If you are not converted, God is
angry with you every day; if you should die in the condition you are now in, you would surely go to hell." Others
were less stern than Edwards, but few went further than
the well-known lines of Wigglesworth's *Day of Doom*, written in 1662 but reproduced in New England primers
through the eighteenth century, which merely reserved to
children "the easiest room in hell." [52] Thus if the "natural" child was "a poor, wicked, miserable, hateful creature," [53] indulgence was absurd. No provincial parent
could reasonably envision childhood as a privileged preserve, an interlude of irresponsibility and innocence, for
children who were obviously not innocent, who were, in
fact, innately depraved. It was contrary to common sense to
trust any impulsions from within, or to authorize their expression. Socialization in New England, in the family, in
religious training, and in education, was a preparation for
sainthood and citizenship by a suppression of the "natural"
child.

The premise of Puritan education was precisely this
conviction of corruption and the consequent necessity to
pour in good things from without. As Edmund Morgan
wrote of the colonial era, there was "no question of devel-

oping the child's personality, of drawing out or nourishing any desirable inherent qualities which he might possess, for no child could by nature possess any desirable qualities." [54] Since any impulse of the child was certain to be sinful, little else was often required of a teacher than a strong right arm; and even if not all teachers relied so crudely on might to make right,[55] the distrust of inner urges was endemic in the education of provincial Massachusetts.

The pre-eminent function of education, whether in religion or the three R's, was restraint: direct restraint in the case of discipline, indirect restraint in the case of instruction. The former was clear to all concerned. Samuel Willard explained the latter in a sermon from which one of his listeners took these notes:

> 1. they are all born in Ignorance rom. 3.17. Without the knowledge and fear of god they must have it by doctrine and institution 2[ly] this ignorance layeth them open to satan to lead them wither he will. 3[ly] holdeth them under the Power [and] efficacy of sin a blind mind and dead conscience are companions. hence they sin without shame ignorance stopps the activity of all the faculties. 4[ly] as long as they remain in their naturall ignorance there is no hope of being freed from everlasting misery. if you have any Compassion for them take Pains that they may know god. 5[ly] Hardness of heart allienation from god Springs from ignorance and 6[ly] they hence are inclined to fulfill their owne evill will.

In Willard's conclusion was the beginning of it all: the child's sinning was due to his "evill will" and the inclination to fulfill it. Education had to be bent to overcoming that will. Or, put more precisely, ignorance was not the cause of evil action—evil nature was—but ignorance did prevent *restraint* of evil action. Instruction was aimed at the elimination of this hindrance to restraint.[56]

From the early days of the colony, instruction had been heavily inclined to the inculcation of obedience "in point of good manners, and dutiful behavior towards all," but even in its other academic aspects Massachusetts education served to suppress self-expression and promote uniformity. The intimate connection of instruction to discipline was explicit in the injunction of the *New England Primer* to the child about to enter upon spelling—"Let him learn these and such like sentences by Heart, whereby he will be both instructed in his Duty, and encouraged in his Learning"—and it was also apparent in other subjects. Reading and arithmetic were taught through techniques of rote memorization, and all education in provincial Massachusetts was subtly shaped by the pervasive influence of the catechism.[57]

The catechism was a summary, cast in the form of questions and answers, of orthodox beliefs. As such, it was the conventional method of religious instruction in most branches of Christianity at the time, but the men of Massachusetts did not cling to it on that account alone. They had, after all, cast off other Christian conventions. Rather, they retained it because it was congenial to them; as Edmund Morgan maintained, "this method of instruction was well adapted to the purposes of Puritan education. It was not designed to give play to the development of individual initiative, because individual initiative in religion usually meant heresy." Children were introduced to the catechism "before they could possibly know the meaning of what they said," and thereafter it was used not only for religious instruction but also in reading and writing drills in school and in regular rehearsals with parents and pastors.[58] And even as a child came to learn the meaning of the words he repeated, he also came to understand that that meaning was fixed forever. The catechistic method assumed that there were "right" answers. The most the student could hope was to comprehend them; he could not amend them.

And many did not even comprehend them, for clergymen themselves admitted that the Shorter Catechism had never been "designed or fitted for Babes." In fact, the largest vol-. ume published in all New England prior to the nineteenth century, Willard's *Complete Body of Divinity*, was based upon the very same catechism the children studied. The Shorter Catechism was aimed at adults; children had to tag along, managing as well as they could.[59]

Children's books, with their effort to provide a seques- tered simplicity commensurate with a child's capacities, were an innovation which awaited the nineteenth century in Massachusetts. "Read no ballads and romances and fool- ish books" went the ordinary injunction before the Revo- lution. One student of the subject has concluded that no period in all American juvenile literature was "so bleak and uninspiring as the first seventy-five years of the eight- eenth century." Children were seen only as ignorant adults, and "nothing was written especially for the needs of the immature mind." Indeed, "the note of fear and repres- sion, which dominated every phase of Colonial childhood, is clearly apparent to the most casual reader of the litera- ture of the young." [60]

Certainly it is apparent in the *New England Primer*, the most widely read item in all that provincial litera- ture and one of the most celebrated schoolbooks in American history. In the *Primer* education was plainly placed in the service of securing uniformity and restraining the Puritan potential for the release of individual expres- sion. The book's center of gravity was the catechism, which no eighteenth-century printing was without; its presence was invariably proclaimed on the title page itself. The sec- ond page was filled with quotations which set the tone of what was to follow: it was studded with injunctions and inducements to fear and obedience. Then came devices for the teaching of reading and spelling, including the rhymed alphabet with the immortal opening couplet, "In Adam's

Fall/We Sinned all." Then a series of precepts in various forms, under such titles as "The Dutiful Child Promises" and including such "Choice Sentences" as "Praying will make thee leave sinning, or sinning will make thee leave praying." Then the names of the books of the Bible, and then the numbers up to one hundred ("for the ready finding of any Chapter, Psalm, and Verse in the Bible"). Then the story of the burning of John Rogers, his wife, and nine small children at the stake, and finally, the Shorter Catechism. Nowhere in all this was any concession made to the child simply for the child's pleasure, never did the *Primer* cater to what the child might enjoy. The only "story" in the *Primer* was the martyrdom of John Rogers, an exceedingly earnest tale even by the standards of the *Primer.* For the standards were adult standards, and what went into the *Primer* was determined entirely by an adult judgment of suitability.[61]

Accordingly, almost no allowance at all was made for childhood. Damnation, death, and depravity—the facts of Puritan life—were impressed upon the youth of New England from such an early age that there developed an entire genre of Puritan literature, the narratives of "precocious conversions." In the *Primer,* death was flaunted before young readers repeatedly, and more than merely as an inescapable eventuality. The *Primer* insisted on death as a very present danger even to children, and consequently it urged them to direct their youthful energies into an appropriate preparation for it. One of the "Verses" was typical:

> I in the Burying Place may see
> > Graves shorter there than I;
> From Death's Arrest no Age is free,
> > Young Children too may die;
> My God, may such an awful Sight,
> > Awakening be to me!

Oh! that by early Grace I might
For Death prepared be.[62]

In the *Primer* a young lad was "constantly impressed
with the fact" that he "was born not to live but to dy," and
that his time and talents were to be focused on the proper
fulfillment of this eternal end. In such popular works as
Janeway's *Token for Children* those were still stronger
preoccupations; typical of its exemplary youth was one
New Engand lass of five who fell sick of consumption and
"would not by any sports be diverted from the Tho'ts of
Death, wherein she took such Pleasure, that she did not
care to hear of any Thing else." [63] And the exposure of children to their own mortality went beyond the literature. It
was in their universal presence at funerals, in the sermons
addressed to them, and in the common conversation of a
family such as Samuel Sewall's. "Sabbath, Jan. 12," one of
the judge's diary entries was dated. "Richard Dummer, a
flourishing youth of 9 years old, dies of Small Pocks. I tell
Sam. [his young son] of it and what need he had to prepare
for Death. . . ." [64]

Depravity too was something which was held before
children constantly.[65] And from death and depravity, the
prospect of damnation followed easily enough, yet no
chances were taken that children might miss the logical development. As Janeway's preface promised, bad children
would "go to their Father the Devil, into everlasting burning; . . . and when they beg and pray in Hell Fire, God
will not forgive them; but there they must lie forever." [66]
The same promise of an infernal future was also made by
proper Puritan parents in the home. A revealing entry in
Sewall's diary recorded the terror of his little daughter
Betty, who "burst into tears," one winter day in 1696
"when she came to fear that she 'was like Spira, not
Elected.' " Edmund Morgan found the significance of the

episode in the fact that her father wept too. "The above descriptions were not fairy stories with which to frighten little children; to the Puritans they were unpleasant but inescapable facts, and the sooner children became aware of them the better." [67] But actually the significance of the story may be carried a bit further. Mortality, original sin, and damnation may have been "unpleasant and inescapable facts" of Puritan life, but facts do not dictate the attitude men adopt toward them or the use men make of them. New Englanders of the provincial period unblinkingly informed their children of unpleasant facts of life because they thought of their children as little adults. They never established separate standards of awareness for children because they were only able to conceive of a single standard for the whole community.

Accordingly, there was a constant condition of earnestness enjoined upon children. One of the girls approvingly offered for emulation by Janeway spent days and nights in tears and prayers, "desiring with all her Soul to escape from everlasting Flame." Another model child was said to be in "Horror," "Anguish," and "trouble of his Spirit," and those were extolled as exemplary states of mind for the young; and indeed all of New England's children were described as "remarkably grave, devout, and serious." [68] There was no age necessarily too young to impose such weights of responsibility and induced intensity, either. Janeway offered one boy who was "admirably affected with the Things of GOD, when he was between two and three Years old," and a girl who was fearful for her "corrupt Nature" before she left the cradle. The adult attitude toward youthful frivolity was epitomized in the common parental injunction to children to "let thy Recreation be Lawful, Brief, and Seldom." [69]

Not every child was as compliant as a Janeway model, of course, but for the disobedient the culture quite approved whatever discipline was necessary to secure their submission. The child's will was to be broken if he would not surrender it of his own accord, and an early start in that affair was essential since "will" was defined as "any defiance of the parents' wishes, at any age." None of the medical advice available to New England parents before the second half of the eighteenth century advocated permissiveness in aggression-training, and the "note of fear and repression" was "clearly apparent" in juvenile literature. The model schoolgirl was "eminent for her Diligence, Teachableness, Meekness, and Modesty, speaking little"; and in still more important situations, not merely "speaking little" but "silence" was extolled. In the *New England Primer* almost all of "The Dutiful Child's Promises"—

> I Will fear GOD, and honour the KING.
> I will honour my Father & Mother.
> I will Obey my Superiours.
> I will Submit to my Elders.
> I will Love my Friends.
> I will hate no man.
> I will forgive my Enemies, and pray to God for them.

—were injunctions to fear, obedience, submission, and control of enmity. They were, in other words, injunctions to community harmony by the control of aggressive and any other self-expressive impulses.[70]

Socialization did not cease when a child came to a degree of competence. Such competence came early to the youngsters of provincial Massachusetts—Ben Franklin was sent to work at the age of ten, and he was the pampered scholar of his father's brood—but in no way did it exempt them from the exaction of obedience. Apprenticeship, into which most of them went, was a relationship of servitude, and the Puritans were quite clear on the obligations of servants.[71]

Law and religion alike, to say nothing of the neighbors, ordained obedience for the servant or apprentice. A standard apprenticeship contract called for a term of seven years, "During all which term, the said Apprentice his said Master faithfully shall serve, his secrets keep, his lawful commandments everywhere obey." Religion similarly supported, by divine sanction, an almost limitless obedience of servants, and the courts too provided for the fulfillment of servile obligation, affirming the master's right to chastise his servants if it was necessary to secure their obedience and respect. Even the complementary responsibilities laid upon masters served only to add a further dimension of authoritarianism to their relations with such subordinates. "God, according to the Puritans, gave masters authority in order that they might use it 'in furthering their Servants in a blameless behavior; and in restraining them from sin.'" [72] Inevitably that injunction meant that the servant was caught coming and going. His obligations to his master and his master's obligations to him amounted to one and the same thing: a demand for self-abasement rather than self-assertion.

Indeed, such discipline may well have been the very essence of apprenticeship, since apprenticeship was not only an economic and educational necessity in provincial Massachusetts, as it was across much of early modern Europe, but also a part of a larger system for which there was no such necessity. Children of the Bay settlement were put out not only to master craftsmen, as was common in many Western societies, but also to schoolmasters or even, in the case of girls, to other mothers, to learn housekeeping. Moreover, and still more revealing, boys were often put out to learn nothing at all, simply being sent for "long visits in the homes of friends, and not always at their own desire." The reason that has been suggested for these removals is that the children were actually put out to learn good behavior, on the assumption that "a child learned better manners when he was brought up in another home than his own"; and Morgan has speculated that control could thereby be continued at an otherwise difficult age, since any potential for renewed self-assertion by the young man could be curbed, in his new milieu, "by someone who would not forgive him any mischief out of affection for his person." [73] But whether or not the removal to another family placed youths in a psychologically more auspicious setting for the application of strict discipline, it certainly placed them in social roles— servant or student—guided by norms of obedience, where sharp correction was the standard penalty for any expression of their own will.

The final phase of the socialization cycle occurred when young men and women established their own families and thus became agents of education for the next generation. That phase too, until its very consummation, was subject to canons of control that were considerably more rationalized, more consistently formal, and more public than those of old England.[74] Indeed, the Puritans attempted to contain the attractions of love much as they sought to govern that other potentially passionate disruption of the social peace, the conversion experience. The choice of a marriage partner was not notably unfree in Massachusetts, any more than men were to be coerced to Christ; but for matrimony no less than for regeneration, the emotions which were aroused had then to be harnessed to a rigid and formal pattern proceeding through specified stages which were to be passed one at a time in the prescribed order. In the words of William Weeden,

the whole business of matrimony was conducted by an economic and practical method of procedure, the forms of which were well prescribed and understood. When people married in those days, they went to the business in regular and methodical fashion. Sentiment might and generally did stimulate the proceedings, but it must enter formally and move according to the will of parent or guardian. The pattern of lovemaking was as rigid as that of their ruffs and collars.[75]

❦ III ❧

The Practice of Peace

THE PRECEPTS OF PEACE were preached endlessly, to old and young alike, in provincial Massachusetts, and they were preached because it was so essential that they be practiced. In other communities and cultures law and order could be conserved by custom or, in the failure of such traditional regulation, by recourse to institutional coercion. In the towns of Massachusetts peace was a preoccupation for the strikingly simple reason that there were no other adequate agencies of enforcement. Without an inner acceptance of the canons of concord by the villagers there could scarcely have been concord at all, since there was no external agency powerful enough to compel compliance. There was, for all practical purposes, only the constable.

The constable represented the formal police power of the town. He was elected annually by his fellow townsmen, and there was not another gift in their power which was less wanted. "Town meeting to choose constables and other officers, the office of constable I narrowly escaped," was the way one Braintree diarist expressed the common sentiment at the beginning of the provincial period, while another, near its end, was "very wroth" about his election as surveyor until he learned that his friends had nominated him to that office so as to spare him a stint as constable, and then he was pacified easily.[1] At other times and in places other than Braintree, the same evasion of the office was the norm.

Plymouth, for instance, chose from one to five constables a year—three in most years—and in only six of the fifty-five years before the Revolution did the initially elected slate of constables serve intact. In twenty-six years at least one (and as many as ten) refused to serve, and in thirty-four years at least one (and as many as four) had to be hired. Altogether eighty refused to serve and fifty-two substitutes were hired, so that in an average year's slate two of the three original choices did not serve.[2] And the plight of Plymouth, though a bit unusual, was anything but unique.*

Refusal to serve required payment of a fine, and the hiring of a substitute too took money, so those who did eventually assume office were generally men who could not afford to avoid it. In Amherst, not a single one of the twenty-five men who served as selectmen of the district from its incorporation to the Revolution were ever chosen constable after they first held the high office. In Braintree only fourteen of the eighty-four selectmen of the first three quarters of the eighteenth century were ever elected constables after their first term as selectmen, and only five of those fourteen ever actually served in the post. In Weston, from its founding in 1754 until the Revolution, only eight of the thirty-six selectmen were ever elected constable thereafter, and six of them hired substitutes. And in towns all across the province there was the same consignment of the constabulary to the lower orders.[3]

The result was that the province had a formal legal system without an autonomous instrument for its own en-

---

* Braintree had every bit as much trouble as Plymouth, and even in towns more typical there was difficulty. In Brookline the original choice served in only thirty-one of the town's seventy years before Independence, while constables had to be hired in twenty-three years and in twenty-seven years at least one and as many as four declined to serve. In Worcester there was at least one evasion of the office in twenty-one of the forty-four years before a collector was added to the constables. *Records of Braintree, Brookline Records,* "Records of Worcester." See also, e.g., Mass. Arch. 116, p. 752; George Chase: *The History of Haverhill* (Haverhill, Mass., 1861), p. 325.

forcement. Constables simply did not have the personal authority to oppose the town if the town opposed the law. They were powerful only insofar as they did what the community wished; they could command compliance only when almost everyone was prepared to give it anyway and so would assist them against any who proved recalcitrant. If most men were not prepared to yield such compliance, the constables could not often compel it. Instead, they stood silently by while public orators openly applauded abrogation of the law, they refused to make unpopular arrests, and they were impotent against the mobs which carried many a day even before the days of the Revolutionary crisis, if indeed they were not a part of such mobs themselves. For open violation of the law was as easily contemplated by communities in their corporate capacity as by a mob itself; and William Weeden caught the character of the New England town's regard for the law quite accurately when he concluded that "loyalty in such a community meant obedience to the law, so long as it did not interfere with their cherished privileges, and those privileges, whether open or secret, were respectable." Against such a conception of propriety, a constable was powerless. Effective law in the provincial community was, ultimately, only what each particular place wished to abide by.* [4]

* A spectacular example of the impotence of the ordinary machinery of enforcement against a determined minority occurred in Easton, where religious dissidents decided to establish themselves in their own meetinghouse in 1751. The orthodox majority opposed them and threatened to tear such a building down, but the pastor of the new church party challenged the townsmen confidently:

> Let them come into my field [the site of the meetinghouse], I will breake theare Heads; when it was answered to Him that the General Cort's Committey might Command Assistance, and he would not be abel to do it, and His reply was this: I do not fear it, I can have anofe to assist me in that afare; Let them Come in to my field if they Dare, I will split theaire braines out.

The pastor's bellicosity was never tested, but the townsmen apparently believed in it. They made immediate attempts at reconciliation, and when

Of course, constables were not entirely powerless nor lacking in capacity for coercive enforcement. When they acted for the community rather than against it, or even when they moved against a few rather than an entire faction, they had sanctions of significance at their disposal, as was explicit in applications for town incorporation for the stated purpose of acquiring such power,[5] and as was implicit in appeals from standing towns for the recovery of that power after they had fallen afoul of the law.[6] Constables could, in principle, imprison a man and levy distress upon his property, and they were also able to employ a number of less drastic penalties. "Before the Revolution," for example, "it was the law and custom to have stocks placed near the meeting-house to deter the disturbers of the peace on the Sabbath, and other public days." [7]

But these powers, and others, were held in abeyance more often than not. In principle, compliance with the law could, perhaps, have been compelled; in practice, towns and the province itself preferred not to do so. In a situation where the agents of enforcement were personally unimpressive and therefore dependent on community support, enforcement was—and was seen to be—inefficient without concord in the community, and efficiency was sought in terms of social harmony rather than, say, the assertion of authority or individual initiative. For what were often quite clearly reasons of reluctance more than of incapacity the province frequently declined to exercise its own prerogatives; and in the towns too the techniques of enforcement were available yet seldom employed. There was indeed a stock in Rutland, but as one old inhabitant recalled, "I

those failed the pastor and his flock split off unchallenged the following year. Goen: *Revivalism*, p. 96. And while few towns confronted such a fearsome opposition, many found themselves equally unable to coerce a coherent minority bent on its own course of action; see, e.g., Mass. Arch. 115, pp. 390–1, 393–6; ibid., pp. 872–5; ibid. 116, pp. 205–6; ibid., pp. 694–6; ibid., pp. 749–50; ibid. 117, pp. 317–18; ibid. 118, pp. 798–801; Francis: *Watertown*, p. 88.

never knew anyone to suffer its punishment." [8] Similarly, communities commonly refused to initiate legal proceedings against inhabitants guilty of infractions, and indeed they never did depend very heavily upon the courts in the decades before the Declaration. Judicial compulsion was always available but not so often availed of, because enforcement in the absence of public agreement was expensive in time, money, and further strains upon the cohesion of the community. The men of Massachusetts had an aversion to lawsuits; they wished to conduct their communities so as to avoid "differences . . . which obstructed a desirable concurrence and unanimity of the inhabitants therein." For the sanctions of the law were no solution to dissension. As more than one town found, "our union being dissolved, our strength was broken." [9]

Contention in the law was costly.* As any number of towns seeking to substitute a "peaceful concurrence" for "vexatious and expensive suits" made clear, harmony was valued on economic as much as on ethical grounds.[10] Consideration of a dilemma such as the one described by some Nantucketers in 1757 is essential, in this regard, to an understanding of the conditions of community in provincial Massachusetts. Nantucket had been managed as a "propriety in common" for more than sixty years, and in that time the islanders had been "very peaceable among themselves." In the months immediately preceding the propriety's petition, however, "sundry persons [had] endeavored to interrupt the peace of the propriety and to throw them into confusion and disorder and if possible to bring them into vexatious and endless lawsuits, which the propriety apprehend they ought not be troubled with." What those "sundry persons" had done was to ignore the limitations of the propriety on the size of each man's herd, releasing their livestock to run loose upon the island, all without a shadow

* See Appendix II for the sole specific account of the costs of litigation in the entire town series of the Massachusetts Archives.

of legal right. The proprietors, for all their moral reservations about the resort to litigation, might still have proceeded to prosecution had prosecution promised an effective solution—but it did not. Moreover, the offenders knew it did not. They had deliberately turned their stock loose not on individual claims but

> upon said propriety at large, without regard to their regulations, with a design that the general propriety should impound them, and so by that means instead of ejecting the particular persons out of the particular share or right they claim in, would put said propriety to the charge and trouble of lawsuits as a propriety to try every man's pretended claim, or else have the said propriety so overstocked that it will be soon ruined and destroyed even by some that have not so much as a colorable right in said propriety. And if they are allowed to go on so, it will end in the destruction of the propriety one way or the other.

The dilemma was cruel but clear. The community would be "ruined and destroyed" by overstocking if the offenders were not coerced, but coercion by lawsuit, even with the propriety's legal position assured, was such "charge and trouble" as to be no less disastrous than a default of coercion. "The destruction of the propriety one way or the other" was the impending outcome, and an important part of the Nantucketers' response was nothing more than a wistful retreat into nostalgic recollection of the previous sixty years of peace.[11]

Peace was precious to the Nantucketers because, even though they had the law on their side, they could not afford to employ it; in many other towns peace was precious because the public course of action was *not* within the law. Such towns proceeded by local precedent rather than the letter of the law. They encountered no difficulty in obtaining compliance by consent as long as there was harmony among the inhabitants, but on just that account they were hesitant to risk judicial coercion when "diverse disputes" threatened. As townsmen of Blanford once explained, "they are unable to collect the residue of said assessments otherwise than by distress, which they conceive they have no authority by law to make." Similar scruples reduced other towns to the same straits, and in all such cases it was evident that the complaints which threatened collection derived less from any abstract regard for the law itself than from a disturbance of local harmony which left men suddenly willing to take advantage of infractions they had ignored for years, sometimes decades, before.[12]

Accordingly, towns attempted quite openly to avoid appearances before the judiciary whenever possible. Committees were often appointed to settle disputes "in order to prevent his Suing the Town," [13] and provincial policy itself abetted such efforts with the enactment in 1734 of "A bill preventing 'unnecessary' lawsuits" and with particular court judgments which revealed the very same purpose.[14] Religious values also discountenanced contention in the courts. The churches themselves opposed lawsuits among members and, much as the towns did, offered their own mediation or arbitration instead; and even the Separatists shared the belief that "Christians ought not to go to law with one another, "but all their differences and difficulties ought to be decided by the brethren.' " [15]

Of course Christians did occasionally go to law with one another despite such expressions and endeavors, but the relatively low level of litigation can perhaps best be suggested by the underdeveloped state of the legal profession in the province. By the eighteenth century most of the original disabilities placed upon lawyers in the colony's first decades had been removed, and yet Emory Washburn estimated that as late as 1768 there were still only twenty-five barristers in the entire province; and at that, ten of them were in Boston alone, and the whole number, small as it was, was double the figure of twenty years before. Similarly suggestive was the paucity of legal publication. Not a single treatise for professional lawyers was published in the province before 1775, and, more significantly, neither were more than a handful of legal treatises intended for laymen. In all the American colonies there were forty-seven such volumes for laymen published between 1693 and 1775, but New England, a publishing center in most other respects, contributed only eight of them, with not even a single Blackstone in the bunch. The practice of law, then, was simply not seen as a suitable social role for a man in Massachusetts. Most provincial towns probably never counted a trained lawyer among their inhabitants, and most could have claimed with a historian of Wenham that their citizens "have always been of a peaceful character, and lawsuits have been seldom known among them."* [16]

Since communities thus required informal accord for their convenient governance, a paradox would seem to be all too apparent: the town was the locus of effective authority, yet the town hardly had such authority. The maintenance of law and order in the province depended on the localities, yet the localities had only the constables and the courts for the preservation of the peace; and the constables could command little more than the townsmen were prepared to obey, while the townsmen's own disinclination to contend in the courts made them loath to use the slender measure

* Of course, litigation did not wait solely upon trained lawyers. Men could and did plead their own cases, and according to the widely quoted observation of Dr. Douglass in 1746, "a very ordinary countryman in New England [was] almost qualified for a country attorney in England." Quoted in Washburn: *Judicial History*, p. 191; see also, e.g., Joseph H. Smith: *Colonial Justice in Western Massachusetts (1639–1702)* (Cambridge, 1961), pp. 173, 183. But Douglass offered only one man's opinion, and isolated impressions can always be set against isolated impressions; for a far better qualified observation of the same year which claimed almost exactly the opposite, see *Journals of the House*, XXIII, p. x.

of coercive judicial power that they did possess. And coercion could hardly have dissolved the dilemma in any case, since the weakness of the constabulary and the courts was only the institutional dimension of the difficulty of enforcement. Beyond the social space defined by the towns themselves, there was always the simple fact of geographical space. In the towns of provincial Massachusetts the disgruntled could always pick up and leave.

The resolution of the dilemma rested in the very cultural patterns which gave rise to it: they reduced its urgency and informed the essential instrument of its solution. The same values which made men reluctant to resort to coercion made the maintenance of authority less difficult: men sought peace, and so they saw the compulsion of the law as inefficient and undesirable. Authority itself was inevitably less problematic among a people disciplined from childhood against dissent and diversity, among citizens who found their historical identity in social solidarity, among men whose public values proclaimed peaceful communion. For such men coercion could not easily be justified, but neither could the conflicts which would have made it necessary.

Accordingly, authority found another form in provincial Massachusetts, and its instrument was the town meeting. The town meeting was more than a mere forum: it was the essential element in the delicate equipoise of peace and propriety which governed the New England town. In the absence of any satisfactory means of traditional or institutional coercion, the recalcitrant could not be compelled to adhere to the common course of action. Therefore the common course of action had to be so shaped as to leave none recalcitrant, and that was the vital function of the New England town meeting. The town meeting solved the problem of enforcement by evading it. Such convocations of the community gave institutional expression to the imperatives of peace; in them consensus was reached, and individual consent and group opinion were placed in the service of social conformity. There the men of the province established their agreements on policies and places, and there they legitimized those agreements, so that subsequent deviation became socially illegitimate and personally immoral as well, meaning as it did the violation of a covenant or the breaking of a promise. In the town meetings men talked of politics, but ultimately they sought to establish moral community.

Choice and necessity coincided almost completely in that effort. Every significant source of public values inculcated exactly what an inadequate engine of enforcement would have required in any case. Government in the little rural communities which were provincial Massachusetts depended upon the maintenance of the public peace through the consent of the governed, and in the eighteenth century such consent meant something less than modern democracy. For government by consent—by reliance upon public opinion—imposes few specific forms; it can comprehend the populism of the mob and the populism of an orderly majoritarian procedure, the most fragmented political pluralism and the most monolithic single party, the political egalitarianism of one-man-one-vote and the economic equity of a stockholders' election. In all of these are techniques for commanding consent from public opinion, but in each of them are group pressures toward very different relations to authority and to others.

In the towns of provincial Massachusetts, government by consent meant something more—and less—than majoritarianism. Majoritarianism implies a minority, and the towns could no more condone a competing minority by their values than they could have constrained it by their police power. Effective action required a public opinion approaching if not attaining unanimity, and public policy was accordingly bent toward securing such unanimity.

That was the prime purpose of the town meeting and that was the essential thrust of its politics of consensus.

The model of this moral community was established at the very foundation of a town, in its civil and ecclesiastical covenants composed "by the whole consent of the plantation." The insistence on mutual consent was so strong that men were denied admission to the town if they "denied any particular in the said agreement," and such precautions produced a heartening homogeneity in the inhabitants. As Swansea explained the initiation of the process, "there was great care taken in the foundation settlement of this town how the ministry should be maintained in this town of Swanzey, by a mutual agreement made and . . . confirmed by all the proprietors of said town; to prevent all troubles discords arising for the future"; and as Swansea examined the operation of that agreement half a century later, the townsmen saw that it had been good. Coercion had never been needed; consent had sufficed, "by free contribution" rather than by compulsion.[17]

Thus consent defined the community at its inception, and thus the same insistence upon unanimity persisted far beyond the settling generation of the community. The original covenant itself was subject to revision, and the moral coercion of participation in an ordinary decision of the town meeting was as binding as the obligations of the covenant anyway. Consent was constant. It was no foundation settlement but simply the community's choice of a minister which Worcester used to rebuff an application of some Presbyterians for separation as "Contrary to their own Covenant with us." It was only an agreement on building a meetinghouse, "made, ratified, and confirmed, and entered on the town books," which the men of Framingham declared so "sacred, that it cannot be receded from without a reflection of dishonor both on religion and the government."[18] For such agreements were instruments of orthodoxy, and from the earliest years of the province to its very end there was a consistent current of affirmation that "harmony and unanimity" were what "they most heartily wish to enjoy in all their public concerns." [19]

Unanimity was, indeed, demanded almost as a matter of social decency, so that a simple majority commanded little authority at the local level and scarcely even certified decisions as legitimate. In communities which provided no regular place for minorities, a mere majority was not deemed sufficient to dictate public policy, and men such as the petitioners from the old part of Berwick were prepared to say so quite explicitly. Since its settlement some eighty or ninety years before, the town had expanded until, by 1748, the inhabitants of the newer parts easily outnumbered the "ancient settlers" and wished to establish a new meeting-house in a place the ancient settlers conceived injurious to their own interest. Those who lived in the newer parts of the town had the votes, but the ancient settlers were icily unimpressed nonetheless. Injury could not be justified "merely because a major vote of the town is or may be obtained to do it," the petitioners protested. They would suffer "great hurt and grievance," and "for no other reason than this: a major vote to do it, which is all the reason they have for the same." Equity, on the other hand, required a "just regard" for the old part of town and its inhabitants: they "ought" to retain their privileges despite the passage of their numerical preponderance. And that principle was no mere moral fabrication of a desperate minority. Six years earlier the General Court had endorsed exactly the same position in a similar challenge to the prerogatives of numerical power by the "ancient part" of another town, and in the Berwick controversy the town majority tacitly conceded the principle upon which the old quarter depended. Accusing the old quarter of "gross mis-representation," the rest of the town now maintained that there had been a disingenuous confusion of geography and population. There could be no question as to the physical location of the old town, but, as to its inhabitants, "the greatest part of the ancient settlers and maintainers of the ministry do live to the northward of the old meetinghouse and have always kept the same in times of difficulty and danger." The newer townsmen, then, did not deny that ancient settlers were entitled to special consideration; they simply denied that the inhabitants of the old quarter were in fact the ancient settlers.[20]

Antiquity mitigated majoritarianism elsewhere as well: in demands of old settlers and in determinations of the Court itself. In Lancaster as in Berwick, for example, a "standing part" could cite efforts to disrupt the old order which had been rejected by the Court as unreasonable. In other towns too, a majority changed nothing.[21] Consensus comprehended justice and history as well as the counting of a vote. In such a society a case could not be considered solely in its present aspects, as the original inhabitants of Lunenburg made quite clear. "What great discouragement must it needs give to any new settler," those old ones inquired,

> to begin a settlement and go through the difficulties thereof, which are well known to such as have ever engaged in such service, if when, so soon as ever they shall through the blessing of heaven upon their diligence and industry have arrived to live in some measure peaceably and comfortably, if then, after all fatigues and hardships undergone, to be cut to pieces and deprived of charter privileges and rights, and instead of peace and good harmony, contention and confusion introduced, there will be no telling what to trust to.[22]

Nor was history the only resort for the repudiation of a majority. Other men offered other arguments, and some scarcely deigned to argue at all. In a contested election in

Haverhill, for example, one side simply denied any authority at all to a majority of the moment. It was, they said,
nothing but the creature of "a few designing men who
have artfully drawn in the multitude and engaged them in
their own cause." That, they argued, was simply "oppression." The merchants of Salem similarly refused to accept
the hazards of populistic politics, though their refusal was
rather more articulate. The town meeting had enacted a
tax schedule more advantageous to the farmers than to
themselves, and the merchants answered that they felt no
force in that action, because "the major part of those who
were present were [farmers], and the vote then passed was
properly their vote and not the vote of the whole body of
the town." That legitimacy and obligation attached only to
a vote of the whole community was simply assumed by the
merchants, as they sought a subtle separation of a town
ballot—sheer majoritarianism—from a "vote of the whole
body of the town"—a notion akin to the general will—for
which the consent of every part of the population was requisite.[23]

Disdain for direct democracy emerged even more explicitly and sweepingly in a petition from the west precinct of
Bridgewater in 1738. The precinct faced the prospect of
the loss of its northern part due to a town vote authorizing
the northern inhabitants to seek separation as an independent town, and the precinct feared that the loss would
be fatal. Accordingly, the parishioners prayed the General
Court's intervention, and after briefly disputing the majority itself, the precinct allowed that, whether or not a majority in the town *had* been obtained, such a majority certainly *could* be contrived. "We own it is easy for the two
neighboring parishes joining with the petitioners to vote
away our just rights and privileges and to lay heavy bur-
dens upon us, which they would not be willing to touch
with the ends of their fingers." Yet for all the formal validity of such a vote, the precinct would not have assented to

it or felt it to be legitimate, "for we trust that your Excellency and Honors will not be governed by numbers but by reason and justice." Other men elsewhere urged the same argument. Perhaps none caught the provincial paradox of legality without legitimacy any better than the precinct of Salem Village, soon to become the independent town of Danvers. After a recitation of the imposition it had suffered from the town of Salem for no reason but superior numbers, the village came to its indictment of the town: "We don't say but you have had a legal right to treat us so, but all judgment without mercy is tedious to the flesh." [24]

Typically in such cases, the defense against this indictment was not an invocation of majority rights but rather a denial of having employed them oppressively. Both sides, therefore, operated upon an identical assumption. One accused the other of taking advantage of its majority, the other retorted that it had done no such thing, but neither disputed the principle that majority disregard of a minority was indefensible.* [25]

---

* On the rarest of occasions a community did propound a thoroughly populistic majoritarianism, but even those few proposals came to nought. The most radical of them, from Sudbury in 1708, was ignored by the General Court, which showed less solicitude for numbers than for mutuality, ordering the parties to reach "a good agreement accordingly, and mutually to regard the peace of the town." Mass. Arch. 113, pp. 447-9, 444. Forty years later in Berwick, men again advanced unabashed majoritarian arguments, but where the Sudbury majority required the rebuke of the assembly, the Berwick petitioners riddled their own position. In the very same appeal in which they insisted that a majority verdict was among "their invaluable rights and privileges," they also asserted their attachment to a settlement which would "accommodate the whole town in general." In the same petition in which they warned that denial of direct majorities would set a "dangerous" precedent and constitute "contempt of the town," they also found it necessary to attempt to discredit the size and character of the minority—ninety men were discounted as merely "a few of their inhabitants," and half of them too poor to meet the voting qualification at that—as if perhaps the extent of minority opposition mattered after all. And finally, twice, they professed the desire to "promote and cultivate peace and harmony among the inhabitants" and "to promote peace and unity among themselves," the very values so incompatible with straight-

This principle was no mere pious protestation. In Kittery, for instance, the parent parish complained that the men who later became the third parish had "long kept us in very unhappy circumstances . . . counter-acting us in all our proceedings" until finally "we were obliged to come into an agreement with them for dividing the then-lower parish of Kittery into two separate parishes," yet it was conceded on both sides that the old inhabitants enjoyed an easy numerical supremacy. Had they been disposed to employ it, almost any amount of "counter-acting" could have been contained and ultimately quashed, so far as votes in public meeting were concerned. But the parish clearly did not rely upon simple majoritarian procedures. It was more than morality that made consensus imperative; it was also the incapacity for coercion without widespread consent. It was the same incapacity which shaped a hundred other accommodations and abnegations across the province, which enabled some "aggrieved brethren" in Rehoboth to force the resignation of a minister, which paralyzed the town of Upton in the relocation of its meetinghouse. "All are agreed that it should be removed or a new one built," a town petition explained, "but cannot agree upon the place." In the absence of agreement they could see no way to act at all on their own account; there was never any thought of constructing a coalition within the town or contending for a majority.[26]

Ultimately almost every community in the province shared Upton's determination "to unite the people." Disputes, when they arose at all, were commonly concluded by "a full and amicable agreement" in which all parties "were in peace and fully satisfied," and the conflicts that did occur evoked no efforts at resolution in a majoritarian manner. "Mutual and general advantage" was the condi-

---

forward majoritarian disregard for the minority. Ibid., 115, pp. 393–6. See also ibid., 116, pp. 276–7.

tion of town continuance in "one entire corporate body." And when disputes did get beyond town borders the General Court itself often insisted on just such settlements. Early in the eighteenth century, for instance, it ordered Watertown to resolve its differences relating to the support of the ministry, the order to remain in effect "until the inhabitants of both parts of town shall mutually agree to support the ministry in any other manner."[27]

Such resolutions were generally arranged, or at least ratified, at town meetings, but they did not really originate there. Rather, they originated in the townsmen themselves, men who genuinely wished to create such conditions of general acquiescence and loving agreement, men capable of the restraint and self-denial which were psychological prerequisites for government by consensus. Thus the petitioners of the western portions of Rutland willingly "conceded" a strip of land they could have claimed when they asked incorporation as a district, "in condescension to the desire of a number of people," and thus they arrived at a 1750 settlement "to which both parties have agreed and are mutually satisfied." The same "peaceable concurrence of all parties" was the purpose of some Framingham proposals a quarter of a century earlier, and the same "necessity of self-denial in all parties in order to an accommodation" was recognized as a precondition of that concurrence. The details of the agreement only made more explicit the profoundly antimajoritarian animus of that psychological set:

> And your memorialists have good grounds to believe that about two-third parts of the town are to this day of opinion that the meetinghouse ought in justice to be erected there. Yet nevertheless your memorialists with others, considering that the affair of building a place for public worship ought to be managed with peace, did prevail with ourselves and others to enter upon agreement wherein as we conceive a very great

concession and condescension was expressed toward
the opposite party . . . and we for our parts apprehend ourselves strictly obliged to use our best endeavors to prosecute and cultivate that agreement.

Still others made the point even more succinctly. "We
think there was a great condescension in the dissatisfied
party in our town, who abated of their own right as to
travel to the public worship of God, purely to make
peace." [28]

In communities which had neither any substantial capacity
for coercion nor any legitimate or structured place for
opposition, in towns which had elaborate entrance requirements and extensive scrutiny of the inhabitants, the absence of actual contention can hardly be considered supris-
ing. Nonetheless, the extent of public placidity must be
emphasized. What decency demanded and the weakness of
the constabulary required was in fact the everyday reality
of public life in the provincial town. All over eighteenth-
century Massachusetts there were votes "by the free and
united consent of the whole" and "By a full and Unanimous Vote that they are Easie and Satisfied With What
they have Done." [29] Town officers were elected "by all the
voters present" or "having all the votes." [30] Town lands
were often alienable only when every man agreed to their
division.[31] Church discipline, and especially excommunication, was by "the united sense of the church," and without
such concurrence it was simply not employed.[32] And ministers in particular were chosen unanimously or not at all, as
in Westborough, where the town offered its pastoral post to
a candidate despite some opposition in the town and he
declined until, a year later, the town could cite its "most
happy union," or as in Wenham, where a minister invited
to fill a vacancy encountered "an unhappy difference"

about salary and declined the offer while the town's next choice was "unanimously" called and accepted.* [33]

Indeed, ministers often gave such unanimity as the only condition of their acceptance of a call. As one candidate coming to terms with the first precinct of Weston explained, though the financial prospects the parish offered were less than munificent, "the Vnanimity of your Call appears matter of Great Encouragemint to me and affords a happy prospect of the good Success of my ministry." [34] And such a man was not moved by whimsy or otherworldliness. A calculation of solid self-interest stood behind the ministerial insistence on unity, for the Massachusetts ministry was no trifling matter. A pastor who accepted a call committed himself to his chosen community for the rest of his life,[35] and on that account he might well have reasoned that a slight difference in salary could hardly be worth a lifetime of harassment and disharmony. If anything, the candidate whose prime consideration was his income was particularly compelled, by his very covetousness, to considerations of the unanimity of his call, for if some significant portion of the town did not support him he was liable to serious loss of effective income due to the difficulty of compelling tax payments from the dissidents. This was so well recognized that ordaining councils "never proceeded to settle a minister who was opposed by a majority or even a large minority of the inhabitants of a town, knowing that he would be denied adequate financial support." The councils simply presumed that, despite the legal liability which would obtain against the minority in opposition, co-

* Also, since few towns in the province wished to be without a pastor for any length of time, and since absolute or approximate unity was essential in obtaining one, consensus upon a minister was one of the fundamental conditions of community in the eighteenth century. Thus "a minister in whom we all may join" or "a gentleman preaching among us to whom we are all well united" was often advanced as the basis for a place's final incorporation. See, e.g., Mass. Arch. 117, pp. 156–7; ibid., pp. 813–14; ibid., pp. 845–6; ibid. 118, pp. 344–5.

ercion would be problematic even if it was not impossible.[36]

Concord was not always so complete in all the affairs of the community, but contention was never common, either. The Massachusetts Archives, for example, contain protests and petitions by the score, yet, in proper perspective, those protests afford a striking indication of domestic tranquility. There were, altogether, 102 local disputes which came before the Court between 1691 and 1775, but they came from two or three hundred settled places in the province and over a period of almost a century. In an ordinary year, then, only one out of two hundred communities carried a controversy before the Court; or, to put it another way, the average town was embroiled in contention which brought it to Boston at a rate of once every 170 years. Even defining internal conflict more broadly, so as to include contention in places which were not yet incorporated, questions over legality, and disputes between towns and their (absentee) proprietors, there were only 308 cases that came to the Court, or less than four a year. Again assuming two hundred settlements, that inflated figure for conflict still yields an average of only one such involvement every fifty-seven years in the typical community.* [37]

Of course, the majority of domestic disputes never went as far as the General Court. The cases which were carried to Boston were those few which could not be settled at home, so they imply an understatement of the extent of disagreement which did occur. A better measure of concord and controversy is afforded by the town records, and for that very reason the town records suggest even more strongly than the legislative archives the placidity of public life in the provincial towns. The minutes of local meetings may be stupefying in their stolidity, but they suggest as nothing else can the substance of social affairs in the eighteenth century; and the picture presented by more than two

* For an amplification of the data, see Appendix III.

thousand such meetings is one of overwhelming agreement among the participants. Not a town among the ten tabulated had much more than a single explicit conflict, however trivial, in the course of a year, and at the other extreme other towns had only one every four or five years. On the average, each town had an overt controversy of any sort but once every other year. On the average, such conflicts arose only once in ten meetings: nine meetings met in agreement on every item of public business for each meeting marked by even a single open discord.

The simple fact of the matter was that the town meeting was not designed to give expression to discussion and division. Its business was transacted more by acclamation than antagonism, and the merest mention of debate in most town records occurred less than ten times in half a century. Considering all the actions taken by all ten towns in the conduct of their affairs, ninety-eight per cent of them were unmarked by any obvious opposition. Indeed, even on a more generous definition of conflict—one in which antagonism is inferred not only from declared clashes but also from negative action or failure to act upon articles on the agenda and from other such uncertain sources—there were still about nine actions out of every ten which were taken without so much as a suspicion of division in the community.* [38]

And still another measure of unanimity may be obtained from the actual figures for voting on a proposal. This is not, strictly, possible for the provincial period, since there is no substantial body of evidence on raw voting returns before the beginning of the Revolution, but there is a comprehensive tabulation of town votes from just beyond the provincial period. In 1778 a constitution was submitted to the towns for their ratification or rejection, and they were required to record the numbers of townsmen on each side so that the numbers for the entire commonwealth

* For an amplification of the data, see Appendix IV.

could be tallied from the returns. One hundred seventy-seven of those returns have been preserved in the Massachusetts Archives; and while their utilization presents difficulties, there is nothing nearly so useful from the provincial period itself, and it is not unreasonable to presume some persistence of styles and structures of community organization a scant two or three years beyond that era.*

In any event, the results of the 1778 balloting could hardly have offered more striking evidence for consensus as community custom. More than half the towns tabulated voted with quite literal unanimity, whether for or against, and almost four fifths reported at least a ninety per cent majority. Only seventeen towns—barely a tenth of those tallied—showed anything less than a seventy per cent majority for whatever position the town took, while almost none of the town votes corresponded very closely to the final division of the vote for the province as a whole. That is to say, the average division of the vote across the province was altogether artificial; there was far more disagreement in the province as a whole than in the towns taken by themselves. And much the same pattern prevailed earlier. Provincial contests were not truly town contests, because provincial issues were rarely received in the towns as issues in any meaningful sense. Controversy at the provincial level neither created nor reflected local contention; divisions in the province were the product not of corresponding divisions in the towns themselves but of local unanimities opposed to contrary local unanimities.† [39]

Unanimity, then, was the meeting-point of expectations and experience in the public life of provincial Massachu-

---

* Of course, it is not impossible that by 1778 the chief dissenters had been driven from the commonwealth, but, if they were, that would simply support the primary point, that the Massachusetts townsmen of that time thought in terms of uniformity as the condition of community.

† For amplification, see Appendix V.

setts. Preaching and practice converged in the structured concurrences of the inhabitants in hundreds of town meetings around the Bay every year and in the sense of strict and sacred obligation which those agreements imposed upon the townsmen. Placing their reliance on their own moral community, the men of Massachusetts not only expected but achieved an enforcement maintained primarily by the consent of neighbors rather than by external compulsion.

They were able to do so because they and their neighbors were so much alike, and the likeness was anything but accidental. Uniformity was carefully cultivated from the first days of settlement, and nowhere more carefully than in the selection and control of the settlers themselves. Under the auspices of the monolithic ideal, fundamental differences in values were rarely admitted within a town, while differences of race, nationality, and culture almost never appeared east of the Hudson River before the Revolution.

Massachusetts was, as a matter of fact, more nearly restricted to white Anglo-Saxon Protestants than any other province in English America, with the possible exceptions of its New England neighbors, Connecticut and New Hampshire. Less than one per cent of the quarter of a million Germans who came to the English colonies between 1690 and 1770 came to New England, and the proportion of the massive Irish, Scotch, and Scotch-Irish migration which went to the Bay was little larger. The province offered no welcome whatsoever to the French Catholics and very little encouragement, according to Governor Bellomont, even to the Huguenots.* [40] And Negroes never attained significant numbers in the settlement either. In 1715 only three per cent of the Negroes in the American

* The celebrated "French Plantation," at Oxford in the Nipmuck territory, was the *only* significant settlement of Frenchmen in Massachusetts, and at that it did not endanger the purity of other places in the province.

colonies were in Massachusetts, though Massachusetts was then the largest colony on the mainland, and only two per cent of the population of the province was Negro; by 1780 the proportions were still smaller, and no states but Delaware, Rhode Island, and New Hampshire had fewer.[41]

This restriction was a product not only of New England's inferior economic enticements but also of the deliberate policy of the communities of the region. Committed to a conception of the social order that precluded pluralism, the men of Massachusetts offered the chilliest of receptions to men who were so clearly not of their own kind. Through a time when Pennsylvania was actually recruiting immigrants all over Europe, Massachusetts often refused even to make provision for the ones who came her way.* In its 1726–7 session, for example, the General Court denied an unsolicited appeal for a township by some Scotch-Irish arrivals while steadily granting lands to aspirants of acceptable Anglo-Saxon stock all through those years.[42] And on the unusual occasion when the Court did grant land to "an unexpected accession" of Scotch-Irishmen, still other patterns of animosity emerged. The newcomers chose a spot just above Haverhill, and some of them set out at once for that town, to pass the winter. Their experience was an unhappy one. As a Haverhill historian put it, the townsmen

---

It was simply a homogeneous French enclave in an otherwise homogeneous English society. But in any case it survived only nine years, from 1687 to 1696. When its inhabitants were driven off by an Indian raid, they did not disperse into the neighboring towns that still stood but instead departed into other colonies altogether. Baird, *Huguenot Emigration*, II, pp. 255–90.
* Such ethnic exclusivity played a part in the general demographic decline of Massachusetts, which had had a quarter of the entire American population in 1690 and which was still the most populous English colony in America a couple of decades after that. By 1780 the people at the Bay amounted to less than a tenth of the American people, and Virginia, Pennsylvania, and North Carolina were all more populous, while New York was well on its way to becoming so. Bureau of the Census: *Historical Statistics*, p. 756.

"thoroughly hated" the Scotch-Irish and "were not at all delicate in making it manifest." The immigrants stayed no longer than they had to, and their momentary mingling with the old inhabitants produced nothing but antagonism and a speedy separation into two distinct and homogeneous local units, the established town fiercely fending off the newcomers, the newcomers accepting those conditions and embodying their own identity and orthodoxy in the very name of their new town, Londonderry.[43]

In the French and Indian War, military and imperial exigencies obliged the province to accept about a thousand of the captured Acadians, or "neutral French" as the legislature called them. Its response to that necessity was revealing. The first shipment of the uprooted victims of war arrived late in 1755, and the House of Representatives took almost immediate action. It clapped them into jail and then appointed a committee of its own "to prepare the Draught of a Bill to prevent for the future the Subjects of the French King going at large within this Province." When another shipment arrived a few months later, they were dispatched to selected towns, which were required to maintain them "in such Manner as shall incur the least Charge," and they were explicitly exempted from any of the privileges of inhabitancy. Later the legislature acquainted Governor Shirley with its feelings—"The receiving among us so great a Number of Persons whose gross bigotry to the Roman Catholic Religion is notorious, and whose Loyalty to his Majesty is suspected, is a Thing very disagreeable to us"—and after 1756 the province accepted no more Acadians at all. As for the thousand already there, almost to a man they petitioned to leave Massachusetts at the earliest opportunity that presented itself when the war was over, and long before the Revolution they were almost all gone.[44]

Except for the Acadians, Europeans had to be induced

to come; without encouragement, they simply stayed at home. The case of the Indians was quite the converse. They were already at home, and the province wished to be rid of them. By the beginning of the provincial period, though, the messy business of extermination was already nearing completion. By the time the Anglo-American forces captured Quebec only one substantial Indian community remained in all Massachusetts, and it was on its way to extinction too. In 1761 the English inhabitants of Stockbridge sought and received a release from the obligation under which they had been admitted to the Indian town in the first place, to carry on all town affairs jointly with the Indians. Once separation was established, white supremacy soon followed, and long before the century was out the Indians were out of Stockbridge. The basis for the appeal of the English inhabitants to the Court had been the old familiar one, still endlessly fertile, to dispel the dangers of diversity. The differences were clearly stated—that in matters of schools, roads, husbandry, and taxation the Indians diverged "in their manner of living from the English"— and as easily resolved, by the division of the community into two separate societies, one English, one Indian. "They therefore pray that they may be allowed to transact all matters and things relative to the premises by themselves, exclusive of said Indians." [45]

But even the situation in Stockbridge was extraordinary, and so were victories in Nova Scotia. Ordinarily, ethnic and cultural homogeneity could be taken for granted in the rural communities of provincial Massachusetts. It simply went without saying that aliens were not welcome. Men who applied for admission to a town were judged by moral, economic, and religious tests, not by their color or their country. For in provincial New England common origins could generally be assumed; it was common ideas which were problematic.

To secure the enclave of common believers that it

sought, a town did not simply deny inhabitancy to out-
landers. It looked carefully into every man who approached its borders, English and American as well as
alien, and its disapproval meant that he moved elsewhere.
For a man did not simply move into a town in eighteenth-
century Massachusetts: he applied for admission. Each community retained the right to accept only those that it
wished, and that right persisted without challenge to the
time of the Revolution. "Such whose dispositions do not
suit us, whose society will be hurtful to us," were simply
refused entry as enemies of harmony and homogeneity.
Men did not move as they pleased among communities
which covenanted "to keepe of from vs all such, as ar contrarye minded. And receaue onely such vnto vs as be such
as may be probably of one harte." [46] Rather, they were received as inhabitants only if they obtained the formal approval of the town or its selectmen. They could not even be
entertained by inhabitants unless such inhabitants obtained the permission of the town. [47]

Such stringently controlled access to the town was given
force not only by direct penalties but also by certain larger
policies. Among them were the early prohibition of the
free acquisition of land or other property in the town by
outsiders without local approval [48] and, even more important, the congregational conception of the church. Edmund Morgan has noted that the original thrust of congregational Puritanism to lodge disciplinary power in the individual churches rather than with the bishops also aimed
at more local control of the membership of the local community, [49] and such congregational autonomy not only provided that control but also quite effectively tied a man to
his own church. He could neither remove to a new congregation without the dismissal of his old one nor even participate in the activities of another church without the permission of his own. And at the same time the minister's
bonds to his congregation were made correspondingly close,

with removal to another place made deliberately more difficult in New England than elsewhere. Each church consequently came to represent an enclosed orthodoxy of its own, an encapsulated consensus whose preservation was a critical consideration in admitting a man.* [50]

Still more significant than congregational solidarity, however, was the practice of "warning out." Under this aegis, anyone who did secure entry to the town and was then deemed undesirable could be warned and, if necessary, lawfully ejected from the community. Such a policy was, in some part, a device to escape undue expenses in the support of paupers, but it was also, and more importantly, the product of the powerful communitarian assumptions of the early settlers, who conceived of their community as a select corporation with a consequent necessity for the consent of the members to any additions. Warning out provided substantial security to the towns that control of settlement rested upon communal, not individual, initiative.[51] And such assumptions did not decline in the eighteenth

---

* In this regard, the opposition of the orthodox to the ministerial itineracy of the Great Awakening is quite comprehensible. Evangelical itineracy not only endangered local harmony directly, setting neighbor against neighbor in an effort to "tell the sheep from the goats," but also jeopardized it more deeply, in its assault upon the self-containment of the homogeneous congregational unit. Itinerants menaced the local monoliths by introducing competing sources of value into the community, and for that reason the constriction of itineracy became a major measure in the campaign against the evangelicals. See Goen: *Revivalism,* pp. 17, 223; Heimert: "American Oratory," p. 145; White: "Decline of the Great Awakening," p. 44.

Moreover, the antagonism to itineracy was no mere transient tactic in the opposition of Old and New Lights. It was the expression of an endemic, abiding assumption of community organization in provincial Massachusetts, a point which the evangelicals confirmed at the earliest opportunity in the revival of 1763. This time the shoe was on the other foot, since the revival occurred almost wholly within the Calvinist camp; and Calvinist ministers reacted quite as vigorously against itinerant competition from the outside as the Old Light ministry had done two decades earlier. For evangelicals as for Arminians, the precepts of local solidarity proved primary. Heimert "American Oratory," p. 164.

century. Despite the contention of Josiah Benton that warning out degenerated into a purely *pro forma* device to evade local support of paupers in the provincial period, town records continued to be studded with such warnings to the time of the Revolution itself, and constables continued to be paid for the bodily removal of undesirables from the towns.[52] And more striking still, communities which could not provide such penalties because they lacked the requisite legal status felt themselves subject to "inconveniences." Ware River Parish, for example, protested in 1761 that in the absence of corporate capacity it could not keep paupers and others out of the precinct, thus implying that incorporated towns *could* do so and that it felt the lack of that power. A few years earlier, the Elbow Tract similarly lamented that it had "neither the power nor authority to carry any of them transient persons out of the place." * [53]

* By implication, however, Benton lodged a larger claim which must be considered more carefully. The warning-out laws provided that men who were once warned were not counted as inhabitants entitled to support in case of poverty merely because they continued to reside there, and a clarification in 1739 declared that there was no legal implication of inhabitancy even in the case of a man assessed for local taxes. Benton: *Warning Out*, pp. 51, 52, 55. The meaning of such measures was that, though warning out was not in fact used as a purely *pro forma* evasion as often as Benton contended, the issue posed in principle was quite the same. Laws which arose out of the expectations of a solidary society simultaneously permitted the separation of physical and legal inhabitancy. A man might, in theory, own property, pay taxes, even hold local offices, without ever formally gaining the status of an inhabitant. And in other areas of local life, most notably in religion, membership in a community was muddied by more than mere conceptual confusion. As early as 1700 men claimed that it was "no unusual thing" for inhabitants of one town to worship and even to be in full communion in a more convenient church in another community. Mass. Arch. 113, p. 280; see also ibid. 114, pp. 622–3, 625–7; ibid. 115, p. 437; ibid. 116, pp. 671–2; ibid., pp. 715–16. And the institution of the independent precinct—a body bound together for church purposes though its members were still attached to their original community in all prudential affairs—dictated an even more complete mixture of allegiance; see ibid., pp. 596–7. (Often, especially in matters of taxation, such separations of allegiance proved problematic; see ibid. 113, p. 280; ibid. 115, pp. 689–91; ibid. 116, pp. 256–7; ibid., p. 626; ibid., pp.

One way to alleviate such inconvenience in lieu of legal authority was by consolidating group sentiment against the stranger, and corporate notions did indeed continue to shape the pattern of new settlement far into the eighteenth century. Goen, for example, suggested that most of the migrants to the frontiers of Massachusetts were "to some extent New Lights," and he cited several instances in which coherent groups of men bound together by a shared religious radicalism unacceptable in their own community de-

---

668–9; ibid., pp. 671–2; ibid. 117, p. 14; ibid., p. 91; ibid., pp. 370–1; ibid. 118, pp. 344–5; ibid., pp. 722–4.)

Nonetheless, all of these abridgements of the close community were, in the provincial period itself, inconsequential. The crossing of community lines occurred, when it occurred at all, only for the few who lived on the outskirts of their towns and parishes, a slippage as inescapable as it was inconsiderable. Yet not even such slippage was always accepted for very long. Arrangements which had to be admitted for a time were often envisioned as momentary makeshifts, to be abandoned as soon as abandonment became feasible. When some Sebascodegin Islanders were attached, "not of our motion and choice," to Harpswell, they were also given the promise that as soon as they were prepared to support the gospel among themselves, they would be set off as a separate society. Ibid., pp. 344–5. Similar promises were made and kept in many other places—see ibid. 113, p. 280; ibid. 116, pp. 437, 439; ibid., pp. 671–2—and the conclusion to which they point is that split allegiances have to be seen in temporal perspective. They were simply stopgaps; the tendency was to their realignment. In much the same manner the independent precincts did not remain independent. Some soon went wholly under the wing of a single town while others pressed on for full town status, but either way the confusion of condition that they imposed on their members was not sustained. Either way the identity of social and legal citizenship was restored. See ibid., pp. 596–7; ibid., pp. 626–7.

At the core of this tendency to restoration was the consensual conception of the community. Loyalties and duties divided into portions rather than attached monolithically to a single society were ultimately incompatible with larger preferences in social policy. In religion men insisted upon the impropriety of any separation of their place of "duty" from the place "where we receive privilege." Ibid., p. 210; see also ibid., pp. 211, 295–8, 336–8, 346–8; ibid. 118, pp. 742–3. In civic affairs the same precepts of propriety also prevailed. When men were taxed where they could "receive no benefit," that very taxation provided an occasion of protest, and the protests were upheld by the General Court. Ibid. 116, p. 626; ibid. 118, pp. 36–7; ibid., p. 392. The true town and its taxables were to coincide.

parted for the frontier, there to establish their own orthodoxy, there to trumpet another verse of the old Puritan roundelay which had begun with the beginning of the migration to New England. Within the province itself other patterns of cohesive settlement persisted, such as that by which Southampton was organized out of the territory of Northampton and under its watchful eye, or that by which a town applied to the General Court for a land grant to which the town's rising younger generation might all go off together. In all those patterns the assumption of solidarity was primary, which puzzled subsequent historians like the one from Watertown who, writing in 1830, came upon just such an application from his town. He noted the obvious implication that the town no longer felt itself able to support an expanding population on its fixed land supply, but he could not comprehend the failure of individualism that the town's appeal represented. "Why a special provision was necessary to procure a settlement for them, instead of leaving them to take care of themselves, it is difficult to discover." Which was simply to say that Jacksonian America was not provincial Massachusetts.[54]

The result of such provincial concern for the members of the corporation was that most of them could be counted upon to share each other's ideas and interests. In the old towns they were not admitted or they were soon warned out if they did not, and in new places their anterior agreement was often a condition of the settlement itself. Nevertheless, public responsibility for the members of the community did not and could not end merely with a man's admission to the community. A man's mind was changeable, and even the best of men were still subject to the sins of Adam. Orthodoxy at the outset was only the beginning of an oversight that had no end. Admission afforded no immunity from inspection, and neither did anything else; for the Puritans believed that the heart of man was tainted and that the knowledge of good was not to be relied upon against the will to evil. Since institutions alone could check man's will—though in the end they too would fail—familial, political, and religious institutions were all bent to the aim of enforcing a monolithic moral unity upon their members. In the little towns of Massachusetts, then, there was no place of privacy, no time of a man's life when he could rest secure from scrutiny.

The demands were most direct in the family, where the authority of the father was acknowledged and obedience was an obligation. Masters were made to feel the same responsibility for their servants, being urged by such experts as Cotton Mather to "Be prudently Inquisitive into their *Experiences,* into their *Temptations,* into their *Behaviours.*" And church and town governments also aimed at the oversight of all behavior. Indeed, such an object was an important reason for a community's formal existence in the first place. When the settlers at Philipstown asked incorporation as a district or town, the request was in order that it might prevent "irreligion and profaneness" and keep up "good order and discipline." Pownalborough petitioned "for the sake of rule and good order," and Whiscasitt and Mounswig Bay "in order to preserve the rules of morality and religion among us." Township Number Four in Berkshire County lamented its lack of proper officers "to suppress wickedness and disorder among us," while in Quabin the connection of moral coercion and the civil authority was asserted still more explicitly: "reformation of manners is greatly wished for among us, and had we power to choose tithingmen, constables, &c, we humbly hope it would in some good measure be effected." [55]

The fact was that moral surveillance was an important part of a town official's job, and in some cases it was the very essence of it. Selectmen had many other obligations, but they were also quite commonly called the ruling fathers of their communities, a metaphor which both reflected and required their exercise of familial discipline.

Ministers were unblinkingly called *"Watchmen,* because they should Watch the Actions of all Men, and with an Aim of Religious Curiosity spy out, how every one liveth, with his Household in his House." In that office they were assisted by the ruling elders of the church, who were also charged with *"Discovering* the State of the whole Flock," and sometimes too by a town committee which helped in the gathering of information on offenders because the "business of a Pastor of a Church is very great and extensive, and particularly the enquiring into Public Scandals and procuring evidence thereof is laborious and burthensome." Constables too were ordered "to inspect families," while the tithingmen had almost no other function. Herbert B. Adams' study set very nicely the division of labor between the constables and these truer overseers of intimate affairs:

> The Tithingman may be distinguished from the Constable by the fact that the former's duties related more especially to the control of family life and of the morals of his neighborhood. The Tithingman's power came nearer *home* than did that of the Constable; it reached over the threshold of every family in the hamlet; it was patriarchal, fatherly, neighborly, in the strictest sense.

And of course such moral scrutiny was tied to a general conception of the community. The tithingman's ultimate responsibility, according to Adams, was to see "that the whole community grew up as one united family in the nurture and admonition of the law." [56]

So too, in the end, did every citizen have the same responsibility, whether he stood in public office or not. Even a *"Scandalous Transgression,"* as Mather called it, was first subject to private policing—"He that knows the Offence, first of all *himself* goes to the Offender, and seriously endeavors to bring him to Repentance"—and only when ob-

stinacy was clear was the pastor or a civil officer called into
the case. And whether private or public means were finally
employed, the end of the sequence of surveillance was always the maintenance of the public morality: the offender
was to be brought to an exemplary correction. As William
Weeden found, "the social and religious atmosphere was
charged with an unattainable ideal of vicarious virtue,—a
conception of duty which exalted each bold scriptural the-
orist into a keeper of his brother's conscience,—a priestly
administrator of another's soul." Citing an assortment of
early prohibitions, such as those on shuffleboard, bowling,
drinking toasts, and taking tobacco, Weeden concluded,
"these are not eccentric notions. . . . The old statutes
teem with the same spirit, seeking by every means to control morals or to enforce a conventional decorum." [57]

The culminating conception to which all these ideas and
institutions tended, the notion that drew them all together
and gave them a coherent, connected meaning, was the
ideal of the homogeneous communal unit. Achievement of
such unity was the ultimate aim of the New England town,
and expectation of it underwrote a consolidated control of
social functions unequaled in any other public body in
English America. In the towns and their town meetings
were vested the political prerogatives of election of public
officials; in them were placed the pivotal economic powers
of taxation, and a range of other regulations of commerce
and trade which would one day be assumed to belong to the
rights of private property; and at their disposal were also
the military defense of the population, its religious affairs,
and its education. The assembled townsmen could select a
schoolmaster as easily as they appointed a highway route,
and just as they instructed their committees or set militia
meetings, so they could instruct their minister or set the
time of a church service. At their dispensation was a unified

authority in the realms of power and values and a very substantial share in the socialization process and the ordering
of property.[58]

Moreover, such authority was almost untouched by any
larger notions of a separation of the civilian and the military, or of the church and the state, or of professionalism
and the political process. Only uncertainly was it touched
by some of the century's new notions of the immunity of
private property from public control. At the level of imperial policy some of these concepts might be acknowledged,
but none of them could be applied at home.

They could not be applied at home for precisely the
reason they came to command American allegiance in
imperial relations: each of them was premised upon a seg-
mentation of the general community. Each of them implied the substitution of structural pluralism for organicism, and the principle of structural pluralism was the acid
by which Americans would one day seek to dissolve an empire; its power for disruption was all too evident to the
men of the eighteenth century. Consequently, organicism
continued to be a real requirement at the local level long
after it had degenerated into mere metaphor at the higher
reaches. For towns such as Southampton, moral uniformity
was the community. As its historian insisted, its citizens
"were not isolated individuals or isolated families; instead,
they were parts of a solidary group." And the same supposition of solidarity obtained everywhere in the provincial
towns. Kinship lines, as Arensberg insisted, stopped at the
town's edge—"fellows of the town were nearer than kinfolk, and kin moving off to another town soon fell away"—
and occupational differentiation likewise left group unity
essentially unaffected—"Yankees were farmers, artisans,
shopkeeper-merchants, seamen and fishermen, without distinction or segregation either in community membership,
political right, or use of living space. They were all townsmen together." [59]

In precisely that insistence upon "townsmen together" the men of provincial Massachusetts shaped a new kind of group life in New England, a communalism whose character was caught quite clearly in John Lathrop's sermon in the Old North Church of Boston six days after the Boston Massacre. In his address Lathrop did of course discuss the violence itself, excoriating "the infinite impropriety of quartering troops in a well-regulated city," but he also dug deeper, and as he did he drew upon the experience of the previous three quarters of a century. His outrage was ultimately rooted in his presumptions of public order, in the light of which the quartering of troops was merely one manifestation of an improper conception of authority and enforcement. "It is time for that magistrate to resign," Lathrop insisted, "who cannot depend on the assistance of his neighbors and fellow citizens in the administration of justice." [60]

The principle that enforcement was to derive from willing and widespread assistance of neighbors rather than from military or legal coercion was, by 1770, well established in the law[61] and in the development of local institutions,[62] as well as in the more mundane affairs which gave resonance to those broader institutional tendencies.[63] It was certainly recognized by the towns themselves as the crucial condition of community. A committee of the town of Dunstable acknowledged it in opposing a 1752 appeal for the annexation of Nottingham, conceding the town's difficulties in the aftermath of a boundary settlement but adding that "we are at present considerably well united," whereas "should Nottingham be annexed to and incorporated with us, we fear it would lead us into very great contentions and confusions." Presuming the priority of public agreement, the committee dismissed the claim of the original application that without an addition to its depleted numbers the town's charges would be "insupportable":

We acknowledge we are but small, but we apprehend a small society well united may more easily go through such business of building a meetinghouse and settling a minister than a greater number when there is nothing but discord and disaffection, which we fear will be the case if they should be annexed to us against their and our wills.[64]

The same assumption that cooperation could not easily be coerced was made in many other communities as well. Just as the Dunstable committee recognized that support of local functions depended on much more than mere numbers and wealth—both of which the annexation of Nottingham would have augmented—so did other townsmen see voluntary consent as essential for the operation of their society. Worcester articulated the necessary connection that many men saw between coercion contrary to its residents' wishes and the dissolution of the conditions of effective community when, in 1743, it answered a petition for separation by some of its inhabitants by explaining that the petition asked the removal of more than thirty families while only eleven had expressed willingness to set off. "Should a major part be obliged against their inclination and interest to go off," the town argued, "unity must subside and then it's plain what will follow." [65]

And in another affair in Dunstable the same appeal to the fear of what would follow informed one of the most revealing threats of the entire provincial era. Angered by the high-handed proceedings of the selectmen at a public meeting, some of the townsmen

expostulated with their neighbors who had done them this wrong and prayed them to desist and that they might come to a friendly and just settlement of their affairs for that what they had done was very unjust and transacted in an unfair and illegal manner, and

that therefore they should not meet with them nor pay
anything towards building a house or preaching at
that place.

In their expostulation was more than the mere menace of
the failure of enforcement. Significant as that standard
warning was, it was not so striking as the fact that, when
grieved, these citizens turned first for relief not to politics
but to friendship. Successful social discipline in Dunstable
depended on the "assistance of neighbors," and the townsmen therefore threatened, fundamentally, the withdrawal
of fellowship. In eighteenth-century New England, there
was no threat more serious.[66]

❧ IV ❧

Healing the
Divisions

ALL COMMUNITIES MAINTAIN a measure of agreement, but in Massachusetts there was more than that mere presence of peace. There was, rather, a *pattern* of peace, dictated by dire necessity and evident in the centrality of its pursuit. In other societies of European civilization the public peace was preserved by tradition or by power; in provincial Massachusetts it was obtained only if there was unity in the town. In the eighteenth-century settlements about the Bay, the sustenance of solidarity was at the very core of community life, because such solidarity was problematic rather than presumed, consciously contrived rather than a resultant of more important forces.

In consequence, social life in the provincial towns was not just dependent upon concord but structured by that dependency. A host of established mechanisms served to maintain consensus, and together those instrumentalities of agreement accounted for most of the conduct of community affairs. Values of harmony and homogeneity governed the political and religious spheres; education instilled the same values in the young; majoritarianism rarely ruled because minorities could scarcely be conceived; and in ordinary times the result was communal control of conflict and town records which reveal no very regular pattern of antagonism.

But not even in New England could every idiosyncratic

impulse, interest, and idea be constantly constrained. Contention did occur, and when it did it confronted the communities of the province with a cruel dilemma. They could neither acknowledge conflict nor ignore it. They could not avow it because they lacked both the intellectual and the institutional implements for its acceptance; yet they could not neglect it because it broke the unanimity on which effective action in the society rested. They had, therefore, to devise other responses to dissidence.

The responses they did devise were in many ways even more revealing than the ordinary absence of opposition in the towns—for in the extraordinary circumstance of contention they still sought peace above all. Even in the heat of local battles the villagers remembered and responded to the values of concord and consensus. They accommodated differences to oblige the disgruntled, separated adversaries who seemed irreconcilable, or submitted disagreements to outside arbitration; they did not drive desperately for conquest of foes, nor did they even derive any evident delight from the contest itself.

Nowhere, in fact, were the contours of conflict in provincial Massachusetts any clearer than in the persistence of the aspiration to consensus even in the midst of contention. Protests and contested elections almost invariably appealed to unity as the chief value which had been violated. Disputes were consistently seen as unnatural and undesirable deviations from the norm. In the absence of any socially sanctioned role for opposition, the dissent that did occur was generally surreptitious, rarely long-sustained, and usually smoothed over immediately upon settlement. And when antagonism endured for any considerable length of time the effectiveness of the community collapsed or declined sharply. Men lived together in agreement or they did not live together at all in provincial Massachusetts.

• • •

Self-denial and sociability for the sake of peace were of the essence of New England town politics, and negotiation and accommodation were its essential means. From the earliest years of the colony, the settlers sought "group agreement by discussion," thereby "imposing a type of local justice by mutual agreement of all concerned," and the same informal arrival at unanimity still prevailed to the very last years of the provincial era, when "prudent and amicable composition and agreement" were urged as the only possible preventive for "great and sharp disputes and contentions." [1]

Such conciliation often shaped the earliest settlement of a society, and especially of a church society, when men were attempting to shape an agreement that would withstand strain for the future. Ola Elizabeth Winslow has given us a vivid account of the establishment of the church in Dedham, which affords a detailed description of this preventive propitiation, the desire for peace which guided it, and the harmonious unity it produced.

> Almost immediately they began to gather in a neighborly group . . .
>
> "Lovingly to discourse & consult together such questions as might further tend to establish a peaceable & co'fortable civill society, & pr'pare for spirituall co'munion in a church society."
>
> No troublesome question arose in connection with the establishment of the civil society, but when they came to the "chiefe scope" of the meetings, namely, "the spiritual house," they struck snags and were confronted by questions which necessitated prolonged discussion.
>
> Fortunately, having expected disagreement, they had prepared for it. The purpose of the meetings was inquiry and all inquirers met on the same level. They met devoutly; each meeting began and ended with a

prayer. Each member came prepared to speak his mind openly on a topic announced a week in advance. When they assembled, the host led off, others following in turn, "as they saw cause to ad, inlarge or approve" what was spoken, until presently a sense of the meeting agreement had been reached. No new topic was proposed until all had taken complete satisfaction in the discussions of the former one. Throughout the discussions objections were welcome, in so far as they came from teachable hearts, and were offered in humility and without thought of "cavilling or contradicting."

Apparently the program justified itself, for according to the record such was the spirit of this free questioning and debate that the "reasonings were very peaceable, loving, & tender, much to edification."

The same procedure that governed the discussions in Dedham, which began in 1637, still governed the gathering of a church in the eighteenth century, when a manual of ecclesiastical organization described "THE MEN who by mutual Conferences with one another, are come to a good Understanding and Resolution . . ." [2]

In civil affairs the townsmen sought a similar understanding. When an issue was in doubt they talked to each other, and the pervasiveness of their prior consultation was apparent in Benjamin Franklin's recollections that even his father, a tradesman too poor to pay an apprentice's fee for his son, was "frequently visited by leading people who consulted him for his opinion in affairs of the town or of the church he belonged to, and showed a good deal of respect for his judgment and advice." [3] Informal accords were often arranged before a town meeting began, sometimes during a meeting itself, and occasionally even after adjournment, when men who felt themselves injured might resort to personal relationships rather than the formal political process for relief.[4]

Accommodation of the amenable was the preferred path to consensus in everything from hogs and fences to the entire management of a community, but the most common occasion of accommodation was, fittingly enough, the very heart of the New England town—its meetinghouse. The location of a local meetinghouse was invariably a matter of intense interest to all the townsmen, since they had to travel to it every Sunday and every town meeting day, yet no one in the province ever suggested that such placement was an appropriate subject for self-interest at the expense of the other inhabitants. A town had rather to take "the greatest care . . . to balance as well as might be the several parts of the town." The building belonged "as nigh the center as could be conveniently . . . so as to accommodate the said town." [5] When a site agreeable to all the inhabitants could not be found in the center of town, committees constructed other meetinghouses for their outlying areas or elected to divide the meetings themselves with their distant centers of settlement.[6]

But even more revealing than these facts of accommodation on meetings and meetinghouses were the evident assumptions which lay behind them. More than one provincial town declared its opposition to an appeal of some of its citizens to set off as a separate society because, by such removal, the meetinghouse would have had to be moved, "to the no Small Cost & Grate Damige of the Town," so as to be "near the center of the then-remaining inhabitants." Yet not a single town ever doubted that the relocation would be imperative, despite the dire consequences, if a separation was admitted.[7]

In a memorial from the east wing of Rutland, in 1759, the absolute accommodative bent of the eighteenth-century townsmen emerged even more explicitly. The wing had already applied for independent incorporation as a town or district when the proprietors of "sundry farms lying between Lancaster and Narragansett No. 2" attempted to attach themselves to the application. The wing wanted no part of them, and to the assembly it explained why. "If the farms should be annexed to said wing it would carry the center of the wing and farms to the very northerly side of said wing, which would oblige the two-thirds of the inhabitants always to travel three or four miles to meeting." In other words, though the residents of the wing would have had two thirds of the voters of the proposed amalgamation, they fully expected that advantage to count for nothing. Location of a meetinghouse was not a matter to be determined by a mere majority vote; it required a regard for, even an obligation to, the common welfare.[8]

The canons of conciliation also shaped the towns' efforts to provide schooling for their citizens. A constant extension of educational facilities kept approximate pace with people who moved off from original village centers; and though specific practices varied from place to place, the principle was the same almost everywhere. Rutland could keep its school in the middle of the town two thirds of the year in 1733, conducting it in the west end only the remaining third of the time, but it did bring the school directly to the west end. Rehoboth could send its school successively through the four neighborhoods of the town a quarter of a century before, twenty-one weeks in one section, fourteen in the next, then thirteen, then nine in the last; but despite the crazy-quilt chronology there was a school directly settled in each district for at least two months. In 1762 Amherst could vote on "Whether it be Best To have two or three Scool Houses," but the town never even considered the possibility of a majoritarian politics in which the various sectors of the town contended for possession of a single town school. And Worcester, which sent its school to four quarters of the town for a while, had five quarters by 1751, seven by 1761, and eight by 1769. If the fractions were often a bit vague, the commitment to accommodation was always quite clear. What was demanded explicitly in 1771 had already been standard practice for four decades there, that "Justice be Done to Each part of the Town." [9]

Of course, justice alone did not control such extensions of the schools—schools were supported by town taxation, which required the approval of the town meeting, which was sometimes obtained only by an accompanying expansion of facilities[10]—but the part played by social values was not negligible in such situations. The political necessity of appeasing some of the citizenry to pass a school tax was not at all the same thing as the felt necessity of appeasing everyone; for if *some* accommodation was obviously essential to secure a majority in any town in which a majority did not live in the center of the settlement, *no more* accommodation was needed, on that account, than would suffice for such an end. That the towns attempted to accommodate all was testimony to their attachment to an ideal of community life.

The same ideal applied in the allocation of almost every other public resource as well. Highways were built or extended on the request of the townsmen they would serve, and roads were repaired "by the united assistance of the whole town." [11] Agreements were made that assured the outlying settlements "a proportionable part of the preaching" if their inhabitants could not conveniently attend church at the central meetinghouse.[12] And for a variety of jurisdictions ranging from those of fence-viewers and hogreeves to those of the militia companies, towns were divided into districts so that men might serve only close to home, where they might derive benefit directly while they did their duty. Moreover, and even more significantly, the lines of these districts were different for different activities and authorities. School districts did not coincide with high-

way surveyors' districts, which in turn diverged from those
of the wardens or the fence-viewers. There was, then, no
stable neighborhood identity; only the principle of extension of facilities was constant, not the geographical units by
which that extension was arranged.[13]

Accommodation was also a constant condition of community even when towns declined to provide their more
distant families with actual physical facilities. A wide variety of other material expedients served to placate men who
could not be gratified more directly. Towns which had
only a single schoolhouse refunded a portion of the rates to
the parents of those children who could not easily attend it,
so that they might make their own educational arrangements.[14] Ministerial taxes were divided when the whole
town could not conveniently meet together.[15] Taxes were
remitted, for villagers furthest from facilities, for the un-
seasonable part of the year; or the remote settlements
were taxed at a relatively lower rate, or they were exempted from taxation altogether.[16]

And all these material measures were but a portion of
the provincial effort to placate potential malcontents, for
accommodation was never merely a matter of money and
meetinghouses. It was a project which pervaded all public
behavior, especially in times of turmoil. In 1732, for example, the town of Dudley met "to see if thaire was aney
thing acted contrary to Law in our proseding in chusing of
a minester at our Last meeting that it may be rectefied." At
the meeting, though, the moderator asked only "whether
any man was disatesfied·with our prosedings at our Last
meeting consarning our Choys of Mr Isaac Richardson."
He repeated the question "several times," but, "there
being no man in the present meting that obgected against
their Choys or Salerey or Settlement," the town went on to
other business. What had been a concern for the violation
of the law when the question was raised in the warrant had

become a concern for the satisfaction of the citizens when it was put forward and answered in the meeting. In abstract logic it might have appeared that the degree of local unanimity was irrelevant to the issue of legality, but in consensual communities another logic prevailed, one in which legality itself could become irrelevant. No town vote could make the truly illegal truly legal, but where there were none who "obgected" or were "disatesfied," that unanimous consent obviously conferred a legitimacy of its own kind.[17]

The real point, nonetheless, was not the logic of legitimacy. The real point was the town's scrupulous concern for the satisfaction of all the inhabitants, and that point was made even more explicitly in an otherwise similar sequence of events in Braintree in the winter of 1703–4. A meeting was summoned on a warrant which ran:

> Whereas there has been some dissatisfaction and disturbance in the Town respecting Mr. Fisks maintenance, there being some of our neighbours who think that that vote which settles 90 Pound @ annum upon him was not so legal & orderly made & to prevent any further Trouble in the Town thereabout we think it needfull that ye Town should meet.

There too, then, the occasion of the meeting was "dissatisfaction and disturbance in the Town" and the object was "to prevent any further Trouble in the Town," while legality appeared only in between and in passing. There too the episode's truest significance was in the solution suggested: "we think it needfull that ye Town should meet." For though the minister's salary had already been settled by town vote, the town could not proceed in the face of discontent simply by citing that prior settlement; rather, it had to return to the issue and contrive a wider confirmation. "A difference and dissatisfaction in divers persons in the Town" required still another meeting a few months later in the effort to eliminate that discontent, but in the end the minister's salary was indeed reduced to eighty pounds annually.[18]

Fitchburg was still speaking in the same accents sixty years later, when it conceded a meeting to "Reconsider their Vote Respecting the placing of the meeting House & Votte to place it near the Center of s[d] Town the better to acomedate Sundry of the Inhabitents who Seam Dissatisfied With the place alredy appointed for Building s[d] meeting House." Framingham met ten different times between February 1725 and July 1726, to reconsider meetinghouse measures, and in its attempts to attain general acceptance the town gave countenance to almost any discontents.[19] And in elections, town separations, and educational issues, there was the same necessity for a new determination when discontent came to the surface. The stated reason for reconsideration was always the same wish to clear up a residue of dissatisfaction, and that disposition always overruled such technical finality as the earlier votes could have claimed. The warrant for a Worcester meeting of 1725 put it plainly:

> whereas it Doth appear that Several of the Inhabitants of y[e] Town are Disatisfied with Reference to the Seeting of y[e] meeting house: That those parsons may have opertunity to make their agrievances known in ye presence of ye Town & give their Reasons therefor, & for ye Town to Consider & Come into Some proper method for Redress wherain it may apear thay are wronged.[20]

By reliance upon these norms of negotiation, it often proved possible for provincial communities to secure the unanimity they sought even out of such contentions. Among men who looked upon initial discord less as a fact to be faced than as an obstacle to be overcome, in discussions directed less to the delineation of differences than to their elimination, a common conclusion quite often emerged from original divergences. Late in 1773, for instance, one town deliberated "with Zeal" upon a communication from the Boston committee of correspondence and then "unanasmly agreed" on a response, including a resolution that the "letters of Correspondence we highly approve of & unanimously consent unto." Other towns in earlier decades also managed to act unanimously despite debate, and the clerks who kept their records saw nothing extraordinary in such juxtapositions as "after much Debate, unanimously agreed," or "long debate and due consideration" in order "to accommodate the matters of dispute" and "to the end that they might be amicably adjusted." * [21]

One way in which such adjustments were arranged was to allow every important interest in the society a voice in the determination of public policy, and in the practice

---

* Another instrument for the promotion of consensus out of conflict was the otherwise innocuous device of adjournment. Towns which were unable to resolve disputes unanimously often preferred to resolve nothing at all rather than impose a majoritarian decision, hoping that an agreement could be arranged before the succeeding meeting. As Berwick once explained, "some difficulties arising about the choice of town officers the said town adjourned their meeting to the fifteenth day of April last and then met, but meeting with more difficulty they adjourned their meeting" once more. Mass. Arch. 116, pp. 43–4; see also, e.g., ibid., p. 107; ibid. 118, pp. 707–12; *Brookline Records,* p. 172; *Records of Lunenburg,* pp. 138–9; "Records of Worcester," IV, p. 16; B. L. Mirick: *The History of Haverhill Massachusetts* (Haverhill, Mass., 1832), pp. 58, 78, 84, 101.

The town returns on the 1778 constitution also testified to the same technique. Forty towns reported at least one adjournment before voting, which, given the magnitude of the matter and the consequent unlikelihood of adjournment for flimsy reasons, would suggest the absence of any initial accord either for or against the document in those towns. Nonetheless, their results were not, in the end, notably different from the unanimity prevalent throughout the province. Almost half of these originally divided communities concluded in agreement, and three quar-

of more than a few towns in the eighteenth century conscious efforts were made along that line. Some communities deliberately chose their officials from the several sections of the town. Others elected more men than were essential, simply so that no sector of the town would be jealous of another. Still others went so far as to ordain, by specific vote of the inhabitants, a balance of neighborhoods in their boards of selectmen and their town committees; and the General Court itself recognized that practice and indeed required it in a few settlements.* [22]

But of course no single practice encompassed all the possibilities. Accommodation could not be compressed so easily into a definitive formula. It was inevitably tentative, experimental, informal; a matter of deft suggestions and clever compromises. Yet it was no less necessary for all that. The collaboration of self-interest and an invisible hand was then undreamed of, and no one in the province would have

---

ters of them reported ninety per cent majorities or more. Not even one in seven declared anything less than a seventy per cent majority. The figures were as follows (figures in parentheses are the comparable percentages for the entire sample):

	No.	Per Cent
100	17	45 (52)
95–99	7	18 (17)
90–94	4	11 (9)
80–89	4	11 (8)
70–79	1	3 (4)
60–69	3	8 (6)
51–59	2	5 (4)
	—	

38 (two of the forty towns reporting an adjournment reported no figures)

* Such balanced boards never represented a developed ethic of interest-group politics. When, as in Dunstable in 1755, selectmen from one corner of the town acted for the benefit of their own corner and ignored the rest, the reaction was one of outrage. Mass. Arch. 116, pp. 702–5. Self-seeking interest groups had no legitimate place in a community that conceived of itself in terms of consensus.

relied upon the public peace to realize itself. Men simply assumed that their own accommodative efforts were essential. Townsmen who chose "a large committee from the several parts of said town" did so in the deliberate pursuit of peace. They openly attributed their action to the "absolute necessity they were under of receding from that spirit of contention and discord," and they charged the committee to "project some method" for so doing. Townsmen who appointed a committee of eight, four for the north part of the town and four for the south, instructed their committee to report "whether there can be any proposals made that may and shall be complied with, on either side, that may be for yᵉ peace and satisfaction of both parts, of yᵉ Town." And the General Court could concur in such sentiments, prescribing agreement and accommodation because "we humbly conceive it will be much for the future peace and well-being of the town." [23]

For the fact of the matter was that the failure of accommodation could "cause great difference" in the community and thereby be "very hurtful" to it. No social system's sanctions are so stringent as to secure absolute invariance—least of all a system so dependent on informal accord as town government in provincial Massachusetts—and nonaccommodative relations between a majority and another significant segment of the town did occasionally obtain.[24] But on such occasions a causal connection was commonly asserted between those dangerous "divisions among ourselves" and the default of conciliation. In the absence of accommodation many men sought a complete disaffiliation from the majority which oppressed them,[25] and in one town where there was no outright appeal for division, men confronted with similar conditions of unconcern responded cautiously, conditionally, equivocally—and even more revealingly. After an extended account of their difficulties some men of Berwick asked for the intervention of the General Court in their case, and their application defined the acceptable terms of communal life in provincial Massachusetts.

> Your petitioners humbly pray that they may be exempted from paying any part of the money voted to be raised for the building the meetinghouse proposed to be built by the town or that the proceedings of the town committee may be stayed and the votes of the town about the same made void, or that there may be a division of the town into two parishes that the lower part may enjoy the meetinghouse which they have built. . . .

Accommodation or separation—those were the conditions of satisfactory community. There were no alternatives.* [26]

There had never been any alternatives. From the founding of the colony men had differed, and those of their differences which could be neither disregarded nor adjusted had ended only with the departure of one party. Circumstances sometimes shifted—Anne Hutchinson and Roger Williams

---

* Of course the integrity of the community was occasionally abrogated, and men did sporadically display vindictiveness, animosity, avowed opposition, or a desire for retaliation. But by far the most striking aspect of such episodes is their infrequency. A faction in Dunstable did indeed tell the town that "they did not care whether they liked what was done or not; what they wanted was their money, and that they would have or they should all go to jail"—Mass. Arch. 116, pp. 702–5—but in all the archives examined, no one ever said anything as antagonistic again. In Haverhill one party cast "odious" and "scandalous" reflections upon some leaders of the other party and refused even to let them see a copy of the original complaint "unless we would pay them for it"—ibid. 115, pp. 349–51—but ultimately that party did allow inspection of its complaint, and the other side turned the other cheek, hurling no countercharges, simply seeking their own vindication against the initial accusation of "partiality." In an Easton election meeting the opposing sides withdrew to some distance from each other—ibid. 49, pp. 398–400—but nowhere else was opposition thus given a physically visible manifestation by overt congregation into separate parties.

left under less amicable auspices than Thomas Hooker's migrants to the Connecticut Valley—but always the final fact of separation had been the same. Indeed, separation as a solution could hardly have escaped the consideration of men whose very lives had been shaped, in that first generation, by a supreme act of separation.

Consequently, there were splinterings of settlements from the very first years of the colony. The culture simply could not contain conflict, as was obvious enough in the larger controversies of the founders, from the Antinomian furor through the halfway covenant, and as was equally apparent in a number of other divisions which arose solely out of the local difficulties of the seventeenth-century villages. One of these is worth rehearsing briefly, both because Sumner Chilton Powell has given us such a superbly detailed account of it and because it will serve as an extended paradigm for the subsequent separations of the provincial era.

In Powell's Sudbury, the pressures of population growth in the first two decades provided a catalyst for divergent English antecedents and competing conceptions of the agricultural order and led, momentarily, to the emergence of opposing factions in the town. Yet Sudbury's difficulties, seen in context and seen whole, did not demonstrate a discrepancy of early rhetoric and reality, nor did they prove the violation of the formal values of harmony and self-suppression when opportunity offered. All they did was confirm the power of those cultural conceptions over the settlers' actions, in the two decades of complete concord which preceded the brief period of animosity and especially in the conclusion of the conflict itself. For Powell found that the resolution of the controversy was "relatively easy," since the leader of the lesser side was able to "turn his dissent into positive political action" by taking his followers off to form "still another town, another religious and political institution with a different spirit." That is to

say, division of the town was not a testimony to conflict but
rather to its opposite. Men of the minority never gave any
thought to accepting defeat by a majority, nor to working
out the uses of a loyal opposition, nor to widening the
scope for dissent; in the end they had been able to conceive
only of separation. The very essence of the affair was the
form a man took to "turn his dissent into positive political
action," the determination to dissolve the situation which
had produced the dispute and to re-establish harmony and
the hegemony of the community under more auspicious
circumstances. In the new community which such men
helped to establish, the expectation of orthodoxy was un-
diminished and relations to authority were unaltered. In
Marlborough as in Sudbury there was still the premium
upon peace, still the reliance upon consensus. A concord
of almost twenty years' standing had been briefly blasted in
the moment when a new generation with disruptive demands arrived to political maturity, but by the partheno-
genetic process which was to continue common in Massachusetts for at least a century, that momentarily shattered
consensus soon became two new and quite whole consen-
suses. Marlborough was every bit as monolithic as Sudbury
had been, and Sudbury itself was restored to homogeneity.
The men who went to the new town went because they
accepted a new set of ideas about the agricultural order;
the men who stayed in Sudbury stayed because they were
satisfied with the old arrangements. In either case accord
was indispensable.[27]

Sudbury's split typified a pattern which prevailed to the
time of the Revolution. So long as the maintenance of an
effective community required widespread consent of the
governed, the unit of government had to be one in which
such united public opinion could be obtained. It was important in provincial Massachusetts to preserve the integrity of the community, but it was imperative to preserve
the peace. When harmony and homogeneity were broken,

the territorial integrity of the town itself often had to be ruptured accordingly. In some towns, such as Sudbury, the division was generational, so that one group had to withdraw to seek a settlement elsewhere. In other towns the division ran along geographical lines, so that the inhabitants could keep their homes and farms while merely dividing the political jurisdiction in two. But in both cases, the technique of turning contention into consensus by a separation of the parties to the controversy was essentially the same.*

Quite simply, discord dictated division because division could restore peace. It was their "many broils, differences, difficulties, and vast expense" which some inhabitants of Framingham cited in an appeal of 1731 which concluded that "although the petitioners are a great deal the smallest in number, yet for the sake of future peace and quietness of the only thing desired, the petitioners pray to be set off and made a separate town." It was a similar stimulus which provoked an earlier demand for disengagement from the men of Watertown, who explained

> 'tis the only method for settling or producing a lasting peace and accord. For while there is a mutual dependence of one part on the other the contest is like to be continued, each will be striving for victory and improving advantages against other, which contest will cease if distinct precincts be allotted.

---

* Needless to say not every separation was an effort to end controversy. In fact, most of them were not. Simple geographic convenience governed far more splits than discord ever did; in a tabulation of all appeals for town, district, or parish status in the Massachusetts Archives, Vols. 116 to 118, it was mentioned thirty-two times in seventy applications for incorporation, easily the most common offering; or see Whitten: *Public Administration*, p. 11, or Nason: *Dunstable*, pp. 55–7, for striking instances. Nevertheless, whether more separations were due to distance than to discord is not a question which has any bearing on whether there existed a pattern of separation as a solution to conflict. The former question does set the latter in perspective, but other than that it is simply irrelevant.

And there were still other spurs to separation later, not all of which by any means were tied to the ecclesiastical cleavages of the Great Awakening. Any discord that endangered the peace was a potential springboard to separation, and such separation, "for the healing the divisions that are yet unhappily subsisting among them," was endorsed by the General Court itself.[28]

The most fertile source of divisions, or at any rate the most self-evident to the men of Massachusetts, was dissimilarity within the community. Where differences developed in religion, occupation, ethnic extraction, or anything else deemed relevant, separation was often seen as the only solution. The communities of the province simply could not conceive of successfully maintaining structural diversity. Harmony required homogeneity; and the appearance of a substantial commercial interest, say, in a town of farmers soon moved such a town to seek its own partition into a monolithic mercantile community and a monolithic agricultural one.

That was what happened in Newbury in 1763, where the petitioners "cited as the basis for their request the irreconcilable breach that had split the two segments of the population," and where the General Court acknowledged the same causal connection when it granted the application and incorporated the "waterside" as Newburyport:

> Whereas the town of Newbury is very large and the inhabitants of that part of it who dwell by the waterside there, as it is commonly called, are mostly merchants, traders, and artificers; and the inhabitants of the other part of the town are chiefly husbandmen, by means whereof many difficulties and disputes have arisen in managing their public affairs. . . .

It was also what happened in Salem a dozen years earlier, and it was what happened in Springfield a decade later; as the Springfield petition pleaded, the citizens being "divided in their interests" prevented "that harmony and unanimity . . . which they most heartily wish to enjoy in all their public concerns but despair of whilst connected with such a large body whose interest is so different from theirs."[29]

The same logic of divergence-dissension-and-division applied elsewhere and to other differences than those of economic pursuits. Ethnic incompatibility was an obvious basis for separation—as a General Court committee once decided in Stockbridge, "Your committee are humbly of the opinion concerning the disagreement between the English and the Indians, their different dispositions, and the manner of conducting their civil affairs, that they be separated into different societies"[30]—but so too were divisions determined by differences among Anglo-Saxons who had lived in different towns.[31] Among townsmen of homogeneous economic, ethnic, and geographic extraction, there were still other sources of separations. Even disputes over the location of a meetinghouse or the choice of a minister occasionally produced breaches,[32] and more often such pragmatic differences derived from deeper doctrinal ones. As a 1711 Swansea petition explained, "ill circumstances" would obtain so long as some men of a "different opinion in matters of religion from our neighbors" remained in the town. The applicants expressed fear that their estates were in their neighbors' "power . . . in all taxes," yet that danger, great as it was, was "little and light compared with the bitterness we feel at present and fear for the future" about the conduct of religion in the town. Disharmony was worse than discriminatory taxation.[33]

The imperative that differences be segregated was no less applicable before the fact than after. Only one modification was necessary: rather than the reality of divergence being used to realign communities, the prospect of divergence was used to prevent that realignment. The concept of the community remained the same; only the tenses were

altered, to suit the circumstances. "Different sentiments
subsisting among us with respect to religious concerns"
were offered as grounds against inclusion in a new town by
men content in their old community in just the same way
they were offered as grounds for seeking a new town by
men dissatisfied with their current situation; and the
danger of difference was the same as well. "Strife and contention will unavoidably ensue," as one group told the
General Court.[34]

Considerations of homogeneous community took precedence, for towns and Court alike, over more mundane
matters of material advantage and even, on occasion, over
the apparent imperatives of nature itself. Towns declined
annexations when they feared religious differences between their own orthodoxy and the religion of the prospective recruits, and they did so despite the broadening of the
tax base and the augmented wealth and population which
annexations would have meant. New plantations also
spurned added complements of land and taxpayers at such
a price, praying instead to the assembly "that we may not
be joined to different opinions." * [35] Springfield managed
to continue as a single corporation for nearly a century-and-

---

* There were, it must be added, limits to the primacy of communal considerations: to take an obviously extreme one, two men could not com-
prise a town no matter how well agreed they were. Splitting, therefore,
made sense only within certain minimal effectiveness. Consensus was a
necessary condition of viability, but it was not the only condition; there
was no point in dividing a contentious society if the new communities
made by the separation could not even meet the most modest material
requirements. Accordingly, voluntarism had generally to wait upon viability. Proponents of a separation were under obligation to show that the
divided units would continue to be operable, while opponents tried to demonstrate their own disability in the event of the removal. See Mass. Arch.
114, pp. 212–14; ibid., pp. 637–9; ibid. 115, pp. 729–30, 741–2; ibid. 116, pp.
392–3; ibid., pp. 529–30; ibid., pp. 602–a; ibid., p. 606; ibid., pp. 607–8;
ibid., pp. 747–8; ibid. 117, pp. 99–100; ibid., pp. 156–7; ibid., pp. 162–3,
165–9; ibid., p. 561; ibid., p. 748; ibid. 118, pp. 613–16; ibid., p. 619; ibid.,
pp. 661–2; ibid., pp. 713–14; ibid., pp. 739–40; ibid., pp. 867–8; ibid. 181,
pp. 128–9a, 130.

a-half after its founding, though the Connecticut River cut
the town almost in two and though it was one of the largest
towns in the province, because during all that time there
were never any good grounds for its division. "They being
well united and happy together," the rare requests for separation that did occur were dropped as soon as the town
declined to support them.[36] And in other towns as well, sev-
erance was often denied to settlements across rivers or
otherwise inconvenienced if such tangible troubles of time
and distance were the only reasons offered against counter-
considerations of the general welfare.[37]

Even when different opinions could be demonstrated
and they were sundered, men still insisted that the lines of
separation be defined by communal considerations rather
than those of sheer economic advantage. There was no purpose whatsoever in dividing one contentious community
into two contentious communities, and so petitioners such
as those of Berwick in 1748 received the town's permission
to form a parish only if that parish was established on lines
limited to their actual adherents, not if it was drawn on the
basis of what the petitioners would have wanted for their
economic well-being. A separation simply had to *separate*
divergent elements, and when it didn't it was worthless. As
Framingham told some of its townsmen who had failed to
draw such lines in 1731, the town was unable to see any
prospect

> that such a division of the town will put an end to
> the divisions and differences in the town, but tend
> greatly to increase and aggravate the same by reason
> of a difficult river in the town (which must then be
> made passable at sundry more places than now it is)
> and the intermixture of the contending parties.[38]

Consent, then, was a clear imperative in the creation of
new communities. In towns and parishes defined by free
consent, a harmonious prospect could be presumed; in

those which included men against their inclinations, that courtship of conflict promised ruination. Or conversely, an absence of consent could itself constitute evidence against homogeneity of attitudes or interests in the community, thereby presenting a powerful argument against divisions under such auspices, an argument which was indeed used by towns to prevent undesired departures. Worcester once dismissed an application for separation by pointing out that "it is against the minds of a majority, so they will be ever a poor, contentious, disunited society," and many other towns also rehearsed a calculus of consent in their declarations against divisions.[39] And the same regard for the degree of voluntary assent was determinative in some of the most interesting dispositions of populations which the General Court made in the provincial era. In one of them, for example, a portion of western Worcester County was sought as a community site by a variety of petitioners from New Braintree, Hardwick, Brookfield, Rutland West Wing, and Braintree Farms. Well over a dozen petitions and other documents rained down on the General Court, yet in that welter of conflicting claims the Court's disposition almost exactly mirrored the apparent agreements among the applicants. New Braintree and the Hardwick inhabitants had asked to be joined, and no evidence ever appeared to discredit their unity; New Braintree and the Hardwick inhabitants were made a parish. Rutland West Wing had attempted to attach itself to the Hardwick-New Braintree men but had been vehemently opposed by them; the West Wing's application was ignored. And some Brookfield settlers had attempted to add their area to the Hardwick-New Braintree contingent only to discover that many of their own neighbors were satisfied to remain where they were; the General Court set off only the seven families which specifically sought connection with the new community. Thus the Court granted incorporation to the two elements which agreed, without the element they did not want, and with only those who consented from the element which they wanted in its totality but from which they could not secure total consent. A knowledge of the range of agreement and disagreement, of consent and discontent, and of almost nothing else, would have afforded perfect predictability of the legislature's decision.[40]

More common than the settlements of such complex and conflicting claims were cases in which men were literally allowed to make their own choice of local allegiance. Applicants for a new community often asked for "those only who shall then be disposed to join with us," [41] and the individuals involved commonly demanded just such an option, much as their towns authorized exemptions for those who did not wish to be set off.[42] The General Court also approved such exemptions, occasionally even specifying that they were "for the healing the divisions that are yet unhappily subsisting among them." [43] And in fact, entire communities were sometimes composed by soliciting the consent of the prospective inhabitants. Agreement as the basis of community was carried to its logical culmination in Dunstable in 1755, in a General Court order which allowed all the inhabitants quite literally to choose their citizenship, simply by submitting their signed preference to the Secretary of the province within three months.[44]

But even such an extension of the consensual basis of community carried curious limitations. The requirement of written notice to the Secretary was one, the confinement of the choice to the citizens of the relevant area of Dunstable another. Still another, still more significant, was the obvious fact that in Dunstable, as in every other place, the petitioners had in fact *petitioned* to be separated from one place or joined to another. The substance of those separations often but their form invariably revealed the profoundly communitarian frame of thought of provincial Massachusetts.

At every stage, men petitioned for permission. First they asked the approval of the communities from which and to which they wished to be set off; those granted, they turned to the General Court for its authorization. At every stage they risked rebuff, but still they asked.[45] A dozen families of Stoughton could complain of their great distance from the nearest place of public worship in Stoughton, and of their still greater distance—"at least eight or nine miles" —from the site of town meetings, with roads "almost impracticable to pass" in winter, and of their "great difficulty as to any school or schooling" in Stoughton for their children; and yet they would actually ask the town to release them to Walpole, where they could find all those facilities far more easily. They did not, they could not, simply *go* to church and to school in Walpole. They stayed in Stoughton until they secured permission to go off. And they did so because even individual convenience was sought within the communitarian framework in Massachusetts.* [46]

The petitions also implied a third technique for the management of dissidence. All those local appeals for legislative authorization of particular compromises and cleavages were efforts to engage the General Court in resolving local disputes, and simply as such, apart from their specific subjects entirely, they indicated quite clearly the disinclination

---

* Such communitarian assumptions in the civic sphere were quite paralleled by those in the churches, where members were enjoined to attend only their own churches. The permission of the church was essential for removal or departure, and going anywhere else, even for ordinary preaching, was deemed a "Disorder." Mather: *Ratio Disciplinae*, pp. 140–1, 62–3; and see also Haskins: *Law and Authority*, p. 87; Mass. Arch. 116, pp. 715–16. And for an episode which clearly revealed certain of these constraints of community—ministerial hostility to the disruption of congregations, willingness to withhold dismissions, and the petitioners' preparedness to *request* transfers—see Heimert: "American Oratory," p. 164.

of the towns to handle determined opposition internally. Not all the towns carried their cases as far as the assembly for composition, but few if any of them hesitated to appeal somewhere for arbitration.

In civil affairs, arrangements for arbitration commonly began with an invitation to men mutually satisfactory to both parties,[47] townsmen if any of the inhabitants stood outside the dispute, "able out-of-town gentlemen" if none did. Disinterestedness was essential; nonresidence alone counted as nothing against a personal involvement in the issue, for as Duxbury explained, in dismissing some it had supposed impartial, "two of the said Committee now make claim to right of Commons with said town, and thereby shew themselves incompetent Judges in that matter." [48] These initial efforts of invited individuals sometimes proved effectual indeed, but if they did not, an elaborate escalation of intercession through more formal offices lay open, culminating at the General Court.[49]

In ecclesiastical affairs the same principles of mutuality and progression obtained. The first step, according to Cotton Mather, was for men to make application to "One or Two wiser Ministers in the neighbourhood," who would hopefully, "by their private and prudent Methods, bring Matters to such an *Issue,* as to supersede the necessity of a Council." If the mediation of the pastors proved fruitless, then a mutual council was called; and if the council could not compose the quarrel, an appeal to the assembly was allowed.[50]

The General Court, then, stood at the pinnacle of an established progression of outside assistance in the solution of local dilemmas, a court of last resort at the disposal of communities in difficulty.[51] Its entrance into a case was not invariable nor even set at the same sequential point in every instance, but whatever the stage at which its intervention was invoked, its function was the same. Local disagreement was antecedent to every such appeal, and the towns carried their disagreement to the Court because they could reach no local resolution.

Peace, therefore, was the prime purpose of outside arbitration. Towns confronted with the paralysis attendant upon conflict went to the assembly as "the only expedient to restore peace or to prevent the various increasing mischiefs of discord and contention among them." Towns which conceded their own impotence to control discordance insisted that, if the legislature would assist them, "it would reconcile all parties and the town be at peace." Controversy simply could not be left to the political processes of the torn community itself; as some Salem men once said, "the peace and quiet of said town greatly depends on what your Honors may do." [52]

Accordingly, application for relief was not ordinarily made until men exhausted all their own resources for restoration of the peace. At an extremity where "no desirable end of the controversy appears," they were quite willing to commit themselves to accept the decision of their arbitrators,[53] a commitment which was an integral element of every appeal outside the processes of town politics. Arbitration was an accepted decision-procedure; it had finality and was to be abided by. As petitioners in Bridgewater promised, if the Court sent a committee they would "be content with their report and determination" on a division of the town. As petitioners from Framingham pledged, if the assembly would pick a place for a new meetinghouse for them, they "would be staked down or determined thereby." As Springfield insisted when some of its inhabitants sought to reopen an issue already decided by arbitration, it would have been "inconsistent with the wisdom and usage of this Court to re-assume the consideration of matters already so solemnly determined as this has been." [54]

Finality was conceded so confidently because the initial applications came from communities at an impasse over everything but their dependence on that arbitration. A united town, not just one party, issued the invitations thus extended to the Court, and so the whole town could promise "that we will sit down by the determination of that committee in reference to matters abovesaid." As Woodstock once asked provincial intervention, "it will conduce to the peace of the town that a committee of this honorable Court should view the same, and they having mutually agreed and consented. . . ." [55]

By 1830 all such behavior was a bit incomprehensible. A local historian of Watertown, writing in the middle of Andrew Jackson's first presidential term, described one plea for provincial assistance, in 1692, and he commented, "This mode of bringing the disputes of a town to an issue would be deemed singular indeed at the present day; but it seems then to have been not uncommon." Describing another, in 1759, he remarked, "Here is another curious instance of an appeal to the Provincial government on town matters." [56] The puzzlement of the Jacksonian historian was easily explicable. He lived in an America which institutionalized competition, even as he wrote of a province which had proscribed it. What he could only call "curious" or "singular," the towns of the eighteenth century had done as a matter of course; even he had to concede that "it seems then to have been not uncommon." But the old premium on peace no longer prevailed in 1830, and from his new perspective he pronounced his inevitable, incomprehending judgment.

If provincial Watertown seemed singular in 1830, it seemed no less so in its own time. But where its singularity from the later standpoint lay in its efforts to secure civic serenity, its contemporary distinction was in its contentiousness. The town's troubles were so notorious that even outsiders knew of them and, at least in Samuel Sewall's case, prayed that the Lord might relieve them.[57] The Lord declined to do so, however, and for three quarters of a century more the men of Watertown continued to contend. For that, in provincial Massachusetts, they paid a price.

The cost of conflict was computed for them by Newton in 1757. Watertown's contentions had become Newton's concern because, shortly before, Watertown lost a portion of its territory to be annexed to Cambridge and asked the General Court to grant it an equivalent out of Newton. Watertown claimed that the original act of annexation was itself "an extraordinary act," but Newton's very first point in rejoinder was that such a separation would have been extraordinary only "had Watertown been then in peace." Peace was, Newton suggested, a preservative of a town's territorial integrity, and the lapse of peace exposed a society to such losses as Watertown had suffered. The theme thus announced at the outset informed Newton's entire response. Again and again the town digressed to contrast its own calm with the conflicts in Watertown, until finally it was clear that these were no digressions at all. The contrast was the very core of Newton's argument. Against its own accommodativeness Newton set the internal antagonisms of its neighbor, and then it drew a crucial conclusion: Watertown's difficulties were to be attributed directly to its discords. Watertown had enviously asserted that Newton was "three times as large and twice as populous as Watertown" and so could easily afford the detachment of one small district. Newton countered that the difference between its growth and Watertown's stagnation was due solely to the social conditions in the two communities. They had each been equally endowed at the outset, or, if anything, Watertown had begun with initial advantages. There had been only one distinction between them, but it had been determinative. "Watertown was once as large as Newton and much richer, and might have continued so to this day had it not been for the wars and animosities among themselves." [58]

Watertown's decline exemplified the dangers to which Massachusetts towns were exposed despite all their efforts at peace. Harmony and homogeneity were the crucial conditions of community in the province, but the norms of harmony and homogeneity did not and could not eliminate conflict everywhere. Even in a covenanted community, men might clash occasionally over scarce resources, much as men did elsewhere. The disposition of conflict was therefore a permanent problem, if only potentially, for people who had no resources for the utilization or the institutionalization of conflict. Their techniques—accommodation of the amenable, separation of the stubborn, arbitration in the case of impasse—were actually attempts to evade conflict, not to manage it. But if conflict could not, finally, be evaded—and occasionally that proved to be the case—then communal functions were not fulfilled, or prosperity ebbed, or both. Conflict which could not be escaped, crippled.

Indeed, such conflict could even, in an extremity, destroy. In the first precinct in Middleborough the death of a minister in 1744 precipitated a battle over his successor "which obstructed a desirable concurrence and unanimity of the inhabitants." Another minister was soon secured, soon dismissed, and thereafter the parish had no pastor for more than four years, sinking the while into "dissensions destructive of our state." In those few years a third of the parishioners departed the precinct "by death and removal otherwise," and near the end the precinct actually asked the General Court's authorization of its continued impotence as a local unit, praying to be excused the support of a minister and permitted to serve instead in the nearest convenient parishes. Culminating testimony to the ruinous effects of unresolved conflict came six months after that request, when the parish asked for its own final dissolution.[59]

The disruption of the first parish was perhaps unparal-
leled in its extent,[60] but the dynamic of its difficulties was
no different in less desperate cases. In Upton four years of
disagreement over the site of a meetinghouse took the town
from a flourishing to an almost forlorn state—in 1766 it
had "greatly increased in the number of its inhabitants"
and improvements were underway in many new neighborhoods, while by 1771 it was reduced to prayer for the remission of a fine for not sending a representative, being
burdened with "many of the poor and indigent" and
others who knew not "of any way to pay the whole of their
taxes"—and all this the petitioners attributed to the debili-
tation attendant upon discord. "Those divided opinions of
the town about a place to set their meetinghouse have been
very injurious and impoverishing to them." [61]

Other towns also experienced damage on account of an
impasse over the location of the meetinghouse or a failure
to find a minister,[62] but ecclesiastical concerns were hardly
the only ones in which discord and the decay of effectiveness were clearly connected. Impotence, or at least impairment of the capacity for action, was also the consequence of
contention in matters of highway maintenance,[63] sending
of representatives,[64] and regulating town meetings.[65] Town
officers elected under the auspices of animosity were sometimes reduced to helplessness; and in at least one town,
after years of intermittent social sparring, there were no
officials chosen at all one year, not even for such an elemental public function as tax collection.[66] In other towns conflict precluded agreement on the terms of a division of the
community,[67] or, worse, was conducive to still further divisions. As Stoughton explained the vicious circle, defections
due to discord left taxes "very heavy" on those remaining,
"which makes all that live near other towns very impor-
tunate with the Court to set them to them that they may
have lighter taxes; but the more there is that get off to

other towns the heavier the taxes to those that remain." [68]

Under such circumstances, towns were simply unable to fulfill public functions or pay public debts. Watertown spoke in so many words of the "vast charge and expense" of contention, and many towns connected peace with prosperity, antagonism with poverty. Worcester spoke generically of "small, poor, contentious parishes and districts," as if the connection of those qualities could be assumed. Natick gave voice to the diffused apprehensions of many when it insisted that the introduction of a cadre of contentious men would be "productive of the most fatal consequences." And Middleborough merely maintained that its "strength was broken" when its "union [was] dissolved." [69]

No elaboration was needed in these cases because the havoc of disharmony was well-established and even self-explanatory. Men in eighteenth-century Massachusetts lived under an unrelenting pressure on that account, and they were aware of it. They knew the consequences of unresolved contention well enough not to require detailed descriptions. Conflict which could not be evaded was disenabling. The ethos was never more eloquently evoked than by those citizens who acknowledged their limited material resources but announced, "a small society well united may more easily go through such business of building a meetinghouse and settling a minister than a greater number when there is nothing but discord and disaffection." [70]

❧ V ❧

The Sense of
the Meeting

CONSOLIDATION OF CONSENSUS and control of conflict were
the essential aims of the eighteenth-century villagers, but in
and of themselves those values did not vouchsafe fulfillment. The broad cultural aspiration to harmony and homogeneity did not convert itself automatically into the tens
of thousands of agreements which were actually reached in
the hundreds of settled places of provincial Massachusetts.
Those agreements had to be hammered out anew every
time an issue arose, and the hewing required an arena and
rules.

At the Bay in the eighteenth century, the arena was the
town meeting and the rules were those that patterned its
structure. In town meetings from Cape Cod to the Connecticut Valley, men gathered to discuss the firewood that the
minister said they had promised him, to consider conditions to be attached to the new town mill that was going to
make a rich man richer, to haggle over the seating of the
meetinghouse; and in the accords they achieved, even out
of initial difference, they deepened their solidarity and
their assurance of union. Each agreement was a real recon-
secration of the community, and so the town meeting
served not only as an instrument of social decision but also
as the institutional site of the translation of larger values
into local behavior.

Meetings were assembled on occasions mundane and

momentous, and the procedures of each of those meetings disclose something of the mechanics of the institution's mediation between wider principles and particular practices. For the purpose of providing a focus, however, the election meetings alone will be discussed directly here. Those meetings in March had, to be sure, a stir of excitement about them that most of the meetings of June or January lacked, but they were not otherwise atypical. Any business that could be brought before an ordinary meeting could equally come before the townsmen on the day they chose their officers, so little is lost in the limitation to March meetings but the quotidian quality of the other assemblages.

In any case, a society's system for determining its leadership affords a vast store of information in its own right about that society. A seventeenth-century account of an English election for Knights of the Shire for Essex County, for example, in which "the freeholders were called upon by the constables to give their votes for the side supported by most of the Justices of the Peace; and there was also a very irregular creation of freeholders, in order to secure the return of Sir Francis Barrington and Sir Harbottle Grimston," shows a society where men voted subject to the scrutiny of their superiors and inclined to the "side supported" by them, and where support was assured anyway by the manipulation of electoral eligibility. An aside in the same account—"Sir Edward Coke and Sir Nathaniel Bernardston have been returned for Suffolk, but they would not have been chosen if there had been any other gentlemen of note, for neither Ipswich had any great affection for them, nor most of the country"—indicates the incapacity of those Englishmen to choose or even to conceive as candidates any but "gentlemen of note." [1]

Similarly, then, the elections of eighteenth-century Massachusetts tell their story—a rather different one—of social structure and decision-making and of the quest for consensus that found its ultimate locus in the town meetings.

There was no such thing as a typical town meeting, so there is no point in trying to reconstruct one, but that very variety is revealing. Towns varied because the province had not the power to prevent it; the divergence reflected the essential isolation and autonomy of the provincial community. If there was considerable convergence as well—a convergence rooted in common cultural values and assumptions together with common imperatives of communal life —such convergence was, in the last analysis, within the discretion and upon the sufferance of the towns. Uxbridge and Attleborough might conduct their affairs similarly, but only to the extent that their convenience was not threatened. In the end they would do what was appropriate to their own needs so long as they were not subject to sanctions which could be made good from Boston, and in the provincial period such sanctions were scant indeed.

By law, town election meetings were to be held in March, elections for representatives in May. Beyond those limitations, and except that elections for representatives had to be held within the dates established by the provincial procedures of notification, the province prescribed nothing for the date of election meetings. Local choice or custom, rather than any imposition of provincial uniformity, governed the determination of election dates.

Such local choice was sometimes prescriptive, sometimes permissive, but always at the convenience of the community. Some towns held their local elections almost as if they had systematically set out to take a random sample of the month of March, while others set a fixed—yet often violated—date.[2] Still others did not meet in March at all, gathering in February or April instead.[3] And even in the more closely controlled elections for representatives, control was not particularly close. Representatives were often chosen around the end of April or at the beginning of June,[4] an open invitation to the rural towns to pack the house once they found out how large a margin they had to supply to counter the mercantile contingent. Nonetheless, no closer control of voting dates was ever contrived before the Revolution.

Election dates were regulated ineffectually by the province. Election times were not regulated at all. They were determined solely by the separate towns, some of them declaring the hour by a formal vote and others relying upon local custom.[5] In either case, the choice was made within the context of local accord, and if it was not, a protest inevitably went up, directed not to any violation of statutory requirements but simply to the breach of the common understanding.[6]

Once the date was decided and the time satisfactorily set, the machinery of the meeting itself was put in motion by the issue of a warrant. This was the one point in the proceedings of the meeting at which agencies outside the town played any role at all, the warrants for May meetings requiring the selectmen's prior receipt of precepts from the sheriffs, who themselves awaited writs from the province authorizing the assemblies.[7] But even that small measure of intrusion occurred only in the elections for representatives—for all other formal gatherings of the group the warrant originated with the selectmen and was dispatched directly to the constables to notify the town of the meeting to be held and of its agenda—and in any case the invasion was more notable for what it denied the invaders than for what it allowed them. The role of the sheriffs in sending the precepts was mechanical and minimal, and the management of the elections for deputies remained entirely with the towns. The very precept itself stated quite explicitly that the selectmen were to direct the meeting, and that was surely its essential significance. For while sheriffs outside

New England generally functioned as presiding and returning officers at all elections, the sheriff in Massachusetts was separated from all effective power. He had no part whatsoever in the actual conduct of the canvass.* [8]

As for the notification itself, nothing else in the entire management of the meeting quite compared, for sheer luxuriant growth of local diversity, with the staggering variety of techniques of warning. The law's only requirement was that the "selectmen, or major part of them, by order to a constable or to the town clerk, are to warn town meetings," a requirement which said nothing at all about how or when the meeting was to be warned and nothing very definite about who was to warn it or upon whose authority.[9] Directives from a unanimous board of selectmen or from a mere majority, executed by the town clerk or the constables or perhaps even by subordinates specifically delegated the duty by those officials—all were compatible with the law of the land, and all were actually employed. So was notification by the selectmen themselves, by the constables at the behest of the town clerk, and by a town crier. In an extremity, even private citizens assumed the responsibility.[10]

Similarly, warrants were set out as little as a few days before a meeting and as much as months. The General Court and the county courts themselves variously allowed eleven, fourteen, and twenty days; and whatever temporal bounds the Court or the counties set, the towns set still other ones. Bellingham allowed a month from the first reading of the warrant to the time of the meeting, Swansea only five days. Others gave notice of a week, two weeks, eight days, ten days.[11] And latitude was still wider when special precepts were issued by the House for elections to fill vacancies created by the elevation of elected representa-

---

* In special elections the precept went directly from the House of Representatives to the selectmen, stripping the sheriff even of his formal connection to the meeting. See, e.g., Mass. Arch. 49, p. 403; ibid. 50, pp. 20-2, 452; *Journals of the House,* XXIX, p. 10; ibid., XXXIII, part 1, p. 7.

tives to the Council. Though the precepts all went out in the last days of May, the new elections, in one short span of years, were held on June 7 in Salem, on July 1 in Kittery, and in Salisbury on August 22.[12]

And the techniques of warning differed even more minutely than the time intervals. Broadly, these techniques may be broken into two central tendencies, public notification and individual information, but within each tendency there was a vast range of applications in particular communities. Public notification was variously obtained by reading the warrant at an earlier town meeting or at the preceding church services or by posting it at public places, variously, the meetinghouse door, a tavern, a stable, a courthouse, a school, a mill, or special notification posts.[13] Individual warning was "by leaving word with them or at their houses," by printed announcements delivered to each house, by verbal notice to inhabitants the constables found at home "or met in the highways."[14] And other towns adopted still other expedients, such as a fixed date for all further election meetings.[15]

An episode in Braintree in 1760, when the town dismissed a meeting because "the warrant for assembling said meeting" had been executed improperly, epitomized the license assumed by the localities. Braintree's impropriety had not been by any provincial standards, for those did not exist or did not matter. The prescriptions that did matter were the ones that had been established "according to the direction of the town," and it was those that had been infringed. The absence of a provincial code meant nothing; local orthodoxy was so strong that its violation required that the assemblage be broken up. Similarly, when a meeting was called upon shorter notice than was customary, that infraction provoked immediate protest. As Bridgewater complained in 1738, the "said warning was so very short that most of the people knew nothing of the meeting." Men might not know how other towns notified meetings,

but they did know how their own community conducted
its affairs. They had probably been parties to the course
adopted, and they expected that course to be continued unless they were parties to its modification.[16]

Ultimately too, the insistence on full warning was an
insistence on inclusiveness. In communities dependent
upon wide agreement for their effective operation, exclusion was impractical. A Plymouth decision of 1732, that the
town "could not proceed" to an announced meeting because the constable for the south part of the town had
failed to notify his neighbors, was compelled not by any
quirk of the Puritan conscience, nor even by the law which
required that the constables return their warrants to signify
that the entire town had been warned, but rather by the
imperatives of consensus.[17] Considerations of conscience
and legality were no different whether a single inhabitant
or half a town had not been notified, but the occasions of
failure to warn one or two eligible inhabitants consistently
met far different fates than those in which more substantial
numbers were involved. The town which voluntarily disbanded a meeting due to larger deficiencies of notification
was completely capable of turning a deaf ear to the protests
of a solitary citizen, despite the fact that the legal issues
were quite the same in both cases. The distinction was on
the dimension of inclusiveness, and it was that dimension
which was determinative.[18]

Indeed, even when the entire town had been lawfully
warned, a measure of inclusiveness still had to be assured
before a meeting could begin. Accordingly, when a storm
caused poor attendance of a Stoughton meeting of 1759,
those who had come voted that the meeting be adjourned
"that the town might be more generally together when the
officers were chosen." When snow or floods curtailed attendance in other towns, the citizens at hand often declined to
convene; and sometimes it was not even necessary for natural havoc to provide a pretext, adjournment being moved

simply "In as much as the meeting is but thin and the affairs to be Transacted of Consequence." In all of these cases the meetings could have been convened with total technical propriety, and the proceedings of such meetings would have had the full force of the law to support them. But mere legal advantage mattered little without the support of neighbors, and so the townsmen in attendance refused to seize the advantage which was technically theirs, and clung instead to the ethic of inclusiveness.* [19]

The procedures of the warning, then, promoted an inclusiveness which in turn promoted consensus. The same procedures also served the cause of communal concord more directly, for the warrant by which the townsmen were notified was also the agenda of the meeting. As such it prohibited action on any affair not explicitly announced on that agenda, and thereby assured not only that everyone would know of the meeting but also that everyone would know, in advance, all the business which would be brought up at that time. Consensus was a quiet business, a business of consultation and compromise, and, as early experience had proven, the cause of concord was not served by free thought on a subject sprung unannounced and unconsidered upon the community. The rigid requirement of full warning precluded the possibility that men might consider

---

* On a few occasions men did avail themselves of their full legal right to convene a meeting in the absence of general attendance. These occasions were marked not only by the inevitable protests—see Mass. Arch. 114, pp. 737, 738, 740–1a; ibid. 116, pp. 373–4; ibid., pp. 702–5; ibid. 117, pp. 494–5; ibid., pp. 647–9; *Records of Braintree*, pp. 302, 303—but also by an extraordinary degree of agreement even in these cases of apparent conflict. In one instance, only a single selectman out of the five chosen by the unscrupulous assembly was in any way displeasing to the aggrieved petitioners who had not been present; and that man, the sole object of complaint, had served quite satisfactorily in the same post on several earlier occasions. In another episode, an accusation of advantage-taking referred only to a vote not to let the swine run at large, though the meeting at issue had been an election meeting in which the entire slate of town officers had been chosen without stirring the slightest subsequent opposition. Mass. Arch. 117, pp. 494–5, 498–9; ibid., pp. 463–5.

an issue on the spur of the moment. Its acknowledged purpose was that matters might be more fully "understood"
and the inhabitants "apprehensive beforehand," and by
thus insuring prior discussion and negotiation it contributed to a climate of consensus.[20]

Consequently, issues not warned in the warrant were
almost never taken up by town meetings. When they were,
a simple protest ordinarily sufficed for their withdrawal;
and in fact the principle was so important that it was
scarcely altered even in cases of imminent inconvenience.
Brookline, on the verge of losing the services of its minister
in 1759, still declined to discuss an adjustment of his salary
when that step was suggested in the middle of a meeting.
"Nothing was acted, as not being notified in the warrant." [21]

Once the warrants were served and the meeting was
called to order, business began with the designation of a
moderator, or presiding officer. And in that too the persistent pattern of local elections prevailed: a dearth of prescriptive provincial legislation and a wide range of local
variations. By implication the law appointed the selectmen
to manage the election, but the provincial provisions were
imprecise and occasionally ignored. In some towns all the
selectmen, acting together as a committee, regulated the
choice. In others a single selectman assumed a primary position. Still other communities substituted still others, especially their clerks, for the selectmen, and a few towns did
not even elect a distinct moderator at all, preferring to
leave the entire management of the meeting to the selectmen.[22]

But the election of a moderator was not merely a procedural matter. It was the first political action of the meeting as well, and from that point forward almost every
aspect of an election meeting was molded by the necessity
for consensus. That necessity began with the nomination

for moderator because substantial power was at least latent in that office.

Although the most elemental function of the moderator was the simple preservation of law and order in the meeting, a number of other parliamentary prerogatives of a presiding officer went along with that duty. Almost inevitably the moderator decided such matters as the opening and closing of the polls, the qualifications of voters, and the outcome of votes, and all of those decisions were subject to shading if he had a partial interest in the results. Indeed, there was nothing but the extent of his audacity to limit even more brazen displays.[23] Tacit testimony to the potential power of the moderator was unmistakable whenever a town protested against the "artifice" a man employed to gain the post, since its employment was worth the effort only if the position carried enough power to justify the risk.[24]

Accordingly, the conduct expected of a moderator was strict neutrality. That expectation did quite commonly obtain, producing elections which were not sought and declinations of the office from men who feared they could not remain disinterested,[25] but there were no alternatives to it in any case, since there was no place in popular expectations for stable parties with which a moderator could have aligned himself. In the normative order of the New England town no concept of a legitimately partial moderator existed because no concept of legitimate parties existed; when the presiding officer at a Chelsea meeting insisted on holding an election for representative despite the apparent vote of the town to the contrary, an appeal was dispatched to the assembly claiming that he had "treated the people more like a dictator or censor than a moderator."[26]

In fact, the standard of impartiality was never more evident than when it was violated. When moderators did infringe the expectation of neutrality, other inhabitants almost invariably complained of their conduct to the General Court, asking the annulment of the election and the appointment of "some discreet, disinterested person to regulate another meeting." [27] When moderators were accused of interested officiating, they bent every effort to denying the charge and displaying their adherence to the norms of neutrality. In Watertown, the selectmen responded to a protest against their regulation of a 1757 election with a vehement denial of any "partial regard" for either of the candidates, insisting that, if anything, they had bent over backward to avoid an open alignment with either side. Likewise in Lexington, selectmen accused of managing a meeting improperly made a reply whose whole design was to deny partiality and demonstrate the most complete accommodation. In neither case did anyone ever challenge the norm of neutrality. Presiding officers accepted it as absolutely as the petitioners themselves, and disputes were confined to the question of its infringement.[28]

After the selection of a moderator was settled, the next order of business was the qualification of voters. Massachusetts maintained a property qualification throughout the eighteenth century, and it was not always easy to determine whether a man met it. Some moderators solved the problem by cutting the Gordian knot, admitting all to the vote who applied for it, declining to turn away even the dubious voters, and characterizing themselves as little more than open conduits through which votes might freely flow.[29] Most men who held the chair found that solution rather too Alexandrian; but almost all of them would have recognized the impulse behind it, for it arose out of a very general preference that the possibility of partiality be removed from the determination of electoral eligibility. If all were not always allowed to vote, at least admission and exclusion did not depend on the whim of the presiding officer or on that "irregular creation of freeholders" by which elite power was sometimes preserved in England. Decisions on the qualification of voters in eighteenth-century Massachusetts were made by the moderator "according to the List and Valuation of Estates and Faculties." The list was prepared for purposes of taxation by the assessors, who were "required to lodge with the clerk of their respective towns and districts an attested copy of such their List and Valuation from year to year, which he shall produce for the purpose aforesaid, as there shall be occasion." If judgments of occasion still varied in various places—in some the List was read at the beginning of every election, in others the unqualified were warned not to vote, and in others still its employment awaited controversy—the crucial considerations were the very existence of a formal voting roll which did not depend on the moderator and the fact that, if differences persisted, the law provided that a man might qualify simply by swearing an oath that he did indeed fulfill the requirements of the franchise.[30]

Thus all questions of qualification became utterly impersonal ones, quite outside the control of a capricious moderator. And this impersonalization had important consequences. For one thing, it insured that, in every dispute over eligibility, the benefit of the doubt would lie on the side of inclusiveness. So long as a man was willing to swear to his qualification, he could not be denied a ballot; the ultimate presumption was in favor of the townsman rather than the moderator. For another, the establishment of impersonal criteria for qualification was consciously conceived as a discouragement to discord. The legislation that established the oath of qualification cited some "doubts and controversies" that had arisen, and it was enacted "for preventing whereof for the future." [31]

The moderator chosen and the voters qualified, the meeting proceeded to the election proper.[32] The order of the election was, like much else, a matter of local opinion: perhaps the most frequent order of election was selectmen, clerk, treasurer, constable, and then the lower officers, though that precise sequence probably obtained in something less than half the local elections.[33] But the order of election was not nearly so important as the simple fact that there were so many elections to be ordered. Altogether, at least forty different petty offices were filled in various New England towns, and almost all of them were filled by elections, even though almost all of them were basically administrative positions. In the English towns from which the men of Massachusetts had come, local government had been "administrative, not legislative." Only the mayor was elected, and not even his election was a particularly public affair; government was a "mystery," not a prerogative of the populace. The communities of provincial Massachusetts, on the other hand, converted the most trivial tasks into public functions exercised by elected agents. Even a gravedigger was an elected public servant in places such as Dudley and Brookline.* [34]

Before balloting for gravedigger, selectman, or any other office could begin, men had to have some idea for whom they were voting. And yet, if they did, there is almost no explicit evidence at all that such notions were ever founded on a formal system of nominations or a preceding period of campaigning. And the absence of evidence is particularly significant since the New England colonies appear

---

* This sense of the extent appropriate to the public sphere controlled the choice of town constables, where it frequently happened that the elected constable hired a replacement. In provincial Massachusetts such a matter was never allowed to stand as a simple private transaction between two citizens. The man elected had to present his proposed substitute to the town meeting for its acceptance, and, in fact, a few candidates were rejected by the assembled townsmen. See, e.g., *Records of Lunenburg*, p. 202; *Records of Plymouth*, III, p. 82; *Weston Records*, p. 171. Of course this was nothing extraordinary in one sense: the constabulary, as a public office, had to be filled to public approval. But in a more important sense that was precisely the point. What was significant was that men did define the constabulary in purely public terms, and that the community did insist on jurisdiction over matters which might have been—and elsewhere were—regarded as proprietary rights or relegated to the realm of administration.

to have originated a system of nomination at the colonial level in the seventeenth century but not to have adopted it for their own local elections.

In England, nominations had been self-announced or propounded by small cliques of the gentry; at the time of the initial settlements, "these were practically the only methods of nomination in vogue among English-speaking people," and therefore the only ones with which the colonists were familiar. In the very first generation in America, however, the men of the Bay Colony had elaborated a far more formal nominating procedure for the magistracy. Their storied system of beans and corn entailed a prior presentation of candidates; and though their biotic ballot itself did not survive beyond the early years, the principle of nominations did. It continued as the basis for the choice of Councilors throughout the provincial period. But for all that, the nomination of candidates was only rarely extended toward the towns, and almost never in matters which touched their internal polity. Where ongoing communal relations were concerned, nominations were rarely resorted to; or at any rate, the evidence for such resort is meager.[35]

Most town records never spoke of nominations at all. The very few which did mention them did not make a habit of it. Braintree, for example, "nominated and chose" five selectmen in 1746, but that was the only time the records revealed such a procedure in the first three quarters of the eighteenth century.* The only town in all the province

---

* On other occasions Braintree did proceed by nomination for moderators, treasurers, minor officials, and town committees; see *Records of Braintree*, pp. 122, 126, 165, 167, 168, 190, 266. But those nominations, far from constituting a technique for the provision of competing candidates, implied if anything an even clearer consensus than the methods employed elsewhere did. Choice by nomination was not far distant from choice by acclamation. Voting was open, "by hand votes," (pp. 165, 199) and the suggestion was strong that election was almost automatic upon nomination. A man "being first nominated was voted Moderator"; others, "being nominated, were chosen" (pp. 126, 167). Such appointments, then, represented no contests among declared contenders for a position. They were

which testified to the regular provision of candidates by nominations was Stockbridge, and its testimony is somewhat less than compelling since Stockbridge was a very singular community in its division between Indians and English.[36]

The evidence against the existence of nominations is inevitably less than direct, but it is both more abundant and more compelling. Any number of accounts of elections said nothing whatever about nominations, and in some very detailed descriptions the entire affair was discussed in terms more appropriate to high espionage than to politics, which was perhaps a revealing attitude.[37] Such descriptions often recorded also "a considerable number of scattering votes" or "single votes," suggesting that there were not just a couple of candidates clearly defined by nomination.[38]

Suggestive too was the fact that no legislation of any kind was ever enacted by the province on the subject of local nominations; and even more suggestive was the almost total failure of the town records themselves to report candidates nominated. If none were noted because none were ever nominated, that would close the case. But even if it expressed only a disinclination to declare openly the actuality of competing condidates, such disingenuity still displayed dramatically the society's desire to display unanimity rather than discord.

Most indicative of all, perhaps, was the occurrence of declinations of office,[39] an occurrence common enough that the law of the province provided for its possibility and codified its consequences.[40] The meaning of such declina-

---

simply plebiscites on the sole candidate up for consideration, and so almost everything depended upon who was nominated first and then upon whether others who had other candidates in mind could be prevented from voting against any but their own. Under those conditions, the absence of acrimony in the town records lends significant support to the supposition that unanimity marked such nominations. Prior discussion and agreement would obviously have smoothed the operation of the system and permitted the attainment of approval for the man first nominated.

tions was almost unmistakable. Unless men were openly nominated and then changed their minds in the few minutes between nomination and election, those who declined offices to which they had just been elected must have had no earlier opportunity, in the absence of nominations, to announce that they did not desire the office. Indeed, even declinations in advance of an election were couched in terms which implied the absence of an established system of nominations. When selectman George Watson appealed to the town of Plymouth—"I don't Know as any person Intends to vote for me as one of the Selectmen for the year Ensuing, perhaps their are some that do, if there any Such I must desire them to give their votes for some other person as I Should be verry Glad to be Excused"—he did not ask the town not to nominate him but rather not to vote for him. The difference was significant.[41]

And yet, without any apparent nominating procedure, Massachusetts towns conducted their elections smoothly and without the catastrophic splintering seemingly inherent in the system. Something must have permitted the orderly provision of candidates and set the stage for the peaceful elections which were held; but again, there is little or no direct evidence on the matter. Much then must be reconstructed inferentially.* And investigation of the material machinery of campaigning, for all that it extends into a murky terrain of suppositions about voting habits and informal politicking, does produce a matched pair of attitudes toward campaigning itself which are most revealing.

On the one hand, there was an antipathy to campaigning altogether. Many towns simply recoiled from the pros-

---

* The simplest inference, that there were local oligarchies to whom such deference was paid that nominations were not even necessary, depends, of course, on the existence of those oligarchies, an existence which will be denied in Chapter Six. Therefore, the inference that a close, consolidated elite could command sufficiently unfailing allegiance to obviate any need for the formal provision of candidates will not be considered here.

pect. Lexington, for one, equated "Canvassing for Elections" with "corrupt influence and open bribery" and condemned them all as having "had the most baleful Effects, to the Subversion of Liberty and the Destruction of good government in Free States; and that in almost all Ages." Sudbury, for another, saw its moderator of a 1753 election defend his management of the meeting by presuming the undesirability of open allegiances and appealing to it: "I never opened my mouth that I know of to said Noyes or any other person since I was born about choosing him." Even in Watertown, the place in the province where conflict was most nearly institutionalized, men still held to the ideal of an unorganized election and a "free, uninfluenced choice" of officials.[42]

In fact, there seem to have been many towns and times which knew no campaigning. Most particularly, the existence of declinations would appear to stand conclusively against the likelihood of campaigning or of close political organization on the occasions of such renunciation, since men rarely organize and campaign for something they do not want.[43] More generally, no provincial legislation was ever enacted to control campaigning, a fact which strongly suggests that campaigning was not a very vivid social problem. And while the lack of regulation did not infallibly prevent factions, it did confine them, by definition, to unorganized and dubious if not entirely illegitimate channels. It did, thereby, retard or even prevent the stabilization of such emergent factions. It did tend simultaneously to starve them to death altogether. And these eventualities were surely to be expected, since the entire apparatus of nominations and campaigning is appropriate only to conditions of political contention, whereas the towns of Massachusetts never could conceive of themselves as divided.

On the other hand, though, many towns of Massachusetts were in fact divided, at least occasionally, and there is ample evidence of the intermittent existence of campaign-

ing for public place. It is true that there was often no need
for campaigning—even the very largest towns of eighteenth-century Massachusetts were still, after all, very small
towns without the impersonality characteristic of a later
American society, and there were always incumbents of the
offices at stake to provide a point of reference for the
voters[44]—but sometimes men did feel a need to campaign.
Many agreements may have been born, but some others
were made. At least as early as 1763, and perhaps for half a
century before, town officers were "regularly chosen" in
the Caucus Club of Boston before they were actually
elected by that town; and while the Caucus Club was quite
possibly the only formal agency of its kind, its techniques
could hardly have been unknown outside the capital. As a
contemporary chronicler described the Club's operation, it
might well have characterized many a rural hamlet:

> When they had settled it, they separated, and each
> used their particular influence within his own circle.
> He and his friends would furnish themselves with bal-
> lots, including the names of the parties fixed upon,
> which they distributed on the days of election. By
> acting in concert, together with a careful and exten-
> sive distribution of ballots, they generally carried the
> election to their own mind.[45]

The use of "particular influence within his own circle"
was probably the most elementary form of campaigning
wherever that art was practiced at all. John Rowe of Salem
recorded in his diary that, despite "blustering weather,
snow and sleet" on the day of an election meeting, he "attended on purpose to oblige my friend Ezekiel Goldthwait
Esq.," and others entered similar expressions. And when
some Stockbridge petitioners informed the General Court
that the Indians were "a people that never form any
schemes or plans of public business beforehand," the unmistakable implication was that the English were not such

a people. In a thousand deeds and designs such as these
must have occurred much of the informal but essential politics of the provincial towns.[46]

Other forms of influence were probably less innocent,
though equally informal. John Adams made a resigned
note of a Braintree election in which "many persons, I hear,
acted slyly and deceitfully," as was, he added, "always the
case." New Hampshire men turned up in Haverhill and
attempted to cast votes one fine spring election day, presumably not without assistance from some sort of political
organization. In Watertown it was openly charged that illegal voters "were brought by an unwearied restless party
to throw us into confusion," and in a singularly frank admission of electioneering in that singularly contentious
town, the selectmen added

> that as to the undue measures said to be taken to qual-
> ify voters and persuade persons to vote for Mr. Hunt,
> although we have no reason to think that such mea-
> sures were ever taken by Mr. Hunt or Mr. Whitney
> themselves, yet as the town is and for some years past
> has been divided into two parties nearly equal in
> number and as their contentions have been so sharp,
> we have no reason to think but that some of each
> party have done everything in their power to procure
> one of their own party to represent the town, and it
> is not so easy to determine which of the parties have
> carried these measures to the greatest lengths. . . .[47]

If few towns were so openly split as Watertown, people
in some others were even more candid about specific techniques of electoral influence. The most common measure
was, of course, bribery, though it was often difficult to dis-
entangle corruption from neighborly courtesy. When one
Mr. Oliver of Chelsea sent a personal letter to an office-
seeker, assuring him of support at the election meeting and
adding that "my son waits on you for that favor you pre-

sented Mrs. Oliver with the other day," the case was not so clear as it was when grosser economic pressures were applied. In Dunstable, for example, the taxing power was turned to partisan purposes in the promise of a controlling clique to another group "that if they would join with them they should be excused their taxes." In Pembroke the constables were accused of threats to make distress upon men who did not vote for their candidate. And at more personal levels of persuasion, indebtedness often proved a powerful inducement to vote as another directed.[48]

And subtler, sweeter cajolery was often even more effective than these heavy-handed threats. John Adams may have grown suspicious "when they are very liberal of their drams of brandy and lumps of sugar, and their punch, etc., on May meeting days," but others were less offended. When Jonathan Edwards petitioned for the purchase of a parsonage, his old enemy Ephraim Williams went to work on the committee "with his Lime-juice Punch & Wine." Edwards, as Perry Miller reported the encounter, "could give them only facts, and so lost the petition." Outside Stockbridge the popular preference was apparently rum rather than punch, but the provision of drink was no less effective for that.[49]

In fact, the resort to rum may have approached regularization in the tavern as a political institution. Unfortunately, the most straightforward statement of that proposition comes from John Adams, whose moral hypersensitivity may have led him into exaggeration, but others have also claimed that "in the inn much of the village business was transacted, and here in the long evenings the political engine was worked to the limits of its capacity."[50] In many towns, moreover, a tavern stood near the meetinghouse and stayed open on election day so that men might "withdraw and refresh." In other towns, election meetings themselves were occasionally held in the town tavern, and business there was said to be done "by some means or other. . . ."[51]

According to Adams, at any rate, the taverns were "the nurseries of our legislators. . . . Here diseases, vicious habits, bastards and legislators are frequently begotten." Of the several paths to power which originated in the tavern, the most obvious, for Adams, was the elevation of the innkeeper himself. "You will find the house full of people drinking drams, flip, toddy, carousing, swearing," he wrote, "but especially plotting with the landlord to get him at the next town meeting an election either for selectman or representative." William Douglass, a contemporary historian, offered Adams some corroboration in his lament that the residence requirement for representatives meant that, rather than a gentleman of affairs and education, "a retailer of rum and small beer called a tavern keeper, in a poor obscure country town," was likely to sit in the House of Representatives. Douglass did not mean to be taken literally, but his choice of a type-figure was revealing.[52]

Nonetheless, the ultimate importance of the innkeepers was probably less as candidates in their own right—though they did occasionally become selectmen or representatives—than it was as potential supporters of other candidates. By 1761 Adams was insisting that "an artful man has little else to do but secure the favor of taverners, in order to secure the suffrages of the rabble that attend these houses, which in many towns within my observation makes a very large, perhaps the largest number of voters." The influence of the taverner traced to rather obvious roots—his wide acquaintance, his liquor, his status as a creditor—which enabled him, if he wished, to hold his patrons "both by gratitude and expectation." And of course implicit in such a system was the possibility of an endless round of selectmen tied to taverners for popular support and taverners dependent upon the same selectmen for their licenses.*[53]

---

* Relatively complete figures for the town of Princeton show a compelling correlation between taverners and selectmen—ten of the twelve licensed

But even if no such circle existed and even if the tavern was not at all the sinister engine of degradation Adams assumed, it is still not difficult to imagine the thoughts of the townsmen lightly turning to politics on an early spring evening at the tavern. A quiet allusion here, a subtle suggestion there would be understood, and would be sufficient. It is not impossible that the tavern was the mediating mechanism of the entire system, smoothing the operation of the political machinery of the town so as to obviate nominations and organized campaigning.

In much the same way it is possible that the distribution of ballots by the candidates or their friends afforded another mediating mechanism which was, in some measure, regularized. Gordon discovered such distribution to be one of the Caucus Club's essential modes of operation in Boston, and if a comparable practice prevailed widely it might have amounted to another middle ground between nominations and electoral anarchy. No nominations would have been necessary in elections in which each interested candidate supplied a ballot with his name inscribed to every voter he could enlist in his cause.[54]

Both these suppositions are, of course, quite conjectural. There is little evidence that ballots were even distributed outside the capital, let alone that such distribution functioned as proposed; and there is not much evidence that the tavern was an important engine of local politics, either. But then, the essential evidence about campaigning in the province is the absence of *any* very substantial evidence. Conjecture is necessary only to a consideration of the specific shape of electioneering; it is clear

---

innholders to 1775 were also selectmen—but the relationship did not begin in the tavern. Only two became selectmen *after* obtaining their licenses to sell liquor; two others gained both positions in the same year, and five were selectmen *before* they became innkeepers. (No date was given for the tenth taverner.) Blake: *Princeton,* pp. 189–90, 355–6.

enough without any conjecture at all that, if the men of
Massachusetts did engage in campaigning, they were reluctant indeed to touch upon it in writing.

However, even if the conjectures are correct—even if
distribution of ballots and discussions in taverns *were* important elements in the provision of candidates—the matter is not as simple as that. Indeed, its lack of simplicity is
crucial to an understanding of the entire issue of campaigning in Massachusetts communities in the eighteenth
century. When Gordon described the Caucus Club's distribution of ballots, he called it "careful." When Adams described his emergence as a Braintree selectman, he spoke in
the accent almost of a conspirator: "Etter and my brother
took a skillful method; they let a number of young fellows
into the design . . . who were very pleased with the employment, and put about a great many votes." The distribution of ballots was no simple business, and its difficulty
was that it had to be managed covertly.[55] Hostility to overt
political organization was apparent among the people and
expressed even by the House of Representatives; and beyond even the antipathy to overt political organization,
there was a more basic structural imperative that militated
against any such machination, since nowhere in the society
were there any legal instruments or formal institutions deliberately designed to sanction and channel campaigning.
Thus there emerged a pair of closely connected attitudes
toward open political opposition in the communities of
eighteenth-century Massachusetts: on the one hand, nothing in the norms sanctioned it and no institutional arrangements accommodated it; on the other hand, such
campaigning as did occur was compelled to run into essentially subterranean streams.[56]

This picture of politicking can be brought to completion with a consideration of local voting procedures, for
nominations, campaigning, and balloting were all aspects

of the same central problem of the town election. The towns of Massachusetts voted by secret ballot, and not a very sophisticated one, either. But all its flaws were outweighed by its one virtue, the virtue of secrecy. The secret ballot in the provincial towns did not necessarily produce a true tally of the townsmen. It did prevent any identification of individual votes; and that was more vital, for the simple fact was that in the Massachusetts towns of the eighteenth century, elections were a potentially divisive force in a society which could not afford division. Secrecy was essential for the prevention of town dissension and the preservation of group solidarity.

The fundamental problem was formulated most clearly in neighboring Rhode Island. That colony had already adopted the written ballot when the legislature went further, trying to prevent plural voting by a bill requiring each voter to write his name on the back of his ballot. The bill met a storm of protest which forced its repeal within a year, and the legislature confessed that the experiment had caused "great dissatisfaction and uneasiness" among the inhabitants. People deemed it "a very great hardship to have their names exposed upon such occasions, to the creating of animosity and heart-burning of their particular friends." [57]

The point of that experience—that a town torn by personal enmities was not a town likely to achieve a public consensus—could hardly have been missed in Massachusetts. At any rate, a secret, unidentifiable ballot was employed in the Bay Colony from early on, and this though there was no warrant for its employment in English practice. In England, where *viva voce* voting was considered "the glory of the British constitution," members of Parliament were not elected by secret balloting until the end of the nineteenth century. The best political theory of eighteenth-century Europe—the pronouncements of men respected in the province, men such as Montesquieu and

Blackstone—inveighed against the secret ballot, yet the citizens of Massachusetts persisted in its practice without
wavering.* [58]

The pressures which permitted this deviation from familiar English principles and practices were the same pressures which proscribed deviation within each local community, the pressures of peace and harmony. Inherent in any
election of import was an explosive potential for contention and even enmity between individuals or between antagonistic camps within the community. Thus in 1757 a
Chelsea selectman who merely *supposed* that some of his
neighbors did not vote for him treated them, "both at the
meeting and since, in so ungentlemanly manner" that
many were moved to protest his very victory. Similarly,
John Adams admitted to a certain residual antagonism despite all the precautions of secrecy, conceding that when he
met a man he had topped for selectman in an election a few
days earlier, "he and I looked on each other without wrath
or shame or guilt, at least without any great degree of either, though I must own I did not feel exactly as I used to
in his company, and I am sure by his face and eyes that he
did not in mine." Of course, no institution short of the execution of all losers could have prevented such exquisite uneasiness as this, but the crucial function of the secret ballot
in eighteenth-century Massachusetts was to confine and
mitigate it, and thereby to preserve the possibility of consensus.[59]

In the context of this premium upon secrecy, the other
pieces of the puzzle fall into place. Nominations and the

---

* Blackstone opposed the secret ballot because he thought it would allow
the poor to combine with the rich, Montesquieu because he felt the poor
ought to be guided by the rich. The failure of either of these reasons to
strike a response in provincial Massachusetts suggests what will be argued
more extensively in Chapter Six, that the conditions of class cleavage
and elite rule, which both Blackstone and Montesquieu assumed, were
not of any enormous significance in the considerations of the eighteenth-
century townsmen.

open commitment they entailed threatened to promote "animosity and heart-burning," so there were no nominations at all. In the resultant vacuum in the provision of candidates there was then bound to be a bit of politicking, a politicking which, of course, violated the requirement of complete secrecy. But precisely at that point the canon of covertness did its essential duty. Ideally the campaign commitments of men subject to its strictures were delicate, and inevitably they were informal since the formal apparatus of campaigning simply did not exist. When John Adams noted unhappily, "I hear that Mr. Benjamin Cleverly has already bespoke Mr. John Ruggles junior against May meeting," he voiced a suspicion he was unlikely ever to transcend; and as long as he could not transcend it, as long as he could proceed on nothing more substantial than rumor, his grounds for any form of retaliation lacked force. The virtual prohibition on overt campaigning prevented the sharp lines of personal enmity and acrimony which could have disturbed the public peace.* [60]

The premium upon secrecy also permitted an astonishing ease in the perpetration of voting frauds. Even in the least complicated of elections, when only a single officer was to be chosen, multiple voting was as simple as stuffing a smaller ballot inside or under a larger one; the law set no standard size for a ballot, and the legal requirement that votes be submitted unfolded was ignored almost at will, not always innocuously. On other occasions voters simply deposited two or three votes without even a subterfuge, and on still others men managed to vote two or three times over, though that was rather more difficult. [61] And when

---

* Of course, it is possible to argue that secrecy itself was calculated to undermine consensus, since it makes easier the mobilization of an opposition. But in the absence of a power sufficient to require the resort to secrecy, there would be no overwhelming reason for such recourse; and so, if Chapter Six succeeds in establishing the absence of such oligarchy or other entrenched power in the towns, it may be assumed that secrecy served other ends primarily.

more than one officer was to be chosen, as in elections for a board of selectmen, all these abuses were available and others besides. In the towns which did not vote for the entire slate on one ballot, voters in such elections were allowed to write a separate ballot for each of their choices, with the result, as contemporaries themselves saw, that "for aught that appears, those who gave in six separate ballots might have given them all for one candidate." And at least one town once permitted its inhabitants their preference, allowing them to put their choices on a common ballot or on individual ballots as they wished, which of course admitted the incredible option under which a single unscrupulous voter could submit, say, five ballots, each of them with five (identical) names on it.[62]

In all of these deceits, success was almost certain if a man once wished to engage in them in the first place. But even for the very few who were ever caught in the act, success was often possible. A man apprehended depositing a fraudulent ballot was required to remove it from the box, but that withdrawal of a vote no more represented an arrest to the original deception than it did an opportunity to compound it. Since the specific ballot he cast could not ordinarily be identified, removal was actually a chance to pluck out a legitimate vote, perhaps a vote cast for an opponent, as was evident in a Stoughton protest against a vote taken out of the hat by a disqualified voter, "whether his or a voter's we know not." [63]

And yet, for all the facility with which fraud could be perpetrated, strikingly slight effort was made to curb it. A few perfunctory laws were enacted, one requiring votes to be put in unfolded, another imposing a fine for multiple voting; but the first was often ignored and the second was apparently never enforced. Similarly, multiple voting could have been checked by comparison between the number of voters present and the number of votes cast, but such recourse was rare, and it proved uncertain even in obvious instances of excess. In a Chelsea election of 1757, for example, "it was suggested that some had put into the hat more than one vote, and it was proposed to poll the voters." Forty-five votes were counted, but only thirty-nine voters were present; the moderator claimed that six who voted had left the meeting, but messengers sent after the six found that there were only three, and those three refused to return to the meeting; and yet, neither the three votes unaccounted for nor the refusal of the three men to leave the tavern induced the moderator to overturn the election.[64]

The same cavalier attitude toward voting fraud and the same sense of obligation to accept any ballot that made its way into the ballot box was evident everywhere. Men who said they saw dubious ballots deposited could do no more than doubt. Their petitions spoke only of suspicion, not of proof, and they *could not* speak of proof so long as secrecy remained primary. Charges of multiple voting, when they were made at all, were made out of doors, not at the meeting. Not even those in public authority possessed any greater resources, as a pair of depositions from Weston, in 1773, made inescapably clear. Each of the deponents was a selectman and each was a direct witness to the deception, yet each ended up certifying his approval of the election in question. One of the men had been "sitting with my eye upon and near the box and saw two votes drop into the box, which appeared to come from one hand"; the other, his suspicions already aroused in a first election which wound up tied, was "more particular in attending to" the suspicious one in the run-off and was "fully satisfied I saw two votes fall from the same man's hand, and have no doubt of it." At the time each of the selectmen independently attempted to call the matter to the attention of the meeting, but there was "much noise and disturbance." Their attempts were "not attended to." And in the end the selectmen had as little regard for vote frauds as the citizenry at large. Each of them signed the precept which ratified the election, and one actually admitted that he had signed "not hearing anything of the above matter and not knowing any person was more certain of the above than myself." [65]

No one was ever certain of a fraudulent ballot—at least no one was ever certain for public purposes—because uncertainty was the price of secrecy. Fraud could have been controlled in Massachusetts as it was controlled in the mother country, by requiring each man to stand up and declare his choice before his peers, but the cost of such control would have been prohibitive in the communities of the Bay. Any form of open voting exposed a town to acrimony and animosity, and none of the protections that did exist against fraudulent voting went to the heart of the problem because none of them authorized any official to scrutinize votes if a dispute developed. Ultimately, cheating could have been prevented only by an invasion of secrecy; there was no middle way. And between an effective policing of elections and the preservation of secrecy, the towns of Massachusetts chose secrecy.

The end of it all was that candidates came before the communities of eighteenth-century Massachusetts in a manner designed to insure domestic tranquility. The reality of local politics rested in a hundred humble conversations, across fences and tavern tables, quietly allusive, subtly suggestive, endlessly tactful. If all went well, an almost silently shared understanding would be reached among the inhabitants, and there would be no contest at all for the office at issue; more often than not, the "sense of the meeting" would be set before the meeting met.[66] And if unanimity could not be obtained, then every effort was bent to the containment and control of animosity in the ensuing electoral test. No man was called upon to confess his commitment in a public nomination, campaigning was sharply confined, and, most importantly, secrecy was assured in the voting itself.

As for the manner of that voting—the procedure of putting in and receiving ballots—local preferences were almost inevitably determinative, since provincial legislation left the subject untouched.[67] Practice varied from town to town and, within the town, from year to year and even from meeting to meeting. But even if an "average" vote cannot be reconstructed, an ideal one can. James Hosmer's rosy recollection will serve to set the scene.

> On a platform at the end of the plain room sat the five selectmen in a row,—at their left the venerable town-clerk, with the ample volume of records before him. . . . In front of the row of selectmen, with their brown, solid farmer faces, stood the moderator, a vigorous man in the forties, six feet straight in height, colonel of the county regiment of militia, of a term's service in the General Court, thus conversant with parliamentary law, a quick and energetic presiding officer.[68]

The moderator would then warn the inhabitants to prepare their ballots, and some systematic provision would be agreed upon for an orderly submission of papers. The inhabitants might bring in their ballots seat by seat, or as they passed through the door of the meetinghouse, or in almost any other manner that was convenient and afforded assurance that voters would vote singly and in turn.[69] Voters had to be present personally in order to vote. No one defended the principle of absentee participation in the governance of these eighteenth-century communities.[70]

Votes would be brought in to the constables or selectmen, or to the particular persons designated for the purpose, who would receive them in a hat or box. As they were received, each voter would be checked against the List and Valuation to certify his qualification, and the name of each voter would be taken down to prevent repeaters.[71] Balloting continued until the selectmen agreed, explicitly or in-

formally, that all the votes were in, and such agreement
was conditional upon the insurance of inclusion of all those
with an interest in the town. Often the clerk was expected
to ascertain whether all who wished to vote had done so
before the polls could be closed. Then, when everyone had
indeed voted, the hat or box was turned over and the decision awaited only the counting of the ballots.[72]

The count was colored by local nuance quite as much as
most other aspects of the election. Generally it was conducted by the selectmen, but sometimes only some of them
participated, sometimes the clerk joined them, sometimes
the clerk assumed the entire task, and on still other occasions the moderator did so.[73] Whoever governed, the votes
were taken from their container and spread upon a table to
be "sorted and counted"; properly, they were to be tolled
off before the assemblage, but once in a while they were
tallied privately instead.[74] At the completion of the count
the winner was announced, and even in this trifle local
particularity persisted: selectmen, constables, and town
clerks variously did the honors in the various communities.[75]

When all the officials had been elected and announced,
and all the other business of the meeting dispatched, there
remained only to adjourn the meeting. Yet adjournment
did not always await the end of all business; not even so
perfunctory an affair as the dismissal of a meeting was ever
automatic or exempt from the canons of consensus. Individual items on the agenda could be referred to the next
meeting rather than discussed as scheduled "in order for
the accommodation of difficulties relative thereto," and so
too, in the end, could whole meetings be concluded without the completion of the warrant when division appeared
imminent. For whatever the stated business written in the
warrant, the real business of a public meeting was always
the consolidation of the community; if the stated business
seemed likely to lead to the open expression of discord, the

gathering would often be disbanded "to prevent such inconvenience as might justly be feared by reason of the heat of spirit" there. Rather than risk contention, men preferred to put their differences aside so that they could attempt to arrange an accord in the interval before the meeting was reconvened.[76]

After adjournment, completion of the meeting required only the recording of its results. Almost every town in the province kept some sort of records, but in regard to elections the most notable feature of those records is the portion of the proceedings that was *not* noted. Robert Brown commented regretfully that his search for middle-class democracy in Massachusetts had been hindered "because the colonists did not consider voting records important," and his laconic complaint might actually be enlarged upon: the men of Massachusetts must have considered such records not only unimportant but also undesirable. Consistently they refrained from listing the votes received by each candidate and even the very names of the candidates, if there were any. Dudley recorded numbers only twice in forty years, neither of them being the occasion of an election; Braintree did so only once in seventy-five years, on the issue of the excise bill; and other towns never did it at all. In fact, most of the records scarcely ever mentioned debate, let alone divulged its proportions.[77]

Not even at the meetings themselves were the numerical divisions disclosed with the announcement of the victor; at most, only the selectmen who counted the votes and the candidates themselves knew the raw results, and even informing the candidates of the actual tabulation was extraordinary. In fact, in a disputed election in Sudbury, a counter of the votes himself could not recall the exact count, and could only give the results "to the best of my remembrance," a bare two weeks after the election. His testimony indicated how quickly all definite trace of electoral divisions might disappear, and certainly it suggested that the results had never been committed to writing, else he might have consulted the record rather than relying on memory.[78]

The record could not refresh his memory because its function was to dampen all memories of division instead. Never would the town records serve as a source for the re-opening of a dispute, never would they legitimate contention. Results were entered without any of the rough edges of discord and diversity, and the very impersonality of the entry identified the result with the entire town, monolithically. It was not the division of the votes which concerned the community but rather the opposite, and so the town records stand as a final mute testimony to the drive for consensus.

❧ VI ❧

A Happy Mediocrity

IN THE ENGLISH BOROUGHS where the provincial townsmen or their fathers were born, political privileges were closely confined. Few men were free burgesses, and the rest rarely mattered. But in Massachusetts, by the eighteenth century if not before, most men enjoyed all the prerogatives of citizenship their society afforded. They could attend and address their town meetings, they could sit on juries in judgment of their peers, they could run for public office, and, above all, they could vote on almost any matter of policy or place.

Modern students of New England have duly described this transformation, and they have not neglected its exemplary and polemical significances. Nonetheless, in their rush from figures on the diffusion of the franchise to labels like "middle-class democracy," they have scarcely considered the social context which conferred meaning on the degree of democracy that did exist. They have never wondered what the *function* of a widely extended suffrage was. They have asked only *whether* most men could vote, not *why*.

Yet in the context of consensus, enlarged access to the ballot is not nearly so extraordinary. A wide franchise could quite easily be ventured after a society that sought harmony had been made safe for such democracy. Most men could be allowed to vote precisely because so many men were never allowed entry to the town in the first place, because those who were there were of like minds. Indeed, within the compass of such conformity, extended participation ceased to be the danger it had been in England and became a source of strength. With wide participation premised on stringently controlled access to eligibility and open elections conditioned on that anterior constriction of the electorate, the votes of the townsmen assembled in their meetings contributed to the maintenance and implementation of their fundamental agreement rather than representing an instrument of choice between competing ideals and interests. And they served that function the more effectively the more townsmen they comprehended.

Thus, in a society in which the consensual mode was customary, a new conception of the social order gradually grew. This conception could not be codified, because it implied certain handsome heresies against English orthodoxy, but its operational premise was that government was founded on the consent of the governed, not descended from the sovereign. Public action rested upon public opinion and accordingly upon the participation of the public in politics. At least in that elemental sense of broad formal participation, then, such a conception implied democracy.

Of course, no matter how many men vote, a society dedicated to concord and devoid of legitimate difference, dissent, and conflict is a society still in transition from assent to a truer consent, a democracy despite itself, a democracy without democrats. But even so limited a democracy has lately been disputed by students who have insisted that franchise rights were more formal than real, because "local pressures for conformity produced a pattern of *deference voting*, in which the lower orders pliantly followed the lead of their superiors." In other words, men might have been free in principle to speak as they pleased, but they were unlikely to exercise their legal prerogatives under the watchful eyes of employers, ministers, and other officials who could give or withhold essential assistance of many kinds. Most men could exercise the privileges of citizenship, but since they were accustomed to bow before their betters, the exercise was an empty one.[1]

Deference itself, however, occurs in some degree in all complex social systems. Its mere appearance cannot sustain a conclusion that franchise democracy was fraudulent. The real issue is whether deference was structured, and if so, how. Deference that follows ability or accomplishment is critically different from deference owed and accorded on the basis of birth or other such accustomed status; deference to the force of an argument is different from deference to the social stature of the man making that argument; and deference to the power of a strong personality differs from deference to the power inhering in a social position. Some forms of deference are innocuous, others are quite incompatible with democracy. The issues are those of fixity and flux, of ascription and achievement, of authority and argument; which is to say, the issue is not deference but oligarchy.*

Oligarchy and inclusiveness, then, are the crucial questions in the context of consensual communalism. They are the issues which have been most controverted among students of the town meeting and provincial America, and they are—if any are—the issues on which the towns of the

* Indeed, much more may be granted and the case still remains the same. Even men who do undeniably defer to "their betters"—and the men of Massachusetts did not do that—may still enjoy a considerable measure of political power. They may lack that sense of personal capacity and competence which marks a genuinely democratic social order, but their deference *per se* does not preclude a certain degree of democracy. For even in a sharply stratified society it is possible that the elite may contend among themselves, in which event, in a society with an extended franchise, the dispute must be carried to the people, who are thereby presented with a choice among persons or policies. Deference in such a society, therefore, can define political competence and impotence for separate strata only if there exists a unified elite; even in circumstances of the most deferential stratification, oligarchy is still the issue that matters.

province may lay their closest claims to having evolved a
democratic order in the eighteenth century. Unanimity as
the condition of effective action demanded that participation be both broad and significant in setting the course of
the community, and both those demands were in fact met.
The politics of the provincial towns was neither reserved
for nor dictated by any meaningful elite.

Any discussion of democracy in Massachusetts must begin
at the beginning: the first settlers came without even a wish
to receive all men, let alone with any larger desires for democracy. Inclusion, the most rudimentary mark of a democratic community, was anathema to men who sought only a
"saving remnant" and had actually forsaken their native
land for the right to reject those they judged unworthy.
Yet, without any English prodding and within about a decade of the first settlements, the original ideals of exclusion
had begun to break down at the local level. Until 1692 the
colonial suffrage extended only to freemen, but by that
time nonfreemen had been voting in town affairs for almost half a century.[2] The ability of the settlers to sustain
suffrage restrictions at the colonial level so long after they
were abandoned in the towns not only indicates the incomplete coincidence of intellectual currents and local conduct
in early New England but also contradicts any contention
that the pressures for democratic participation derived
from Puritan theology or thought. The New England Puritans were pressed to the popularization of political authority only in grudging adjustment to the exigencies of their
situation.

But the popularization so reluctantly practiced in the
seventeenth century was openly accepted by the eighteenth. Governance by concord and consensus required inclusiveness. In communities in which effective enforcement depended on the moral bindingness of decisions on

the men who made them, it was essential that most men be parties to such decisions. Not the principled notions of the New Englanders but the stern necessities of enforcement sustained such town-meeting democracy as there was in provincial Massachusetts. The politics of consensus made a degree of democracy functional, even made it a functional imperative. Men were allowed to vote not out of any overweening attachment to democratic principles *per se* but simply because a wide canvass was convenient, if not critical, in consolidating a consensus in the community.

Under this incentive to inclusion, the town suffrage in the eighteenth century was never set so sternly as to keep any considerable proportion of men from the franchise. Property and residence qualifications were neither negligible nor neglected, but as Robert Brown's very determined study has demonstrated, most men could meet those qualifications in provincial Massachusetts. If the democracy of adult males was something less than universal, it was not *very much* less. In principle the franchise remained a privilege rather than a right. In practice that privilege was accessible to most men.* [3]

* Brown's research, for all the energy and occasional ingenuity on which it is based, ought not to be regarded as definitive, though it goes without saying that his findings must be preferred to any others until someone even more energetic and ingenious proves otherwise. His conclusions, however, overreach his evidence on occasion, and his evidence is not always as complete as it might have been. The mercantile port towns probably provide the most prominent counterinstances to his claims, and many other communities also had less impressive percentages of qualified voters than Brown would have wished. See, e.g., Mass. Arch. 8, p. 279; ibid. 113, p. 270; ibid. 114, pp. 550–2; ibid. 115, p. 144; ibid., pp. 168, 169; ibid., pp. 316–17, 319–20, 321; ibid., pp. 392, 397; ibid., pp. 448, 469–71; ibid., pp. 619–22, 625, 706–6a; ibid., pp. 864–5; ibid. 117, pp. 647–9, 651; ibid. 118, pp. 523–4; ibid., pp. 734–5a, 762; ibid. 181, pp. 122, 133–4; Blake: *Princeton*, I, pp. 76–7. Cases such as these may damage Brown's thesis, but they do less harm to the argument advanced here, because the present perspective on inclusiveness is not so deeply determined to demonstrate "middle-class democracy" as to discover the extent and the patterns of that condition and the direction of the deviations from it.

Even in the towns where a substantial proportion—
sometimes a majority—of the people were not technically
entitled to vote, the ineligible were quite commonly admitted to the ballot box. For the same imperatives impinged on towns where few were legally qualified as on the
others, and the same results of wide political participation
obtained because of the same sense that inclusiveness promoted peace while more rigorous methods threatened it.
The town of Douglas, with only five qualified voters in its
first years, flatly refused to be bound by a determination
confined to those five, declaring its conviction "that the intent of no law can bind them to such ill consequences."
Mendon, in its "infant state" in 1742, voted "to permit a
considerable number of persons not duly qualified by law
to vote . . . being induced thereto by an apprehension
that it would be a means of preserving peace and unity
amongst ourselves." Princeton, incorporated in 1760 with
forty-three adult males but only fourteen eligible to vote
according to provincial regulations, established a formal
"agreement among themselves to overlook" those regulations, and the General Court upheld that agreement. "The
poor freeholders" in the early days of Upton were also "allowed liberty to vote in town meeting," and it had produced "an encouraging harmony" in local affairs until
1746, when a few of the qualified voters, momentarily possessed of a majority of the ten in town, sought to upset the
customary arrangements and limit the franchise as the law
required. The rest of the town at once protested that "such
a strenuous method of proceeding would endanger the
peace of the town" and begged the General Court "to prevent the dismal damages that may follow" therefrom. The
Court did exactly as it was asked, and at the new meeting
the town reverted to its old form: "everyone was admitted
to vote, qualified or not." [4]

The principle which governed such universalism was
not deliberate democracy; it was merely a recognition that

the community could not be governed solely by the qualified voters if they were too few in number. Such a situation was most likely to occur in new communities, but it was not limited to them. Middleton had been incorporated for almost a quarter of a century when it was conceded that in the local elections of 1752 "there was double the number of votes to the lawful voters." In other established towns the requirements for the franchise were also ignored and admission of the unqualified admitted explicitly.[5] Thomas Hutchinson's wry lament that "anything with the appearance of a man" was allowed the ballot may have been excessive, but it was not wholly fabricated.[6] And even towns whose political procedures were more regular resorted to universalism in cases of conflict or of major issues. Fitchburg, for instance, agreed in 1767 that "every freholder be a votter in Chusing of a minestr," while twenty years earlier, in a bitterly contested election in Haverhill, "there was not any list of valuation read nor any list of nonvoters nor any weighting of what name or nature whatsoever by which the selectmen did pretend to show who was qualified to vote in town affairs."[7]

The question of inclusiveness itself sometimes came before a town, not always without challenge but generally with a democratic outcome. Dudley, more than a decade after the incorporation of the town, voted "that all the freeholder of sd town should be voters by a graet majorytie and all agreed to it." In Needham in 1750 it was also "put to vote whether it be the mind of the town to allow all freeholders in town to vote for a moderator," and there too the vote carried in the affirmative. And that verdict for inclusion was not even as revealing as the method by which that verdict was reached, for in voting *whether* to include all in the election, Needham *did* include all in the procedural issue. Every man did vote on the question of whether every man was to be allowed to vote.[8]

Of course, absolute inclusiveness never prevailed in

provincial Massachusetts—women could not vote at all, and neither could anyone under twenty-one—and property and residence qualifications, introduced in 1692, were probably adhered to as often as they were ignored, so that even the participation of adult males was something less than universal. Yet these deviations from a fully democratic participation were revealing. The men who were not allowed legitimately to vote with their fellow townsmen were commonly tenants or the sons of voters; as Brown discovered, it was those two groups against which the property requirement primarily operated. And against those two groups sanctions were available that were far more effective than those of the generalized community. Stringent property qualifications were clearly self-defeating in a society where consensus was the engine of enforcement, but overly generous ones were equally unnecessary. Where some men, such as tenants and dependent sons, could be privately coerced, liberality on their behalf, from the standpoint of social control, would have meant the commission of a sin of superfluity.

Similarly, almost nothing but disadvantage could have accrued from a loose residence requirement enabling men not truly members of the community to participate in its decision-making process, since voting qualifications in provincial Massachusetts were connected to the concept of community, not the concept of democracy. The extensions and contractions of the franchise were significant to the townsmen of the eighteenth century primarily as a means of consolidating communal consensus. All those whose acquiescence in public action was necessary were included, and all those whose concurrence could be compelled otherwise or dispensed with were excluded, often very emphatically. Sixty-six citizens of Watertown, for example, petitioned against the allowance of a single unqualified voter in a 1757 election because he was "well known to belong to the town of Lincoln." In many towns such as Sudbury, the town clerk "very carefully warned those that were not legally qualified not to vote and prayed the selectmen to be very careful and watchful that nobody voted that was not legally qualified." [9] Even in disputes over specific qualifications, both sides often agreed on the principle of exclusion of the unqualified; contention occurred only over the application of that principle.[10]

Consciousness of voting qualifications colored the conduct of other town affairs as well as elections, as indeed was natural since the meaning of the franchise went so far beyond mere electoral democracy. Protests by men recently arrived in a town could be discredited, as they were in Haverhill in 1748, without any reference to the justice of the protest itself, simply by stating that "many of their petitioners are not qualified to vote in town affairs as may be seen by the selectmen's list of voters, and some of them were never known to reside in town or did we ever hear of them before we saw their petition." Similarly, in the creation of new communities, qualification for the franchise could be crucial. Inhabitants of Bridgewater resisted their own inclusion in a precinct proposed by thirty-seven men dwelling in their vicinity by pointing out that "there is not above eleven or twelve that are qualified to vote in town meetings as the law directs." Many towns in their corporate capacity made much the same plea when confronted with an appeal for separation from the community. As Worcester once noted in such a case, more than half the petitioners were "not voters and one is a single Indian." [11]

Such consciousness of qualifications sometimes appeared to be nothing more than an insistence on a "stake in society" in order to participate in the society's deliberations and decisions, but the stake-in-society concept, despite its popularity in the West and its convergence with certain conditions of public life in the province, was not precisely the notion which controlled those restrictions of the franchise which did persist after 1692. It was not out of any

intrinsic attachment to that concept, but simply out of a
fear that those without property were overly amenable to
bribery and other such suasion, that the men of Massachusetts clung to their voting qualifications. As the Essex Result was to state the principle in 1778, "all the members
of the state are qualified to make the election, unless
they have not sufficient discretion, or are so situated as to
have no wills of their own." [12] Participation in community
decisions was the prerogative of independent men, of *all* a
town's independent men, but, ideally, *only* of those. Indeed, it was precisely because of their independence that
they had to be accorded a vote, since only by their participation did they bind themselves to concur in the community's chosen course of action. The town meeting was an
instrument for enforcement, not—at least not by design—a
school for democracy.

This logic of competence governed the exclusion of
women and children from the franchise and also accounted
for the antipathy to voting by tenants. The basis of the prohibitions which were insisted upon was never so much an
objection to poverty *per se*—the stake-in-society argument
—as to the tenant's concomitant status of dependence, the
pervasive assumption of which emerged clearly in a contested election in Haverhill in 1748. There the petitioners
charged that a man had been "refused as a voter under pre-
tense that he was a tenant and so not qualified, when the
full reason was because he was a tenant to one of their [the
selectmen's] opposers and so at all hazards to be suppressed," while another man, a tenant to one of the selectmen themselves, had been received as a voter though
"rated at much less in the last year's taxes than he whom
they refused." The protest was thus directed primarily
against the abuses of the selectmen; that tenants would do
as their landlords desired was simply taken for granted.[13]
And naturally the same sort of assumption controlled the
exclusion of sons still living with their parents. The legal

voting age of twenty-one was the most rudimentary expression of this requirement of a will of one's own, but the legal age was not very firm around the edges. Like other laws of the province, it could not stand when it came up against local desires, and the age qualifications were often abrogated when unusual dependence or independence was demonstrable, as in the case of the eighteen-year-old who voted in a Sheffield election of 1751 because his father had died and he had become head of his family. As the town's elected representative was able to declare on that occasion, quite ignoring the legal age requirement, the lad "had a good right to vote, for his estate rested in him and that he was a town-born child and so was an inhabitant." [14]

Of course the townsmen of the eighteenth century placed no premium on independence as such. Massachusetts townsmen were expected to be independent but not too independent; ultimately, they were supposed on their own to arrive at the same actions and commitments as their neighbors. Any genuine independence, excessive *or* insufficient, was denigrated if not altogether denied a place in the community. Thus, when a number of inhabitants of a gore of land near Charlton faced the threat of incorporation with the town, they submitted "one word of information" about the townsmen who had asked for that incorporation. The note said only

Baptist signers	— 7
Churchmen	— 3
Tenants	— 4
Neither tenants nor freeholders but intruders upon other men's property	—15

The whole of the petitioners in Charlton consisting of 35 in number.

In other words, tenants were tainted, but so too were all others who were their own men, such as squatters and those who dared to differ in religion. In denigrating them, the inhabitants of the gore drew no distinctions; tenant and Baptist were equally offensive because they were equally outside of orthodoxy, beyond the confines of consensus.[15]

Ultimately almost *any* taint on membership in the homogeneous community was a potential basis for derogation. Some inhabitants of Rutland once even attempted to deny the validity of a town decision merely because many of its supporters were "such as were and are dissenters from the public worship of God in the old meetinghouse." And though Rutland's religious orthodoxy was a bit exquisite even for eighteenth-century New England, it was so only in degree. For example, when Sutton opposed the erection of a new district out of parts of itself and several other towns in 1772, the town actually deducted the Anabaptists from the number of signatories to the application—Baptists simply did not count as full citizens. Worcester did the same thing and indeed went even further. Several of the signers of the petition for separation were not heads of families but mere "single persons, some of them transient ones," and so, said the town, were not to be "accounted as part of the number of families the petitioners say are within the limits of the proposed district." Whereas excessively reliable bonds confined the tenant, no reliable bonds at all attached a single man to the community, and either alternative evoked suspicion.[16]

For all that, though, the insistence on orthodoxy did not directly exclude any excessive numbers, and neither did the property and residence requirements disqualify any great proportion of the province's adult males. In the perspective of the English villages from which the New Englanders came, these very dimensions of disqualification may be better seen, in fact, as defining a much broader qualification than had previously prevailed in English practice. The criteria of exclusion were, much more truly, measures of the inclusiveness of the communities of early Massachusetts.

Thus the property qualification that kept some men from the franchise provided a basis for admitting all of them, for while only a few men were taxed in the English towns from which the Bay settlers departed, "every inhabitant was declared liable for his proportion of the town charges" in Massachusetts, as early as 1638. Thus, more fundamentally, the residence requirement also extended the electorate, for with it went the shift from property to residence as the irreducible basis of town citizenship. In England several classes of property-holders were "technically termed inhabitants even though they dwelt in another town"; property defined political citizenship, and only those who held the requisite property in the community directed its affairs, whether or not they lived there, whether or not they had ever so much as seen the town. In provincial Massachusetts such stake-in-society notions never prevailed, for reasons that had little to do with any abstract attachment to democracy or antipathy to absentee ownership. They never prevailed because the point of the town meeting was not so much the raising of a revenue as it was political government, especially the maintenance of law and order. In Massachusetts it was necessary to act only on the individuals living in each town, and it was imperative to act upon all of them.[17]

And thus, most fundamentally of all, the very elections in which such action was secured were dramatically different from those of England. Regardless of the precise sweep of the suffrage, the institution of regular elections itself was a thing unthinkable in the mother country. In English towns such as Sudbury, on the eve of the migration, the mayor alone was chosen by the citizens eligible to vote. All other public positions were assumed *ex officio* by the outgoing mayor, appointed by the incoming one, or continued in long terms. "Consequently, the yearly elections were in no sense public affairs . . . The mayor, aldermen, and burgesses conducted the 'mystery of government' up in the moot hall, quite apart from the commoners, and only now and then appointed a particularly worthy citizen to be privy to their secrets." [18] In the towns of Massachusetts, on the other hand, there was never such a sense of the "mystery" of government. Officials did not hold office *ex officio*, or by appointment, or for extended terms; and almost every single office was elective. Selectmen and hogreeves, assessors and fence-viewers, all were elected annually by their neighbors assembled in town meeting. For the men who elected them no less than for the men elected, that meant a vastly different degree of participation in the governmental process.*

The notion that the New England towns were deferential societies is, then, an essentially unhistorical one. New Englanders had once been Englishmen, and there they had known the most genuinely deferential communities they would ever know. In America they were moving away from those patterns of political deference, substituting broad popular participation for elite prerogatives over the "mystery of government." † Of course, participation was still a privilege rather than a right, but it was a privilege open to far too many for the restrictions to define an elite. If eighty per cent of the townsmen could participate in public decisions, they were likely to find scant satisfaction in the deference of the remaining twenty per cent, especially when they could compare their situation only with the one they

* Also indicative of an important difference is the fact that the management of public affairs was collegial rather than individual in Massachusetts. The office of mayor was unknown in the provincial towns, all of which were governed by a *board* of selectmen.

† It is ironic in this regard that the most unreserved advocacy of the deferential conception has been that of Thernstrom, whose work was, to a significant degree, angled toward a strident attack on "ahistorical social science." By missing this larger movement away from elite privilege toward broad popular participation, Thernstrom achieved something very like ahistorical history.

had known in England. For that reason the franchise restrictions which remained could hardly, in and of themselves, have encouraged Massachusetts townsmen to acknowledge their betters and defer to them.

And little as the legal conditions of participation contributed to the creation or continuance of an elite, the formal regulations governing access to office contributed even
less. Other than a requirement of attendance at the election meeting[19]—a requirement which could have disqualified no important groups of men but absentee owners and
gentlemen of quality—a candidate for local office had to
meet no stated regulations at all, beyond those for the franchise itself, so that there was no formal distance whatever
which was demanded between officials and the electorate.
The mass of men who were entitled to vote were, by that
very token, eligible for office.[20] Representatives, in fact, had
only to be resident freeholders in the town which sent
them, a requirement which was actually *less* stringent than
the terms of the suffrage.[21] And in the elections themselves
the ballot was a secret one, which removed a man's preferences from the scrutiny of his more powerful neighbors and,
as the Massachusetts Supreme Court declared one later day,
was deliberately "calculated to insure an independent
suffrage." [22] Under such conditions of eligibility and conduct, oligarchy found scant support in the formal structure
of elections in the provincial towns.

But of course institutional calculations and legal declarations were only a formal framework for the town meeting, and even a government of laws must still be adminis-
tered by men. In its actual incidence, oligarchy is less a
question of rules and regulations and the formal organization of offices than it is of operative structure and, most
immediately, of the occupancy of positions of power in the
society. It entails a patterned concentration of power in an
elite of considerable numerical constriction and significant
stability of membership. It requires that these notables

maintain a style of life set off at a distinctive distance from the rest of the community, and that their authority be acknowledged and unchallenged by those subject to it. If such things can be demonstrated, oligarchy can be considered effectual; but for provincial Massachusetts they cannot be demonstrated.

The very membership of the official class was generally far too extensive to sustain an oligarchic elite. The "extreme numerical limitation" that Simmel stipulated as essential to its existence rarely prevailed in the province,[23] where even a town as small as Topsfield chose 102 men to the post of selectman in the years between the issuance of the new charter and the break with England. In a single year in the little village of Norton there were twenty-one men actually elected as selectmen. Many others might have been chosen as well, had the town not grown "discouraged of proceeding any further" in the face of declinations from almost every man among the first twenty-one, yet even if no others at all expected an election in their turn, it was still quite clear that in 1751 Norton judged at least 21 men suitable for the town's highest office, a number rather cumbersome for genuine oligarchy in such a small society.[24]

Substantially similar figures could be afforded for other towns,[25] but the dispersal of offices of importance was actually even greater than would appear in the number of selectmen chosen in each place. Assessors, when elected separately from the selectmen, were also major officers of indisputable consequence, and so were the town treasurers and, sometimes, the town clerks; yet some of these men were never elevated to the board of selectmen. Moderators, militia officers, and church deacons had honor and authority, but they too did not infallibly attain to the board. Other men never elected to any of these less lofty offices nonetheless served on town committees of obvious consequence.[26] And still others, some of them squires and merchants, sought to avoid rather than to acquire office, so that the circle of leading citizens was often still wider than the most extended definition of important public positions.[27]

Even if only the selectmen are considered, however, the seats on the board were ordinarily scattered rather more widely than a real oligarch would have wished. John Adams once denied this, insisting in the strongest possible terms that "in every village in New England" there were "three or four families at most" among whom the town's highest offices "generally descended," [28] but in his own town of Braintree the four family names which accounted for the most terms in office attached to only thirty per cent of the terms served. In other towns the percentage was commonly higher than that, but it was not very much higher. The median proportion for thirteen towns tallied was forty-one per cent, and even the mean average was well under half the seats on the board for the four leading families in each town.* [29]

* In the calculations on which these conclusions are based, family is construed very narrowly: only common surnames are considered to constitute a common family. This construction doubtless includes together a few men who were unrelated though they shared surnames, but it surely excludes more who might have been included as related by marriage. This definitional decision was ultimately determined by necessity—the lack of the requisite genealogical information—but it was also in some degree deliberate. For a variety of reasons it may be safer to discount than to discover those larger kinship connections.

For one thing, they may have spread so far as to include almost the entire town, thus rendering the entire question of kinship almost meaningless. Consider a community of 300 people, and consider it to have been relatively isolated, so that marriage would be within the town. Allow fifty families, figuring four children in each, though this is, if anything, an underestimation of family size, since the average household still had 5.7 members as late as 1790, when family size was already declining; see Conrad and Irene Taeuber: *The Changing Population of the United States* (New York, 1948), p. 170. Then in that town of fifty families, and allowing interrelations solely by marriage of children, there would be one chance in twelve that any two families in town were interrelated, even in the first generation of marriages. And of course that would be just a beginning. For many men and women there would be multiple marriages, due to the relatively high mortality rate, while for all the townsfolk the web of kinship connections would grow more densely intertwined in any

The point of such proportions is not, obviously, that these offices were obtained in an egalitarian setting. The figures assuredly show that there *was* concentration of high public office along lines of kinship, rather than its random distribution. But concentration, as such, is not the essence of the case. The essence is oligarchy, and oligarchy is something more than a deviation from random distribution. Oligarchy requires stable, coordinated control by a very few, and control is something more than concentration. Or at any rate it is a greater concentration than prevailed in these towns, where the leading families could not even command a majority of the selectmen, let alone secure dominion on the board.

Also, oligarchy is much more than mere contraction of the official class. Another of its indispensable attributes is a relative stability of tenure among its elite officials, for rapid replacement of leaders is inherently inimical to oligarchic domination. Defenders of the deferential conception of eighteenth-century society have recognized this requirement, and they have accordingly claimed of New England's

---

case as succeeding generations married. And since the Puritan conception of kinship was extended indeed—see Edmund Morgan: *The Puritan Dilemma* (Boston, 1958), p. 23—the question of who was related to whom in such a society may prove to be not merely a difficult one but also an insignificant one. For with the probability so strong that almost everyone was related to almost everyone else, the mere fact of family ties ultimately enjoined very little on conduct. In every family there were, in all likelihood, rich relations and poor relations, and for that reason relationship, *per se*, would not have been crucial to political advancement from the standpoint of the social system of the community. It is worth mentioning too that, as a matter of fact, kinship connections do not correlate well enough with political positions to permit wholly reliable inference even from common surnames which did represent a single family. Families themselves were often divided, sometimes on generational lines, sometimes on sundry other bases; see, e.g., Mass. Arch. 114, pp. 227, 228; ibid. 115, pp. 288–90, 292, 295, 296, 297, 298, 299, 303, 305–8, 309; ibid., p. 625; ibid., pp. 630–1; ibid. 116, pp. 668–9; ibid. 117, pp. 302–5, 306–7; Francis: *Sketch of Watertown*, p. 78; Greven: "Family Structure," pp. 234–56; Powell: *Puritan Village*.

leadership that "these gentlemen or their fathers had ruled the colony since its founding, and the people were conditioned to return them to office almost automatically." [30] Yet the fact of the matter was that virtually no one was returned automatically in the eighteenth century, and that fact was recognized more clearly by men of the time than it has been since. One handbook for local officers simply took it for granted that "as most of them are frequently changing, it cannot be supposed that they should be so well acquainted with their duty as if they had had a longer time to inform themselves of it." Another author insisted that "there is such shifting and changing of men in authority that before a man knows what part he has got to act, he is dismissed, and another placed in his room, and thereby the affairs of government are continually managed by new, and inexperienced men." [31]

This "shifting and changing" showed most starkly in specific episodes. In a Brunswick election of 1742, for example, an incumbent of one of the town's major offices was found to have insufficient estate even to vote in the elections for his successor and other officers, while another man, whose merest eligibility to vote had been in doubt the year before, was not only admitted to the franchise but also elevated to the board of selectmen. In other places elections often marked the reduction of once-prominent public officials to the most demeaning of public services, in the passage of a very few years.[32]

But the same shifts were still more powerfully apparent in the prosaic town records, year after year. Reversals such as those of Brunswick were merely the more dramatic eruptions of an endemic instability of leadership in the provincial community. There was simply no substantial basis in extended tenure, in the towns studied, for an elite cadre of local officials.

Of course it is possible that a larger sample of towns than the one used here might tell a different tale, but that hardly seems likely. The fifteen towns investigated—Amherst, Braintree, Brookline, Dedham, Dudley, Fitchburg, Lunenburg, Manchester, Plymouth, Princeton, Tisbury, Topsfield, Watertown, Weston, and Worcester—bore no very great likenesses to each other except that they all subsequently published their provincial records. Certainly in time and in space they were broadly dispersed. Eight were founded in the seventeenth century and seven in the eighteenth, and even in more minute detail they were spread extraordinarily smoothly across that temporal span. Situated in Dukes, Essex, Hampshire, Middlesex, Plymouth, Suffolk, and Worcester Counties, they included towns as far west as the Connecticut Valley and as far east as Cape Cod, towns south to the Connecticut border and Martha's Vineyard and north to within a few miles of New Hampshire. Among them were port towns and island villages, agricultural communities and inland commercial ones, and proto-suburbs within the orbit of the provincial capital. They are not an altogether random sample, but, given the rampant localism of the era, they will do.[33]

In only three of those fifteen towns did selectmen average as many as five years' service in the course of an entire lifetime, and the median term for all fifteen towns was three years. The median dipped as low as 1.5 terms for each selectman in Fitchburg, where the mean tenure was 3.6 years, and in Princeton the mean tenure was still lower, 2.9 terms for each selectman. Even in Plymouth, where the figures were half again as high as in any other town, the mean for men elected to this highest of local offices was but 7.6 years and the median only 4.5. In more personal terms, such figures meant that men elected to the board of selectmen held their places of pre-eminence, on the average, only a tenth of their adult lives; the median selectman served in no more than one of fifteen of his adult years.

Of course some men served longer. In Weston, where the average term was 3.7 years, one man served seventeen;

in Worcester, where the mean was 4.7 and the median a
meager two, one man remained in office for twenty-eight
years. In Watertown, unless the records failed to distin-
guish between a father and a son, one selectman was a
member of the board for a total of forty-three years. In fact,
the selectman with the longest lifetime service in each of
the fifteen towns averaged a little over twenty terms. But a
tenure of twenty years, though obviously substantial, was
also revealing precisely because it marked the outer bounds
of oligarchy: not even the most politically pre-eminent
man in the entire community was likely to be on the board
as often as he was off of it.

Moreover, even these men who were returned half the
time—*semi*-automatically, as it were—were unusual. In
eleven of the fifteen towns, at least one man served twenty
terms or more in the course of his life; in eight of those
eleven towns, that man was the *only* one to do so. All told,
only one man of every fifty ever elected selectman in the
first place was among those elected for twenty terms or
more. Only one selectman in ten was ever elected for ten
terms or more, and less than a third of the selectmen served
even as many as five years.

Simply in terms of total tenure, then, an entrenched
elite could hardly have sustained itself in these towns. In
the more demanding—and more appropriate—terms of
consecutive service, the absence of oligarchy was even more
obvious. In theory, a genuine oligarch's eminence would
have been conceded; he would have been maintained constantly in office, not shunted in and out at the pleasure of
the electorate. In the practice of the provincial towns, even
the relatively brief periods the selectmen served through
their entire lives were unlikely to be consecutive. Only
three men among all the inhabitants of all these towns ever
saw twenty years' consecutive service as members of the
board, while the selectman with the longest steady service
in each town averaged less than fourteen years. In Amherst

no one ever served more than five years in a row, in Princeton and Lunenburg no one served more than seven, and in most towns few men served as long as that. Little more than a sixth of all the men ever elected to the board served so many as five years in a row, and barely one in twenty-five continued in office for ten terms at a time, though that figure itself was but a quarter of a man's adult life.

With few if any men maintained in office in the style of oligarchs, the turnover in the boards of selectmen was, of course, considerable. The "self-perpetuating oligarchies" that governed the towns and counties of England were unknown in its province at the Bay, where elections were annual, co-option unmentioned, and officials removed easily and, in fact, often. In Topsfield three of the five selectmen were likely to be newly elected in any given year; in Amherst the mean turnover was almost four out of five selectmen each year, and the median amounted to the full complement of five. For thirteen communities together, almost half the selectmen were replaced with every election and, as often as one year in eight, the entire board of selectmen was supplanted at a single swoop.* [34]

At the same time, such dispersal and instability of the leading local offices also shaped the pattern of politics and political ascent at the provincial level. In a number of other American colonies, election to the assembly represented a filtering stage beyond induction into the local elite, and the assembly itself served to complete the consolidation of local authority.[35] But in Massachusetts the absence of entrenched elites at the local level largely precluded that possibility. There was simply no sufficient, stable predominance in the communities which could have been reflected in a relative stability of tenure in the provincial legislature; and it was, accordingly, no accident that the House of Representatives at the Bay was never able to constitute itself a provincial oligarchy in its own right.

* For an amplification of the data, see Appendix VI.

Pamphleteers spoke slightingly of the "native obscurity" of the delegates,[36] and the town records told much the same story of instability. In none of the towns tallied did representatives remain in the House longer than the 5.1 years averaged in Braintree, and the average delegate for the six towns together served only two or three times in his life. Of course a few men served longer, but just a few. Only two men in all six towns served more than twenty years in the assembly, and only three among all the representatives ever elected served so much as ten years in a row.*

More persuasive than the tally of a few towns or the pronouncements of pamphleteers is the evidence that can be compiled for the entire province. Beginning in 1715 the Massachusetts House of Representatives printed the records of its sessions, and at the head of each year's record was a list of the delegates, from which the degree of discontinuity in the lower house can be computed. The degree was always a substantial one. There was not a single year of the first fourteen for which there are records in which even as many as half the deputies were incumbents, and in the years after 1728 still another seven Houses met in which there were more representatives who had not been members the year before than representatives who had. Altogether, from 1715 to 1774, more than three out of every seven elections for representatives installed men who had not seen such service in the previous year; "new, and unexperienced men" were of necessity engaged in provincial affairs. In 1831 the noted New England historian Jared Sparks would be able to claim of his own era that, though

---

* Meaningful evidence could be secured for only six of the fifteen towns. Most of the others simply did not elect representatives often enough to permit a tabulation of any value—Dudley, for instance, sent a deputy only four times in forty-four years—or did not send representatives at all—Amherst, for one, was formally a district until the Revolution and so could not have sent anyone even had it desired to do so. For the data on the six towns, compiled from their local records and from Mann: *Annals of Dedham*, pp. 79–81, see Appendix VII.

representatives then too faced annual electoral tests, "it is recognized by experience that three quarters of them are always returned to the chambers by re-election." [37] In the provincial era no such stability ever prevailed. The turnover of new men in the House was twice as great through the 1750's as the rate "recognized by experience" in the age of Jacksonian democracy, and even in the last decade and a half before the Revolution, when discontinuity declined sharply, there were still only three provincial legislatures of the last sixteen in which as many incumbents were returned as the proportion claimed by Sparks.

Of course, fifty-seven per cent continuity from year to year is rather more than random; a degree of continuity was never unknown in the provincial era. It was simply not substantial enough to sustain anything approaching an oligarchy. Even on the very topmost rungs of the ladder of public life in the province, apart from the handful of men around the governor and in the council, there were still three men who were removed for every four who stayed, every year. And these removals recurred: forty-three per cent was the *rate* of removal. It was repeated year after year. Not only were only fifty-seven per cent of the members of any legislature likely to be back the following year, but also only another fifty-seven per cent were likely to be back the year after that. Thus the unlikelihood of a provincial oligarchy consolidated through the House of Representatives may be even more clearly indicated by a somewhat wider view of the rate of change. Turnover every other year amounted to five eighths of the membership of the assembly; only thirty-eight per cent of any given House were likely to be sitting two years later, including even those who did not continue through the three years but rather served terms separated by someone else's election in the intervening year. Not one assembly in ten had as many as half its members still sitting two years later. And at longer intervals instability was even more apparent. With three years intervening, and again including those who did not sit continuously as well as those who did, no House *ever* had a majority of its members return, and only one House in forty had so much as a forty per cent return; on the average, little more than a quarter of the representatives at any session were back four years later. And at a distance of a decade—itself an almost insignificant span under truly oligarchical conditions—not even one town in ten still had the same representative serving in Boston. With turnover so nearly total in a mere ten years, it was quite out of the question to establish an oligarchy that could sustain itself in the provincial assembly, and that impossibility, in turn, reflected the chronic instability of leadership in the towns from which those delegates came.*

Even more revealing, perhaps, than the dispersal and instability of authority in the province was the failure of the local leaders to find a distinctive style of life. An entrenched elite must stand at some social distance from the rest of the citizenry if it is to exert oligarchical influence, yet there was rarely any such distance in the rural towns of the eighteenth century. Even in the case of the highest public official the community was impowered to choose— the representative—the very definition of the role denied any sharp separation of an oligarchic elite from the rest of the society. Communities which insisted on annual elections, "to the End that those who are unfit for their tasks may be easily dropped," were not communities bound by any vast deference to their elected officers. When John Adams insisted that there was not "in the whole circle of

* The figures, presented in detail in Appendix VIII, are compiled from the *Journals of the House,* currently being republished by the Massachusetts Historical Society. For the dozen years not yet republished, the printed Journals in the Massachusetts Archives were consulted. The figures do not include Boston, which was deliberately excluded because of its distinctively metropolitan situation and its disproportionate allotment of representatives (four a year). For Boston, sixty of its 240 delegates, or twenty-five per cent, were not incumbents.

the sciences a maxim more infallible than this, 'where annual elections end, there slavery begins,' " he spoke for a
provincial refusal to concede secure pre-eminence to anyone, a refusal which would have been quite unthinkable
in the mother country.[38]

In much the same manner, mandates to representatives
also revealed a refusal to acknowledge unequivocal authority. Attorneyship of representation not only afforded lever-
age to the communities in their external relations with the
province, but also spoke still more eloquently of the internal polity of the towns, where constraints unknown to the
English gentry who sat in Parliament were imposed almost
without thinking about them. Implicit in the mandate was
a denial of autonomy to representatives which was, above
all, a very direct denial of their separation from their constituents. Representation in provincial Massachusetts was
conceived in terms which men sensed to be appropriate to
their social order, and, in a society with no substantial economic specialization or historical tradition as a basis for
differentiation, that sense of the social order was a sense of
rough equality. Representatives were admonished to recall
their "natural dependence" on their communities, and occasional instructions even informed them explicitly that
"all officers are nothing more, than Servants to the
People." [39]

Others in apparent authority were similarly servants.
Agents were dispatched to the General Court and told
what they were to say there.[40] Selectmen and other citizens
were also sent with some frequency to perform delegated
duties before their county courts of general sessions.[41] And
the concept of agency was maintained even more persist-
ently and more pervasively within the towns themselves.
Town officials at home were expected to act in accordance
with the "duty and trust" they owed their fellow townsmen, quite as much as when they went to Boston or the
county seat; and whatever their legally assigned jurisdic-

tions, they were ultimately subject to the assembled citizenry.[42]

Thus the town meeting instructed local officers just as it instructed representatives, and far more often. Town committees were subject to instructions in almost every conceivable area from the town meetings which constituted them, and if they provoked any suspicion of independence their instructions were supplemented with a warning that they were "hereby wholly forbidden to act any Thing to yᵉ Conterary whatsoever."[43] Assessors, though legally authorized to make assessments in their own right, were commonly instructed by the town on the execution of that office.[44] Even the selectmen discharged their duties at the direction of the town meeting in such spheres as the appointment of innkeepers, the warning-out of undesirables, the laying out and altering of roads, and the provision for education, though all of these were formally within their own official prerogatives. The subjection of the selectmen was generally secured by the end of the seventeenth century; thereafter the board was broadly bound by the determinations of the community.[45]

Instructions, moreover, were barely the beginning of communal constraints on civic leaders. After an officer acted, his recommendation had still to be authorized, so that, for example, selectmen could lay out roads and bridges and assess taxes for them but the assessments had no standing and the roadwork did not begin until the townsmen did "signify their satisfaction" in a public meeting.[46] The accounts of town committees were consistently examined, and town votes were taken on the allowance of committee claims for expenses;[47] and so too were the accounts of town treasurers audited everywhere in provincial Massachusetts, though in this era in England an official pressed for an accounting of his bills could refuse with haughty indignation, insisting that "it is a very unpleasant thing to have one's bill handed round for everyone's inspection."[48]

It was unpleasant indeed at the Bay, because there such inspection was quite serious. No deference to persons or their places prevented townsmen from referring committee reports and recommendations back to the committees for amendment or for more careful execution of their original charge. Rather often, in fact, committee reports were rejected entirely.[49] Selectmen were subject to the same control and correction,[50] and their subordination was typified in a Worcester order of 1746 directing the board to ascertain the boundaries and value of each plot of public lands, "So yᵉ Town may better know how to proceed in Said affair & they desired to be as Speedy as may be." The selectmen were simply sent on an errand; they as much as constables or committeemen or cullers of hoops and staves were the servants of the town meeting, which reserved its right to make any actual decision.[51]

Of course, officials did not always submit tamely to such subordination,[52] but their boldest efforts to assert their authority were often the occasions which best revealed its boundaries. Local leaders in provincial Massachusetts were never the "independent, self-perpetuating bodies" which provided the local government of eighteenth-century England and even of Virginia; and when they attempted to establish themselves thus, they encountered resolute resistance. The expressions of resentment, and the effectual opposition which accompanied such expressions whenever a few men moved to "perpetuate themselves" in office, openly implied a distinct lack of deference on the part of the populace. In fact, opposition to these scattered efforts to initiate official immunity may stand as one small index to the social structure of the provincial community. The protests, *per se,* suggest that public expectations of official conduct had been flouted, and those expectations were not the expectations of a deferential society. Official immunity was, as a Brunswick petition announced around the middle of the century, "contrary to reason." The attempts to secure it were seen as brazen seizures of illegitimate power, and they were seen that way because the men who made them had no particular claim to special privilege conceded by the community.[53]

Thus the efforts to establish an elite testified to the absence of any established elite among the officers of the towns. Men expected themselves to matter in eighteenth-century Massachusetts, because in communities of consensus the opinions of many men had to be consulted. And where many men mattered, social distance was slight. Status could not be sharply distinguished. Near the bottom, not even servitude set a man much apart from his neighbors,[54] and at the top no oligarchy enjoyed a separate style of life either. Some men did possess more power than others—it could hardly have been otherwise as long as only three or five selectmen were chosen annually in towns of two hundred adult males—but social sequestration is not proven simply by the failure of an absolute equality; and it is social sequestration which is crucial, because a community in which some men matter more than others is not incompatible with a community in which many men matter, unless there is some significant social distance between the elite and the rest. Oligarchies require more than just the stable confinement of privileged positions to a severely limited few; they require also the separation of those few from the other inhabitants. Elite offices must be limited to the elite, menial offices to the menial, and the lines must be sharply drawn between them.[55]

In Massachusetts, the lines were hopelessly blurred. Men might serve as precinct committeemen five times in less than a decade, as one Amherst man did, and subsequently be chosen to sweep up the meetinghouse, as that man was.[56] And if that was an isolated and unusual incident, as it was, then more regular denials of social distance can also be compiled from the town records. Study of the leading local officials of thirteen towns shows that no social distance sufficient for oligarchy separated them from their fellow townsmen.

Positions such as selectman, assessor, treasurer, and, often, clerk were places of honor and esteem in the local establishment. But for each of these elite offices there were, every year, at least two or three minor posts to be filled— hogreeves, haywards, sealers of weights and measures, and many more of the same sort—and those were predominantly the preserve of men who would never in their lives sit on the board of selectmen. Such positions carried a slender status at best, and at their worst, they were altogether oner- ous; yet selectmen were commonly compelled to serve in these inferior positions quite as easily as they were elevated to their seats of pride, and hardly any selectmen ever es- caped such lowly service.

Among the thirteen towns investigated, nine of them elected more than ninety per cent of their selectmen to menial office at least once (and generally many times). Even in the four which did not, none installed less than eighty-four per cent of the selectmen in an inferior posi- tion for at least one term, so that nowhere in these towns did so many as one selectman in six escape such duty. In Manchester, only one selectman in thirty-seven never served; in Brookline, only two of forty-eight; in Topsfield only four of 102. And the few who escaped service were hardly an inner circle of the elite, supreme oligarchs ex- empt from attending to the town pound or viewing fences. The one Manchester selectman who never held a lesser office was a selectman for only a single term, in a town where the average service for selectmen on the board was almost five years. The two Brookline selectmen who never did menial duty also never did much service as selectmen; each was chosen to the office twice, while the average Brookline selectman sat slightly more than five years. In only one town of the thirteen were selectmen who did not hold office in the lower ranks elected more often than those who did. For all thirteen towns, the average tenure of the selectmen who never served in subordinate positions was about a term and a half shorter than the tenure of those who did.*

Social distance was similarly negligible in several other spheres. Civic obligations such as the maintenance of roads were obligations upon the entire citizenry, without distinction; any man who failed to perform his few days' work on the town ways was subject to fine. In some communities comparable terms were imposed on the clearing of the brush on the common and the killing of an appropriate quota of blackbirds.[57] In others, every man was compelled "to serve either as a constable or surveyor"—burdensome tasks both—"or to pay a fine." [58] In almost every town the schoolteacher's birch rod fell on the children of the rich and the poor alike.[59] And even where status was apparently acknowledged, as in the allocation of pews in the meeting-house according to status—that "hierarchy of dignity and property" so often cited by historians as visible symbol of social stratification in the provincial towns—such arrangements were, in the end, only another indication of the utter absence of oligarchical social separation.[60]

In the first place, such separation as did exist in the seating of the meetinghouses was altogether without stability. Social place could barely be presumed constant for longer than three or four years at a time: Weston rearranged its pewholders four times in sixteen years, Watertown revised its seating as often in fifteen years, and Lunenburg as many times in a mere three years. In Amherst the meetinghouse was seated in 1749, re-seated the following year, and re-seated again nine times in the next two decades. Such rearrangements were neither necessarily nor invariably very radical, of course, but the degree of difference from one year to the next is not nearly so important as

* The figures are presented in detail in Appendix IX, compiled from the town records.

the simple fact that differences were deemed likely. There was no expectation of stable status, not from generation to generation and not even from year to year. Towns such as Worcester undertook a complete redistribution of seats six times in less than two generations and also maintained a standing committee on the matter to make lesser adjustments in the continuing revision of visible status which was represented by the occupancy of church pews. And perhaps there was no more significant symptom of the expectation of unstable social separation than the failure to project or perpetuate positions into the succeeding generation; children were simply "huddled together into a common pew, without any regard at all for differentiation according to parental status." [61]

Secondly, and still more significantly, not even the momentary status made visible by meetinghouse seating was apparent anywhere else. The hierarchy of the pews was an artificial imposition overlaid upon the life of the community. When Westborough allotted its pews in 1749, it did so on the basis of tax payments, but it required a committee of townsmen "to find who were the highest payers." When Dudley voted to install pews in 1738, the inhabitants also had to vote that a committee "sarch the lists to find who is highest in the charges of the town and make return thereof to the town." [62] In the villages of England, men had known their places; in the towns of Massachusetts the notion of social stratification took on a radically different meaning when men had to institute inquiries to find out who occupied which strata.

Of course men continued to contend for position, but their very contention was vastly significant: status was no longer self-evident. Everywhere there was controversy over the seating of the meetinghouse—Weeden maintained that "court chamberlains could not have adjusted all their subtile claims and conflicting rivalries" [63]—and decisions on seating generally had to be submitted to committees rather than made in open town meeting. Such submissions, and the contention that caused them, themselves signified that there were in these towns no well-defined and clearly conceded elites; and the same submissions made the matter clearer still when the committees reported back to the town. For then, if the report was rejected or ordered back for reconsideration,[64] the townsmen were repudiating the authority of the committee as well as its recommendations; and even if the report was accepted, the fundamental fact remained that social status was thereby placed at the conscious disposal of the entire community, in town meeting assembled, rather than being accorded automatically.[65]

Oligarchy, then, was a virtual impossibility in provincial Massachusetts because there were virtually no oligarchs in towns such as Bridgewater or Southampton, Topsfield or Tisbury, none whose scale of living or style of life set them off at a secure social distance from their neighbors, none whose civic and economic and intellectual superiorities were known and acknowledged by all. There were leaders, of course, but their authority was fragmented rather than unitary, tenuous and temporary rather than firmly fixed. It sprang from no necessity of social and economic arrangements in the society.[66] In communities an ocean apart from England—communities which were, likely, several days' travel even from Boston, and communities which had no staple economy—the skills by which one man sustained himself and his family were much the same skills by which other men around him did the same. Few were possessed of anything sufficiently exotic as to separate themselves very far from their fellows, and few sought such separation anyway. If political and economic inequality existed, definitive social distance did not. Deference in such a society was just a dimly remembered dream from the mother country.

❧ VII ❧

War and Peace

IN APRIL OF 1776, British and provincial soldiers fired on each other across Lexington green in a shadowy engagement that began a battle that would ultimately transform America—and the towns of the old province too. With sovereignty in the society wholly in native hands again, and with a new central government able to command a confidence that the one tied to England had never held, an attrition of local authority would set in. Men would set their sights more broadly for the first time in almost a century. Consequence in the community would cease to be the consummation of men's ambitions, and local aspirations would turn steadily into cosmopolitan ones. From the very first statewide elections competing candidates from outside the town would enter in quest of votes, and a decade later national politics would provide another element of division; and the accustomed political peace of the communities would be no more.

Before the Revolution, such opportunities for external allegiances had been almost entirely absent, and their absence had underwritten the coercive moral authority of the town. The town had been able to define and establish the morally legitimate community because, against the orthodoxy of the organized group, an individual had almost nothing with which he could align himself. His reference groups had been wholly within the town, and there were none outside to support his sense of moral personality.

After independence, no New England town would remain the sole source of value for its inhabitants. A subtle shift in local political practices would set in, and the premium on peace would find other foci in response to other forces. For more than anyone foresaw at the time, the Revolution marked the commencement of a new career for the communities of Massachusetts.

Increasingly, it became difficult even to remember how powerful they had been, and how homogeneous. Increasingly, it became natural to tell the story of the eighteenth century and the Revolution it produced in terms more appropriate to the national politics of the nineteenth and twentieth centuries, terms of central initiative and local dependency, terms of struggle and strife. The origins of the final conflict were sought in the running battles of governors and assemblies, or in the grand designs of imperial strategists; the Revolution itself was explained as if those other revolutions in industry and agriculture, transportation, and communication, had already occurred when it broke out.

The result of such assumptions has been an extended series of historical explanations of the eighteenth century that are, ultimately, unhistorical. Accounts that concentrate on Boston and Whitehall cannot comprehend a society in which almost all men grew to maturity under the auspices of local institutions, for it was in the towns and from their fellow townsmen that the overhelming majority of men learned the rules and roles by which people lived together then. In their relations to each other and to authority, the men of Massachusetts were almost untouched by governments which came and went across the ocean or even in their own distant capital. Their primary experiences of public life throughout the provincial era—the experiences they caught up, codified, and enshrined for time to come in the course of building a new nation—were the experiences provided within the context of the community. An understanding of those experiences and the expectations that attended them requires an understanding of the communities in which those men lived.

Concomitantly, an understanding of those communities illuminates their wider setting quite strikingly. With so much power in the province lodged in its localities, a plausible bridge can be built between the study of those towns and villages and the study of the province. Local history, which has heretofore resisted most efforts to make it more than local, can be endowed with a larger significance, for in the instance of eighteenth-century Massachusetts it provides a prospect of actually accounting for developments instead of simply describing them. From the vantage point of 1775 it is possible to look back over almost a century of public affairs under the second charter, and to see that many staples of the traditional story of provincial politics can be explained in terms of the conditions of community far more fruitfully than they can explain such conditions. Episodes such as the Great Awakening and the excise controversy, broad tendencies such as the spread of democracy, and, indeed, many of the most important patterns of provincial stability and the most momentous changes from such patterns in the public conduct of the province were all connected quite closely to the conditions of local life. Almost every aspect of the established system of eighteenth-century politics—its tension between governor and legislature and the outcome of their clashes, its factionalism and the failure of organized parties, its issues and their ephemeral nature—was molded more by the demands and assumptions of the towns which sent men to Boston than by the institutional pressures of the government they found there; while the alterations in the system—the decline of doctrinal rigidity, the emergence of a new conception of the derivation of legitimate authority—were even more tightly tied to the needs and notions of the towns.

And in the end the Revolution itself is illuminated by an understanding of the provincial pattern, for the Revolution was largely formed in the towns and sustained by the towns. It was their attachment to the canons of concord that was threatened most immediately by the British edict against the town meeting in the Intolerable Acts of 1774, and it was their defiance of that edict—an edict which would have destroyed the essential instrument of local consensus—that ignited the rebellion. In the end the townsmen went to war to preserve their old patterns of peace and harmony, and those patterns persisted through the war and governed its conduct in every crucial regard. Muted, modified, yet in more ways than one, they are with us still.

The persistence of peace in the towns conditioned the conduct of provincial politics throughout the first three quarters of the eighteenth century. It tipped the balance of power between the assembly and the royal governors, it set the size of issues that did extend beyond the towns, and, perhaps, above all, it produced the peculiar pluralism of public life in the province at large.

As every account has made clear, provincial politics was fragmented almost beyond accounting. No stable parties structured Massachusetts politics, and no great issues provided men with a sense of provincial political identity; there were only individuals seeking special privileges. And if it was true that individuals fought quite as strenuously for the favors of the government in other colonies on the continent, it was also true that in other colonies such promotion was less primitve. At least a rudimentary political organization arose to express the regional rivalries of Rhode Island, the family dynastic aspirations of New York, the land company antagonisms of Virginia, and the more complex ethnic, religious, and proprietary politics of Pennsylvania. Massachusetts, in contrast, was politically underdeveloped. Its shifting alignments deserved the designation factional only in the most kaleidoscopic sense of Madison's term.[1]

The relative retardation of political organization in Massachusetts was not inevitable in the general nature of the case. The province was populous, and the privileges and powers its government could confer were not contemptible. A stable partisan politics was precluded instead by the particular conditions of consensus at the Bay. Independent towns, each straining for its own internal accord, could not support political parties which cut across town lines. The very same premium on peace which precluded pluralism within the towns almost assured it in the capital, where pluralism ran rampant because any larger organization was almost impossible.[2]

For almost all practical purposes, then, consensus closed the towns to provincial politics. There was simply no steadfast opposition which could be mobilized and no standing issues with which to mobilize one. Even the issues important enough to strike a few provincial sparks—the land bank, for example, and the excise—were more illuminating for the rapidity with which they blazed and then vanished. Provincial political issues were invariably ephemeral, and that was their truest significance. Even the Great Awakening "lost its unity as a mass movement and degenerated into eddies of local fervor" within two years of its inception; by Whitefield's second visit, less than five years after his first, "most of his appeal had disappeared."[3] And in the absence of any organization that could reach into the towns, no provincial party could sustain itself, while in the absence of any such rudimentary political structure, no issue could be sustained. The result was a milling and pushing politics of individuals in Boston which was prob ably dignified rather than demeaned by the label of factionalism.*

The same social system that accounted for the failure of provincial political organization also explained the general course of the conflict between governor and assembly in Massachusetts. The royal governors entered the political arena as emissaries of a great European power, but the rude provincials who sat in the House of Representatives sat for the real seats of power in the province. As every governor discovered as soon as his intentions crossed those of the Court, the assemblymen spoke for the only agencies of effective enforcement in Massachusetts. A deputy from Dedham or Rehoboth might lack the social graces of London, but he did not lack connection to a local consensus that could elicit compliance with provincial policy. Governors learned quickly that they could proclaim the royal instructions but that they and their administration were incapable of coercion across the colony. Effective authority in the eighteenth century was local authority, and a governor had to accede to it if he wished to govern effectively.

If he did not accede, if he attempted to pursue a policy of independence, he was doomed to emerge from the effort isolated and impotent. To govern at all he required revenues; since he could not obtain imperial aid he required the appropriations of the province; and for appropriations he had to have the approval of the assembly. The assembly, of course, preferred to conceive his necessity in more elevated terms—it spoke loftily of the traditional authority of

* The premium on communal consensus did not, however, preclude *every* form of provincial political organization. What it did deny was the legitimacy of open political parties professing distinctive values in a distinctive rhetoric and appealing to those values as a basis for the internal division of communities according to party programs and labels. What it in no way prevented, and what in some small measure did apparently exist, were political alliances of unified towns with other unified towns to do battle with still other unified towns.

the popular house to originate all money bills, the authority that was a standing prerogative of the House of Commons in England—but tradition was not really the essence of the issue. Sheer constitutional authority did not infallibly survive the sea-passage. The House of Representatives of Massachusetts enforced its claim upon the power of the purse by its influence with the only people who filled that purse. The towns were the units of taxation, and the townsmen alone could give effect to provincial levies. In the provincial government, only the representatives had ties to the townsmen.*

The point was driven home whenever a royal governor neglected that elemental fact of his official life. Governors did not neglect it often, but the occasions when they did were illuminating. In the 1731–32 session of the General Court, for example, the governor and his council engaged the lower house in a dispute over the governor's salary and the government supply bill. In itself the issue was by no means a new one—salary and supply constituted an almost annual occasion of conflict at the time—but in that session the governor clung to his royal instructions with an unprecedented insistence. The dispute dragged on while the deputies waited for the governor to give in graciously, as others had done, but eventually they exhausted their patience and had to recall their executive to provincial political realities. First, and pointedly, they requested a recess so that they could canvass "the reply of their constituents in town meetings." When the governor still refused to yield, the representatives informed him of the results of his ada-

* One thing the governor could do was minimize, to the best of his ability, the number of representatives, thus keeping the assembly as manageable as possible. Accordingly, the alignment within the legislature on the creation of new townships is revealing. In almost every case of conflict within the Court, it was the Council, with its close connection to the governor, which opposed additional votes in the assembly, while the representatives welcomed them. See, e.g., Mass. Arch. 114, p. 52; ibid., pp. 732, 733a; ibid. 115, pp. 477–8; ibid. 117, pp. 870–1.

mance: "only two towns in the Province had given direction to supply the treasury as required by the thirtieth Royal instruction." [4]

Ultimately, then, the power of the purse was no mere affair of ideology; its roots were in the realities of provincial power far more than in the traditions of the English constitution. Similarly, the men of Massachusetts insisted upon legislative supremacy less from any abstract attachment to radical whiggery and the rights of Englishmen than from an immediate attachment to their own interests. As Morison maintained, "it was only natural to wish to entrust power to a body, every member of which was elected in town meeting and subject to its instructions." [5] The assertion of legislative supremacy was ultimately an assertion of local supremacy.

Ultimately too, the governor's primary power was in his capacity to confer legitimacy. When that too was called into question, at the approach of the American Revolution, the impotence of his administration was exposed for all to see. [6] The governor's authority now embraced little more than Boston; the royal treasurer soon failed to receive payments or recognition from the towns; by the towns had been brought about the end of the royal legislature; at their instance the royal courts had been abolished; and it is significant that in this general collapse the town system, and that alone, had maintained an existence that was practically continuous. The town system alone preserved its continuity through the Revolution, because its connection to the provincial government had always been tenuous. There was nothing remarkable in the smooth transformation of a royal province into an American commonwealth; the towns installed the new government without chaos and without great confusion because they had provided the genuine government of the province all along. Even the most powerful arm of the provincial government, the House of Representatives, had been a creature of the communities.

Actual representation, especially when set so deliberately against virtual representation, implied what was actually the case, that the House had no distinct identity. When the towns sent their agents elsewhere, as they did in 1774, power went with them.

The pattern of peace also shaped a more pervasive development during the provincial years, one which transformed the very power that the towns transferred in those late days of the imperial crisis. Through four generations the canons of legitimate coercion had been subtly shifting, touching institutions and inclinations alike, altering the relations of localities to the central government and the expectations men maintained about the appropriate exercise of authority; and in the Revolution and its aftermath the shifts were caught up and codified.

Out of the transition from colony to province at the end of the seventeenth century had come a meaning of local government utterly unlike the meaning of local government in the mother country. In England the institutions of town and county and village "reinforced the authority of the king and parliament, thereby enhancing the tie between the people and the central government." [7] In America, local government contributed almost nothing to the ties between the people and the central power. Direct communication was minimal, and crucial mediating mechanisms such as the county were weak or nonexistent in New England. To most men it was not even clear whether the relevant central government was in Boston or in London.

Other differences also unhinged the accustomed connections. The unitary authority of king and Parliament in England became, in American terms, the antagonistic authority of governor and assembly; and while the powers of king and Parliament pertained to the same constituency in the mother country, that was not the case in the provinces. In England the king concerned himself with the entire English people, and, according to the theory of virtual representation, members of Parliament did the same. In Massachusetts neither the governor nor the assembly attended directly to the common welfare. The governor regarded his responsibility to the people at one remove, because his job depended on his allies and enemies in London, not on his performance in the province. The representatives owed their essential allegiance to their own particular communities, an allegiance implicit in the deputy's role as attorney or agent and explicit in the colonial argument for actual representation.

Accordingly, all questions of a constituency larger than the immediate community were hopelessly muddled in provincial Massachusetts. Representative self-government, which quite broadly contributed to the decentralization of English dominion across the continental colonies,[8] more basically promoted decentralization within the province itself. For whatever the confusions at the provincial and imperial levels, no man of Massachusetts could mistake the locus of the coercive power that affected his own daily life. He knew that the powers of the province and even of the county were not entirely negligible, but he knew far more profoundly that it was the community which counted. And he knew that he was a part of that community.

Such knowledge was the ineluctable outcome of a new experience of authority. In eighteenth-century Massachusetts power did not descend mysteriously from above. Power was personal, and it could be seen close up. Power was neighbors talking around a table at the village tavern, and the agreements at which they arrived. It was something in which every man mattered and any man might participate. Even as poor a tradesman as Ben Franklin's father was courted and consulted "by leading people," [9] and across the province thousands of men as obscure as Josiah Franklin had comparably to be considered. In the towns and villages of the eighteenth century, authority was dispersed by the very homogeneity of the inhabitants. Effective action and the merest maintenance of order required harmonious relations among all the inhabitants, and this unanimity could not be imposed from above because no one had eminence enough to do so. In the absence of oligarchy, accommodations to which all citizens could accede had to be carefully and consciously constructed, by bargaining and by mutual concession. The experience of power, in a town of one or two hundred adult males, came in conversations with fellow townsmen; and men who grew up in such towns, surrounded by these mundane mechanisms of power, could hardly help developing a certain sense of competence. Men could be sure that they counted, because few of them failed to meet the minimal requirements for political participation and consensus comprehended all participants in the political process. A politics of consensus was a politics of the compromises necessary to come to a consensus. The power requisite to regulate livestock, allot land in the town common, or elect a minister was a power susceptible to the ideas and interests and influence of the townsmen. It was a power which was manipulable and, more often than not, benign.

By the time of the American Revolution, this new experience of power had given rise to an entirely new orientation to authority, an orientation which pervaded the province and was, in a sense, what the Revolution was all about. In the environment of eighteenth-century America, the meaning of legitimate government had diverged drastically from the English acceptation. In Massachusetts legitimacy did not derive from the assent of the sovereign but rather from the consent of the governed. Power was drawn from the mass of the people; the loftier reaches of central authority were servants, not masters.*

Countless petitions and resolves underscored that submission, and their thrust was always the same. Men who had only half-consciously diverged from the political practices of the mother country were groping to draw the distinctions consciously, groping, in essence, for a certain self-discovery. Out of the decades of democratization of power, out of a dozen devices designed to bind in their representatives at the central government and secure that government's subservience to local desires, they were attempting to distill their political identity. And on the eve of the Revolution, their success was substantial. Dozens of towns spoke in the same accents as Worcester, protesting the Tea Act of 1774:

> We apprehend that all officers are nothing more, than Servants to the people, for whose Good only they were appointed, for which Service, they ought to Depend

* The Handlins have anticipated an important part of this argument. They too took as a premise the deepening difference in the European and American meanings of legitimacy—"discussion and practice both reflected the assumption that legitimacy was a consequence not of royal assent but of the consent of the governed"—and they also acknowledged that the divergence had not always existed—"sometime in the century before the Revolution there must have been a change in the American view of the derivation of authority." And the Handlins also expected that the roots of this radical change would be found in the conduct of politics in the colonial communities:

> We know too little as yet about colonial political theory or political practice to account fully for that change. The dynamics of the process will no doubt emerge from more careful study of the ways in which power was exercised at the town or county level and of the relation of local to provincial government. . . . [This] conception of popular authority . . . established the basic procedures within which power was to be used in the United States.

See Oscar and Mary Handlin: *The Dimensions of Liberty* (Cambridge, 1961), pp. 31, 32–3.

on those they Serve for their pay: and we are constrained to Say, that to have those who are to Judge,
and Determin, on our lives, property, paid by a foreign State, imme[d]iately Destroy, that natural dependence, which ought to Subsist between a people,
and their officers, and of consequence, destructive of
liberty.[10]

By the beginning of 1776 the General Court itself proclaimed that any act of government "against, or without
the consent of the people, is injustice, usurpation, and tyr-
anny," and the constitution of 1780 elevated that principle
into the fundamental law of the commonwealth: "ALL
power residing originally in the people, and being derived
from them the several magistrates and officers of Government, vested with authority, whether legislative, executive,
or judicial, are their substitutes and agents, and are at all
times accountable to them." [11]

The placement of original authority in the people was
the culmination of a century-and-a-half of thought and action in hundreds of towns around the Bay, and in that line
the constitution of 1780 was the culminating statement of
the provincial period. It codified the eighteenth-century
experience of authority that the framers and their fathers
had known in their own communities, proclaiming popular sovereignty and proclaiming too the forms that such
sovereignty ought to take.

Foremost among such forms was the rule of accommodation. In the "Address of the constitutional convention,
to their constituents, 1780," the norms of negotiation were
accorded the same pre-eminence that had long prevailed
locally, among townsmen seeking a consolidated popular
opinion and the public peace. For the Address was no visionary document. It was designed to win votes for the
work of the convention, and it was directed to the assumptions accepted most widely among the voters. It began with

the statement of the delegates that they had "endeavor'd to act as became the Representatives of a wise, understanding and free People; and, as we have Reason to believe you would *yourselves* have done, we have open'd our Sentiments to each other with Candor, and made such mutual Concessions as we could consistently." It declared its disbelief that success was even possible "without such mutual Condescention." Proclaiming consensus as a premise of the convention's efforts—"The Interest of the Society is common to all its Members"—the Address maintained that that premise had shaped the delegates' deliberations because it shaped their aspirations.

> The great Enquiry is, wherein this Common Interest consists. In determining this Question, an Advantage may arise from a Variety of Sentiments offer'd to public Examination concerning it. But wise Men are not apt to be obstinately tenacious of their own Opinions: They will always pay a due Regard to those of other Men and keep their minds open to Conviction. We conceive, that in the present Instance, by accommodating ourselves to each other, and individually yielding particular and even favorite Opinions of smaller moment, to essential Principles, and Considerations of general Utility, the public Opinion of the Plan now before you may be consolidated.[12]

Such explanations, the rest of the Address, and the frame of government which followed, would all have been inconceivable to the men who founded Massachusetts. Few of the founders had seen any advantage whatsoever in "a Variety of Sentiments," and the master of invective among them had once insisted that "polypiety is the greatest impiety in the world." Openness to other opinions and any valuation at all of diversity were antithetical to the very mission on which they had arrived. By 1780, on the other hand, the sense of mission itself was dormant among their descendants. In a single sentence the Address of the convention brushed aside its barest possibility, saying "we may not expect to agree in a perfect system of Government: This is not the Lot of Mankind." Where Winthrop and Ward had hoped to establish God's ideal commonwealth at the Bay, their sons abandoned the ancestral heritage in bland resignation to imperfection. Where Winthrop wished for an almost absolute agreement in his consecrated colony, and had banished Williams and Wheelwright and Hutchinson and a hundred others to achieve it, his inheritors cooperated in the Revolution with the very communities of Rhode Island to which the heretics had fled, and with the polypietists of Pennsylvania and New York and Virginia as well. A politics of accommodation precluded the assurance of the settling generation.[18]

Concomitantly, the abandonment of assurance introduced the possibility of legitimate change. The settling generation, contemning democracy, had attempted to institute a set of eternal decrees. The sons of the selfrighteous, embracing a measure of democracy, actually incorporated allowance for amendment into their constitution in 1780, and they left the direction of such alteration very largely to the vagaries of popular whim.

In the interval the assumptions of life in New England had shifted profoundly, and while a large part of the change was explicable in terms of external developments, another large part remained beyond such accounting. The brute facts of change in the new American environment had indeed demanded some sort of intellectual confrontation with the issue of innovation, but they did not demand capitulation. They did not require that innovation—which had once, in the days of the jeremiads, been seen solely as deviation from the desirable—come to be seen as, in some measure, desirable in itself. They did not force men of Massachusetts to feel that what had happened was, as Bernard Bailyn has put it, "good and proper, steps in the right direction." [14] Their own experience alone brought them to that conclusion, and in their own experience novelty had rarely been the menace their fathers had feared. Innovation had, basically, been domesticated in the provincial villages. The priority placed on widespread acceptance of alterations enlisted a united public support for them. It was such accommodation for the sake of consensual change to which the convention urged its constituents—"by accommodating ourselves to each other . . . the public Opinion of the Plan now before you may be consolidated"—and it was such consolidation that shaped an emergent American attitude toward social change itself. Townsmen of the eighteenth century came to expect innovation that proceeded by placating evey substantial interest in the community, innovation in which few men were ever very deeply damaged because most were bought off, innovation that was almost inevitably slow and rarely very radical. If such change did not go to the root of a problem, it was because problem-solving, *per se,* was not primary. Solutions took second place to maintaining a community that moved together, without any deep pockets of resistance.

Historical change, then, did not derive entirely from outside the province in the eighteenth century. Some changes, such as the introduction of religious toleration, were indeed imposed at the outset, but they were also accepted and even, in the end, embraced. No English power compelled Cotton Mather, in 1726, to condemn men much like his seventeenth-century forebears as "unreasonable Sons of Procrustes, the Narrow-soul'd and Imperious Bigots for Uniformity." [15] In their passage from absolute conviction to a degree of accommodation, the men of provincial Massachusetts were accomplices as well as victims; and in their complicity inhered the essential significance of town meeting politics at the Bay.

The town meeting, as it existed in scores of eighteenth-century villages, provided the prime experiential basis for the new orientation to authority. Unbending conviction was incompatible with the peaceful and prosperous development of the community. So too was disdain for the democracy, for the democracy was not the depressed and deferential mass of men known to the towns and villages of the mother country. Consent was the condition of success in the American community, because enforcement was inefficient if not impossible without wide participation and widespread agreement among the participants. Widespread agreement, in turn, was impossible without a resignation to the imperfection of men and a readiness to make the changes that they variously wished.

The result was that the stern necessity of enforcement sustained town-meeting democracy in Massachusetts and undermined the doctrinal rigidity of the men who had once sought to set a city upon a hill. The politics of consensus made a measure of democracy functional; under its aegis, men of "untolerable pride" bore sons who expected to submit their judgment to the judgment of the peers.[16] By the middle of the eighteenth century concord was secured by settlements "to which both parties were agreed and are mutually satisfied," and they were based on voluntary concessions "in condescension to the desire of a number of people." Such settlements marked the Puritan passage to a new pattern of politics, a politics whose novelty was as much a matter of psychological style as of institutional arrangements. Where their fathers had known that the gate was strait and few passed through, the provincial villagers aspired instead to settlements of differences which almost everyone could accept, or at least live with. Denying their own utter rectitude, they sought coalitions that subordinated ideological clarity and blurred all borders of contention. They learned to take seriously another man's attitude. Within their communities of co-believers, they set negotiation and conciliation as their new norms. The "mutual Concessions" and "mutual Condescention" reported by the constitutional convention of 1780 expressed quite accurately the developed provincial sense of the appropriate employment of authority, and that sense and its attendant expectations persisted far beyond 1780 in America.[17]

Indeed, in the decades before the Revolution, a few auguries even appeared of the extended accommodativeness that was to come. Townsmen who refused to allow their neighbors' applications for separation began for the first time to assail not just the practicality of particular separations but also the very principle of separation in cases of conflict. As Worcester declared in 1772, "the cutting up, slitting and dividing old towns in order to make little, small, poor, contentious parishes and districts is attended with ill consequences, has a tendency to discourage learning as they cannot support school and gospel among them as they ought to be supported." Such statements were not common, but their importance was as much in their possibility as it was in their prevalence. The very proposal itself indicated that, for a few men in provincial Massachusetts, the perils of pluralism were no longer prohibitive. Men whose whole lives had been lived under conditions of accommodation had glimpsed the prospect of an accommodation that could secure concord even out of genuine conflict in the community. They had managed to transcend their tradition. Separations in situations of social divergence had always been an aspect of the monolithic unity of the Massachusetts town; proposals such as Worcester's would have prevented many of the fissions which fostered such homogeneity. It would have confined differences within the community, and accordingly it would have forced men in Massachusetts to do what they had never done before: find ways to live together without absolute anterior agreement.* [18]

---

* What Worcester urged was, of course, what did subsequently occur. The town network was largely completed by the time of the Revolution in Massachusetts, and as population increased thereafter, the concentration

But in the provincial period itself, Worcester's way was not adopted. The old ideal of uniformity was affirmed as often in the last decades before independence as it had been earlier, and the commitment to harmony and homogeneity assured the continued legitimacy of local fissions in

---

of people per political unit rose and a different pattern of problem-solving in the community emerged. There were only half again as many towns added in the next century and three quarters as already existed in 1779, while population increased more than twelvefold over the same span. See Commonwealth of Massachusetts: *Historical Data Relating to Counties, Cities, and Towns in Massachusetts* (Boston, 1948); Taeuber and Taeuber: *Changing Population*, p. 14.

What Worcester presumed elsewhere in its petition, however, betokened a change already well underway by 1772, when that petition was sent. The original settlers' ideal of the compact community had referred not only to values and votes but also to settlement patterns. The town's ecology was to be the physical embodiment of its idea system. But by 1772, and indeed for some time before, dispersal of settlement had been the actual condition of affairs in most towns, and the Worcester petitioners actually accepted it as inevitable: "Your respondents are sensible in country towns where people get their livings by husbandry they cannot live compact but must be scattered over a considerable tract of land. . . ."

Worcester's sense of the situation was the more significant for being so casual and truistic, for the maintenance of the monolithic communities of Massachusetts had depended very heavily on such social structural supports as close contiguity and the extended family. The original ideal of homogeneity and the very preservation of peace had been conditioned on the prohibition upon impulse-gratification of the crowded household and on the high visibility and sustained scrutiny of the closely settled village. But though those supports sufficed for more than a hundred years, though the extended family and the compact community remained functional far into the eighteenth century—see Bash: "Family and Community Organization," pp. 24–5, 39–40, 41–2—they did decline in its latter portions. By the second half of the century, if not before, the extended family ceased to be the standard unit of socialization of the children of Massachusetts— see Bailyn: *Education*, pp. 24–5—and about the same time the spread of population produced recognitions such as Worcester's of the emerging dispersal of settlement.

The norms of nonaggression, on the other hand, persisted throughout the provincial period, and to all appearances they were almost wholly unaffected by the erosion of their social structural supports. Harmony and homogeneity were affirmed as often at the end of the period as they had been at its beginning; and if the Puritan patterns of family and settlement

cases of conflict.[19] Within the community itself, pluralism never did prevail before the American Revolution.

Summarizing the several strands of local activity in the last years of the province, Harry Cushing found that "then, as earlier, the chief care of the towns was to secure the utmost scope and freedom to local action." Few towns went so far as Attleborough did in that concern, formally declaring its independent sovereignty unto itself, but from the fall of the old provincial assembly in 1774 the towns of Massachusetts had neither a legally constituted central government nor any apparent need for one. It never mattered that the political theory congenial to the time claimed the commonwealth suddenly plunged into a state of nature. So long as the towns operated unimpaired, society remained stable. Offenses against it were as competently controlled in Massachusetts as in any of the other erstwhile colonies which had established constitutions and legitimate central governments. The towns maintained law and order as well without the provincial legal machinery as they had done with it, because the community rather than the county courts had been the essential instrument of law and order all along.[20]

Indeed, though a few communities did feel the need for a judicial system of their own devising, most required neither new institutions nor a new status. The old armory of authority was quite adequate for them. Their local regulations and the informal sanctions of small-town society "reduced the refractory to obedience," so that, as an early legal historian of the commonwealth summed it up, "the defect of courts of justice was in some places supplied by the es-

---

shifted but slowly, the movement of cultural values in the province was glacial. Implicit in that lag, of course, was the prospect that the old values would not survive unimpaired the ideological adjustments inaugurated by the Revolution.

tablishment of local tribunals for the trial of causes, but more by the spontaneous action of the people in restraining crimes and enforcing justice." [21]

The pattern of restraint and enforcement was, in other words, the pattern of consensus politics. In this respect, as in so many others, men behaved in the era of the Revolution much as they had grown accustomed to behave before. Public opinion was still their essential engine of control, and they still assumed the canons of consensus because they lived in communities of consensus and knew no other norms. What they had done for almost a century, they continued to do for the few years of the Revolution.

Long before battle itself broke out, massive majorities were binding themselves to a common course while exerting no sanctions against the few who failed to comply but the sanctions of exposure. In the nonimportation agreements of 1770, for instance, towns such as Newburyport resolved not to use or buy foreign tea, and, according to a town historian, "public opinion was the principal means of enforcement [of their resolution] by the threat of publishing the names of unrepentant offenders as 'pests of Society & Enemies of ye Country.'" Newburyport did appoint a committee of inspection to give effect to the agreement, but even its efforts were essentially appeals to publicity, being basically the circulation of "a pledge to be signed by all the inhabitants determined not to buy, sell, or use India tea," with those who refused to sign "to be reported to the next town meeting." Fully ninety-four per cent of the town's adult males did sign that pledge, and the few who refused were disproportionately the older men of the town, men perhaps no longer so solicitous for the esteem of the entire community.[22] Similar sanctions applied in other towns, and they continued to apply until the very eve of armed rebellion. In Braintree, for example, a committee of observation was constituted to inform itself of violators, if any, of the nonimportation and nonconsumption accords of 1774, "that in such case they publish his, her, or their names that they may be known & esteemed as Practical enemies to our rights & Priviledges." In Dedham the committee to enforce those engagements was instructed only that "if any one should be so devoid of patriotism, his name was to be posted up in the several parishes, and declared an enemy to his country." [23]

Of course exposure was no empty threat—moral isolation was not easy to maintain in a town of two or three hundred families—but the essential point is that exposure was often the only threat. The committees of inspection in such cases were given no police powers, only the powers of publicity; and even the few who refused compliance were at first urged only to reconsider their recalcitrance. The truth was that town discipline in the Revolution resembled nothing so much as church discipline throughout the provincial era. Reform rather than retribution was its primary purpose, because punishment could, at best, purge the community, whereas repentance restored its moral integration. A confession acknowledged and even reaffirmed the morality of the community, and so the design of discipline was the extraction of that acknowledgment, under the pressure of the moral condemnation of the community.

Formal censure was the simplest expression of that pressure, and its power carried far beyond its ostensible objects because, like every other exemplary punishment, it threatened everyone. For every man explicitly disciplined, there were a hundred others on whom the lesson was not lost, a hundred others who were also reminded to consider the consequences of defiance. But formal censure was certainly not the only instrument of intimidation nor the only technique to dispel dissent. In other towns accusation served, and in still others, interrogation and scrutiny or the drafting of statements to be subscribed by all inhabitants deemed dubious in their loyalty. [24]

The essential point is that in every case it was publicity

which was the purpose, and even when men went beyond moral suasion to physical coercion, exposure was still their ultimate intention. The routs and riots of revolutionary mobs were characterized by what Arthur Schlesinger called "a singular self-restraint," in which the rioters relied on "horror rather than homicide." [25] Tarring-and-feathering too lacked any basic intention to inflict bodily injury for its own sake. The crucial part of the penalty occurred *after* the application of tar and feathers, when the culprit was carted about the town so that his disgrace might serve "as an object lesson to others as well as himself," for "the shame and ridicule of carting acted as a more effective deterrent . . . than either imprisonment or stripes." Physical force simply could not compare with social sanctions. The same didactic design also guided the hanging-in-effigy, a sanction even more obviously exemplary in its intention than the tar brush. In some communities a "suit of the modern mode" became "the favorite discipline for those of low degree" while the erection of effigies "was reserved for offenders of higher station," but either way, as Schlesinger observed, exposure "advertised the enormity of their misconduct to the public." [26] Indeed, the militia itself, according to John Roche, performed its primary service in a task which was "not so much military as para-military: it kept anti-British opinion dominant in the countryside by quasi-vigilante activities." [27]

Exposure, isolation, and a bit of vigilantism were the sanctions set in the service of unanimity everywhere. In this sense it did not matter that some towns tarred and feathered and others hung in effigy, that some accused and others inquisitioned or insisted upon sworn statements. These were only vagaries of town taste in tactics, not indications of deeper-lying differences in strategy. Dissent was conceived as a danger in every town, and everywhere men were discontent with a simple majority. Dissident minorities were to be eliminated rather than merely outvoted, for no town aimed at anything less than perfect unity.

Thus the unanimous votes that characterized the years of revolutionary crisis[28] were consciously created, often with exquisite artistry. In June of 1774, for instance, the Boston Committee of Correspondence circulated a nonconsumption covenant to the towns. Some of them adopted it at once, unanimously, but in others the compact found only a substantial agreement, not a complete accord. In those communities the inhabitants preferred to hold on to it for a while rather than ratify it immediately by a mere majority. Brimfield spoke for many of them when it explained:

> Gentlemen, we should have sent you a copy of the Covenant at large, and a List of the Few that as yet have not signed it, But under Expectation of our Uniting to a Man and the great Reluctance we have in holding up to the world a Brother a Fellow towns Man, as an Enemy to his Country till we have the best evidence of his Vileness has determined us not to publish their names at present. We would still think we are all of one Mind in the grand american Struggle for Liberty; but if any should long continue to oppose, by their Fruits we shall know them, you may depend on having Their Names in our next.[29]

An important instrument of agreement was the town committee. The fundamental function of a committee, ordinarily, was the formal arrangement of its community's internal accord. An *ad hoc* committee might give voice to the common feelings of the townsmen when they wished explicitly to instruct their representative, a committee of correspondence might articulate the town's agreement in specific terms when word arrived of the Boston Port Bill, a committee of inspection might define the bounds of a boy-

cott; and in all such circumstances the recommendations
would be adopted without opposition. But if the
community was in fact divided, committees could also be
established in many places, to create common feelings
where none existed before. In those cases they were composed of representatives of the contending factions, and
they were set apart so that their differences could be composed and a common ground discovered. Thus, in Decem-
ber of 1773, the town of Fitchburg attempted to take action
upon some letters from the Boston committee of correspondence but found itself stymied after men "Dilibrated
there on with Zeal and candor." The townsmen then
"unanasmly agreed to Chues a Committee" to consider the
matter under circumstances more favorable to conciliation,
and when the committee emerged with an answer for Boston the townsmen consented unanimously to its resolutions.[30]

Occasionally the committee itself could not conciliate
all factions, but even then it did not despair of a solution
satisfactory to all. Instead, it established within its ranks a
subcommittee, in much the manner the town had already
established the committee and with much the same ultimate intention to eliminate diversity of opinion and erase
individual responsibility. The committee or its subcommittee was almost always able, eventually, to submit a report which was a model of impersonality, a direct expression of the ideal of homogeneity, with all the rough edges
of dispute and dissent removed. The report, then, could be
identified only with the committee as a committee, not
with the victorious and the vanquished factions which had
composed it, just as, after the report was adopted in town
meeting, it was identified with the whole community, not
a mere majority.[31]

If the gentle methods of committees and publicity
failed, then more rigorous ones were used. Sometimes they
entailed only an attack on the appearance of protest, as

when town records were adjusted or falsified.[32] But on other occasions they aimed at the protest itself, and even at the protestants. In Stockbridge, for example, a man had to flee for the mountains, "where his family fed him until the worst of the excitement died down," after he cast the town's lone dissenting vote against national independence.[33] In other places other disabilities and dangers confronted dissenters, particularly those who professed loyalism. They and their families were isolated within the community—the very term "Tory" was one of obvious opprobrium, its effect not much different than a hanging in effigy[34]—and then, often, they were driven from it, by demands for a conformity beyond their capacity. The demands were rather commonly enforced by an impetuous populace suddenly mounted as a mob, and mobs sprang up all over the province. Boston's was merely the most notorious; it was not the only one, nor was it a noticeably more natural phenomenon in that urban environment, for the mob was indigenous to rural communities too, and perhaps a bit more natural as it existed outside the metropolis. It was, after all, the country towns which drove the mandamus councilors to Boston and the protection of the British troops there, and it was in the country towns that the mob was most clearly the ultimate expression of a community consensus, for no mob could have existed for more than a moment in those towns without the toleration of the people. It was in the accents of local pride that a countryman could proclaim that "it is more dangerous being a Tory here than at Boston," and it was in despair that the cosmopolitan Peter Oliver, as much a connoisseur of the mob as any man in Massachusetts, concurred. After he had witnessed his first mob scene outside Boston, he confessed, "I never knew what mobbing was before." [35]

Of course, it was not every dissident who was menaced by a mob—although many were—nor every loyalist who lost all his local property in confiscation proceedings—although many more did. But it was the case, quite commonly, that the cost of safety was silence. It was a fact that open opposition to the communal course was apt to irritate or even enrage a band of men bent on an appearance of absolute agreement, and it was a fact that, inexorably, dissenting impulses were extinguished, in high places and in low. Late in 1774, for instance, one of Newburyport's leading lawyers—a selectman of the town—addressed an open letter to his fellow townsmen in which he lamented his lately lagging patriotism and "atoned for his sin." A few months earlier, a far less prominent citizen of the same town took similar refuge in an even more revealing recantation. Daniel Bayley, a potter, proffered his apologies in a letter in the *Essex Journal,*

> ". . . exculpating himself from sundry reports, which have been spread to his prejudice, that he has been inimical to the town & has propagated many stories against their liberties," reports which he insisted were entirely groundless. "Notwithstanding," Bayley continued, "he readily acknowledges that he has (considering the spirit of the times) been too free in speaking his political sentiments which have (perhaps unfortunately for him) been somewhat different from the major part of the people; but this consolation he has, that (if he has been in an error) he has ever spoken his honest sincere and unbiased sentiments— but is determined in future, not to converse on politics which seem so greatly to disgust."

Bayley had never even expressed himself in a town meeting —he gave offense only by his conversation around town— and yet he found it prudent to silence himself rather than provoke "disgust." [36]

This was the way in which the broad social imperatives of consensus impinged on particular men in particular places and drove dissent from the community. This was the coercive power of common attitudes and expectations, lifted from the individual to the social level by a score of similar confessions. And this was the way in which so many towns such as Weston could be fully in favor of the British empire in, say, 1772, and as utterly opposed to it by 1775, while remaining always united. As late as the winter of 1773–4 the community was so complacent as to refuse, "by a very great majority," even to choose a committee of correspondence. Eight months later it set itself squarely astraddle the political fence by choosing delegates to both the General Court at Salem and the Provincial Congress at Concord; and eight months after that, in May of 1775, the town came to conviction on the magnitude of the peril confronting the commonwealth and chose a representative to the Provincial Congress "to save this People from Ruin." [37] Within sixteen months Weston occupied almost every point in the political spectrum, and it occupied them all with wide agreement among its inhabitants. Only a community accustomed to consensus could have managed the shifts so easily. It is quite inconceivable that every man in town could have gone through the same gyrations and arrived independently at the same conclusions at the same times. And yet it was precisely that pattern of unity which, at a price, permitted an easy passage into the Revolution and independence, without the social disruption that would have attended more genuinely independent individual decisions.

Indeed, the uniformity that obtained in the towns not only permitted the passage into rebellion but, in a very real sense, produced it. Such unity had secured the towns' power to order their own affairs, and it sustained their dominion of the province as well. "The towns were in fact the several sovereigns of Massachusetts-Bay," as Morison said,[38] and the preservation of their sovereignty was, more than anything else, what they went to war for.

Townsmen who identified liberty with their accustomed local practices and prerogatives had been disposed to distrust England's attachment to the sacred cause ever since the beginning of the English effort to establish an American episcopate, around the turn of the century; and as the Anglicans expanded their efforts the distrust of the townsmen deepened, coloring their every interpretation of events after 1763. The icy antagonisms that grew out of that menace to the congregational autonomy of the towns probably played the crucial part in the creation of a revolutionary situation in Massachusetts.[39]

And in that revolutionary situation, it was another English assault on the customary conduct of the communities which triggered armed resistance itself. For a decade after the subsidence of the turmoil attending the Stamp Act, there was restlessness but there was no rebellion. It was only when Parliamentary demands went beyond customs duties and abstract obligations, only when the provincial communities themselves were more directly threatened, that the imperial crisis came to a climax. The Intolerable Acts of 1774 were the first which truly touched the pattern of sovereignty in severalty, and they precipitated a revolution.[40]

The Intolerable Acts affected every level of local life. They eliminated the elective jury, an institution tied totally to the shared prejudices of peers and one which had proven itself a splendid shelter for the townsmen from imperial regulations.[41] They altered radically the provincial legislature, the central governmental agency of the towns at one remove. And above all, they required the approval of the royal governor for the convocation of an ordinary town meeting, a requirement which represented an almost un-

precedented imperial intrusion on local autonomy and an
intolerable impairment of the villagers' essential instrument for the consolidation of their communities. According to one authority, it was that prohibition of the town
meeting which "was long remembered as the most damag-
ing act, short of armed coercion, that could possibly be
made on the liberties of the people." * 42

The very core of their community life thus threatened,
the townsmen turned their attention outward for the first
time in almost a century. In villages all over the province
men who had barely ever bothered with anything but their
immediate affairs took up with zeal the unaccustomed issues of Massachusetts and America and the empire itself.
In a town such as Tisbury—where less than one item in
every eight that came before the meeting had been in any
way beyond the town in the previous eighty years—more
than three of every five such items concerned external
affairs in 1774 and 1775. In Amherst, seventy per cent of
the public business was external in those two years, where
little more than seven per cent had been so before; and in
Dudley and Fitchburg, though the proportion of business
outside the town was but thirty-six per cent in 1774 and
1775, that proportion was still almost ten times what it had
been in the years preceding. For seven towns tallied, about
forty-five per cent of the town meeting entries of the two
years after the Intolerable Acts engaged issues alien to the
town, against a bit more than nine per cent of such entries
in all the time before.†

As the townsmen entered the imperial arena, they
moved ineluctably toward insurrection. In August and

---

* It is perhaps significant that the only comparable interference with the
town meeting before 1774 occurred during the brief regime (1686–89) of
Governor Andros, and that he and the Dominion of New England too
were overthrown by force of arms.
† The figures are presented in more detail in Appendix X, compiled from
the town records.

September of 1774, in the wake of the Intolerable Acts and their restriction of local gatherings, there was actually "an unusual frequency of town meetings" across the province, at first slipped through a loophole in the new law, then increasingly assembled in open defiance of any necessity of the governor's permission. Before the year was out the townsmen had come "plainly and uniformly" to sanction "the blunt resolve 'to pay no regard to the late act of Parliament, respecting the calling town meetings, but to proceed in the usual way.'" And the determination "to proceed in the usual way" that drove communities to contemn the authority of Parliament in 1774 led them to armed opposition in 1775 and declared rebellion by 1776.[43]

Almost paradoxically, the entry into war occurred according to eighteenth-century canons of concord; it was to preserve the prospect of peace that the townsmen entered the battle, and it was with their accustomed agreement that they did so. The communities that joined to declare their independence were not deeply divided when they did so, and neither were they dragged unwittingly into a declaration or a war they did not want, by the artful propaganda of a few cunning men. They could not have been thus deceived, because they themselves installed and maintained the "propagandists." The town meeting itself created the committee of correspondence in each community, and the committees of correspondence were, as a recent student of the subject concluded, integral elements of their communities. They were, at bottom, the town committees in charge of politics and constitutional theory, and as such they were subject to all the sanctions and controls that other committees of the community were.[44] Their organization was, ultimately, an easy outgrowth of an extended experience in the contrivance of consensus among the inhabitants of the various villages of the province.

The towns were also the essential instrument of insurrection after the battle with the British began. In organizing resistance as much as in inculcating it, they supplied the sinews of opposition. Soldiers of the Massachusetts military companies were recruited by requisitions upon the towns. Salaries for the troops were provided or supplemented from the same source. The ammunition with which the army fought was supplied locally, and the towns were called upon for provisions as well. The men, the money, and the matériel which repulsed the imperial army all came from the communities of the new commonwealth.[45]

And ultimately the commonwealth itself came from those communities, constitutionally as much as militarily. Three times it was recognized, during the early days of the Provincial Congress, "that the ultimate source of power was in the towns," and the General Court, once it was reconstituted, similarly recognized the people, acting in their town meetings, as "the possessors of constituent powers." Thereafter that constituent power of the towns was acknowledged, in one form or another, in the aborted efforts at a constitution in 1776 and 1778 and in the successful one of 1780. The constitution of 1780 was drafted by a convention in which the towns were the units of representation, approved by a procedure in which the towns were the instruments of ratification, and kept flexible by a provision which established the towns as the essential agents of amendment for the future.[46]

The constitution reflected the commanding position of the community in the substance of its final form as well as in the vicissitudes of its formulation. It maintained a large measure of local autonomy despite concessions to the new central government, and, in the central government itself, it installed the towns at the very center, expressly asserting the priority of towns to population as the basis of representation in the popular house of the legislature. Morison has maintained that that basis "sacrificed size to equality," risking an unwieldy number of representatives in order to preserve the principle of representation for every town; but in fact the constitution sacrificed both size *and* equality, to the primacy of the towns considered simply as semisovereign units entitled, each and all, to representation. As the Address of the Constitutional Convention explicitly resolved, "Representation ought to be founded on the Principle of equality; but it cannot be understood thereby that each Town in the Commonwealth shall have Weight and importance in a just proportion to its Numbers and property." The commonwealth was conceived in terms of a protofederalism of communities, and the protests of the more populous areas, that the town basis of representation was flagrantly biased against concentrations of people and property, fell on deaf ears. Not until 1857 did Massachusetts recognize the principle of regular representation proportional to population in its House of Representatives.* [47]

* Even more indicative of the pressures of the past were the demands which were not met in the final draft of 1780. By far the bulk of them were applications for a still more extensive local autonomy than the constitution ultimately accorded, such as the famous Berkshire County remonstrance of 1775; see, e.g., Elisha Douglass: *Rebels and Democrats* (Chapel Hill, 1955), p. 150. Many of the actual powers claimed by the communities were former powers of the prerogative, which was, of course, a symbolically revealing transfer of dominion. Various communities asked that the towns be authorized to review all legislation pertaining to them, that administrative authority be vested in the towns by local election or nomination of registers of deeds, probates of wills, and military officers, and that judicial powers be placed in local hands in "all Contravarsies what Soever Exept in the Case of Murdor." See Taylor: *Colony to Commonwealth*, pp. 43, 18, 19, 71, 122, 153, 158; Douglass: *Rebels and Democrats*, p. 150; Cushing: "Political Activity," pp. 110–11; and, for a clear exposition of similar tendencies in similar terms in New Hampshire, Daniell: "New Hampshire Politics," pp. 167–8, 168–9, 190–2, 207. Other claims which did not derive from the former powers of the royal establishment did, nonetheless, arise out of the same sense of local independence. Some towns sought sole determination of the qualifications for representatives, and some—enough to constitute a "party"—insisted upon the "competency of the town to control all matters of religion." As late as the drafting of the constitution, one town seriously threatened to declare its independence of the state if its demands were not met, and even in the struggle for ratification in 1780 there were a num-

. . .

In their constitutional convention and in the rebellion before, in forced flights and in confiscations, in tarrings and
featherings and in hangings in effigy, in committees of correspondence and in committees of inspection, the communities of Massachusetts were only doing, under revolutionary pressures, what they had always done in the ordinary
conduct of their affairs. Surveillance and moral suasion in
the interest of uniformity were not new things—they had,
in fact, come over on the *Mayflower* and the *Arbella*—but
all that had happened in a century and a half had not undone them. Men of Massachusetts could not yet conceive of
conflict as anything but intolerable even in the placid years
around the middle of the eighteenth century; in a society
at war, in the revolutionary communities of 1775, there
was no legitimate place at all for fundamental opposition.

Of course, the iron inflexibility of the seventeenth century had edged steadily into the accommodative character
of the eighteenth, but in respect to real dissent accommodation only blurred the bounds of the unacceptable a bit.
Men had indeed supplanted absolute by accommodative
agreement, but still the community required agreement
and still there was no patterned place in the community for

---

ber of objecting towns which, according to Morison, apparently considered themselves "distinct bodies politic in their relation to the state" and
"passed a vote to the effect that they would accept the constitution without
their favorite amendments if two-thirds of the people so voted." Morison
called their concession "wholly superfluous, being merely a promise to submit to the will of the majority," but the superfluity was apparent only from
the perspective of the twentieth century. The townsmen themselves, at the
time, did regard themselves as distinct bodies politic; it was not clear *to
them* that they had to submit to the will of the majority of the commonwealth. Nor was it entirely clear even to advocates of ratification, for a
vote such as the towns passed, so far from seeming superfluous at the
time, was actually urged by one "Philopatriae" in the *Boston Gazette.*
Cushing: "Political Activity," pp. 110–11; Morison: "Adoption of the Constitution," pp. 397, 397n.

the man who questioned the basis of its accord. Just as the new democracy was still the old democracy in principle—a democracy, a full participation, of the like-minded—so the new modes of accommodation permitted the presentation of differences only so long as they were small differences. The dark demon of Puritan xenophobia still slumbered fitfully; it was dangerous to go beyond the bounds of the substantive sentiments of the society.

Localization of authority was the prime political development of the provincial decades, but localization was not, in and of itself, liberal. As John Roche has written, "the centralized state is not the only institution capable of oppression; the parish can be as coercive as the state, and decentralized authoritarianism can be as severe in its impact on the individual as the centralized variety." [48] The treatment of the Tories was a touchstone, but it did not differ in kind from a hundred other dismissals of dissidents before. The hounding of the loyalists was ultimately of the same order of indifference to individuality as, say, the derision that Dunstable heaped upon a small minority—"a mere amusement"—in 1739,[49] and both bespoke the moral totalitarianism of the Massachusetts town.

That town was still a very small place in the middle of the eighteenth century, and most relationships among men were face-to-face relationships, where the pressures of propriety were sternest. The Puritan had always considered himself his brother's keeper; in such communities the opportunity for scrutiny was omnipresent. Even as the Massachusetts villager of the eighteenth century made his encounter with power, he learned the limits of his freedom. The very same conversations among neighbors that controlled the community also confined all impulses and ideas within the limits of what that community and the men and women who composed it defined as decency and propriety.

The definitions were strict in the eighteenth-century

towns, as they had been strict before. The peculiar genius of the Puritans had always been outward and external rather than inward and spiritual—as Edmund Morgan has observed, the settlers of the seventeenth century "did not differ from their contemporaries in their views about the importance of salvation as much as they did in their views about behavior"—and it had always displayed itself in zeal for the right conduct of others rather than in any willingness to allow them the liberty of their own desires and destinies. Thomas Hooker had merely been more explicit than most when he explained the obligation of "the true convert" to labor the removal of "What ever sins come within his reach" in his family, his community, and indeed in all "the companies and occasions, with whom he hath occasion to meet and meddle at any time." [50]

The seventeenth-century community had been a veritable coliseum for meddling men, and the provincial town preserved almost intact that "loving watch" of neighbors. It elected local officers to the task specifically, it set its selectmen and its minister to the same service along with their other duties, and ultimately it charged all its inhabitants with the same responsibility. Husbands had to watch their wives, parents their children, teachers their pupils, masters their servants; and in the sum of those domestic subordinations and institutionalized self-suppressions, the Puritan potential for individual discovery was drained. The societies of Massachusetts, in the century before the Revolution, were still societies governed by the canons of community rather than the individualistic canons of contract. The identities and purposes of their inhabitants were still expressible in the homogeneity of the town meeting and the church covenant; the villagers required no rich panoply of voluntary associations and displayed no particular desire for the variety that elicits the existential decisions by which an ego grows.* And where the public character of the

* The psychological issues are still controverted, but substantial empirical

eighteenth-century townsman did diverge from that of his fathers—in the repudiation of the ancestral conviction of utter rectitude and the new-fledged capacity to imagine another person's perspective that together made accommodation possible—his character had only grown more profoundly other-oriented than it had been before, and more self-suppressive.

Self-suppression for the sake of social harmony has rarely been so sternly prescribed since the eighteenth century; but it has persisted ever since as an organizing force in the small towns of America, and the small town has been the forge of the American character until well into the twentieth century.[51] The homogeneity which characterized the community at the time of the Revolution has continued to constitute the condition of acceptable group life in America, and it still survives in our modern country clubs and secluded suburbs, in our demands for "neighborhood schools," our fears of "outside agitators," and our fond hopes that we can "reason together" and be "well

---

evidence is accumulating to support the clinical insights of such students as Else Frenkel-Brunswik, whose writings would suggest that the New England character matured under conditions very little likely to produce "inner-direction" or a strong personal identity. Frenkel-Brunswik has insisted that authoritarian demands for external conformity and for unquestioning acceptance of the punishments meted out by parents is "ego-destructive," interfering with internalization of the rules being inculcated and therefore with "the development of a clear-cut personal identity." They prevent the emergence of self-reliance and independence, and instead make the child feel weak, helpless, worthless, and depraved. See Else Frenkel-Brunswick: "Differential Patterns of Social Outlook and Personality in Family and Children," in Mead and Wolfenstein: *Childhood*, p. 384.

Another, no less revealing, perspective on the paucity of institutional scenes of social life in the provincial towns has been offered by Page Smith. Comparing the covenanted communities of pre-revolutionary New England with the small towns of the mid-nineteenth century, Smith notes the explosion of associational activity in the later age and insists that "such a plethora of organizations is obviously a disease of the body politic in communities which have lost all sense of an integrated community life." *City Upon a Hill*, p. 174.

liked." It survives because we wish it to survive, because we are that kind of a people, and its survival belies the belief that we are a liberal society which, in Louis Hartz' phrase, has always known "the reality of atomistic social freedom." [52] Such a belief deliberately disregards the shared understandings and the covert social compacts that have shaped American society, and that derived from experiences and expectations such as those consolidated in the communities of eighteenth-century New England. Groups in America have rarely made more than an uneasy place for those outside their covenants and the community they defined—freedom has generally been construed as the privilege to be like everyone else around, to belong to a community of co-believers[53]—and in provincial Massachusetts the towns made almost no place at all for men who differed from their orthodoxy.

Indeed, in the last years before independence, the massive coercion of the monolithic community even came to expression in the conduct of the legal system. Routine litigation remained largely unaffected by the revolutionary crisis, but, as a student of "law under pressure" has recently remarked,

> it is not in its treatment of the ordinary affairs of *meum* and *teum* that a judicial system receives its ultimate test. Even the most arbitrary government arranges to have private disputes decided routinely. The true litmus of liberty is the availability of unfettered justice to every litigant or accused criminal, including men who may be unpopular or even demonstrably dangerous to the social structure. It is a test which no society ever passes; there are only degrees of failure. The evidence suggests that in pre-Revolutionary Massachusetts that failure was complete.[54]

Under pressure, then, the men of provincial Massachusetts performed much as their Puritan ancestors had done.

The Massachusetts of Adams and Warren was not the Massachusetts of Winthrop and Ward, and the accommodative authority of the eighteenth-century community was not a sham, but accommodation was, in the end, sharply limited. The communities which sustained the politics of consensus were still, ultimately, communities of common social values. The bounds of commonality had been stretched, but they were still stringent. The dissident in these little hamlets of homogeneity still, finally, had the options of his forebears: he could conform or he could leave. Revolutionary Massachusetts, a society at the center of the conflict which ushered in a measure of modern liberalism, never itself sanctioned the value of conflict in the community; and least of all did it bequeath to us a principled notion of legitimate differences among men.

Appendices,
Bibliographical
Notes,
and Index

Appendix I

A GENERAL MEASURE of localism was drawn from the town records of eight towns by a tabulation of town concerns as they appeared in the business considered by the town meeting. The towns were: Amherst (1759–75), Braintree (1701–75), Brookline (1705–75), Dudley (1732–75), Fitchburg (1764–75), Lunenburg (1728–64), Tisbury (1692–1775), and Weston (1754–75). The categories in which town actions were classified were: land distribution; appointment of town officers, including miscellaneous official town procedures; economic regulations and taxes; church affairs; schools; military affairs; public health; division of the town; personal quarrels in the community; admission of men to the community; relations with other towns; relations with the Indians; relations with the Massachusetts government; relations with a council; relations with the county, including the courts; intercolonial affairs; imperial affairs. In broad outline, these are the categories used by Powell: *Puritan Village,* p. 5 (expanded and subdivided where necessary for the somewhat different communities of the eighteenth century), though obviously common categories are useful for comparison over time only if the rules adopted for tabulating the entries were also similar.

The rules adopted here can be explained rather easily, though the compilation is almost inescapably subjective, at least at the edges. Many entries in the records are marked by a mingling of two or more categories, and in all such cases judgment must be made on the primary concern of the action.

In those instances where an unequivocal decision was deemed too difficult—e.g., a vote to lay a tax of fifty pounds to build a new bridge, in which it is virtually impossible to determine whether the relevant issue was the amount of the appropriation or the question of building the bridge at all—the unit was divided between the categories involved. (Obviously, subjectivity in such an assignment is sharply limited: the item could not plausibly be tallied under relations with Indians, or church affairs. Another tabulation might produce figures differing from those offered here, but it seems unlikely they would differ very widely.) A few other special rules, besides the division of a unit, were also adopted for the tabulation. Votes to adjourn and to elect a moderator were not counted at all, and neither were entries which were solely for the record, such as notations of livestock markings or strays, or "warning outs," which never came before the town meeting as actual business. Also, the entire slate of officers elected at a March election meeting was counted only as a single unit, even though a score or more posts were filled, each in an individual election. The result of these exclusions was, of course, a minimization of the proportion of business which appears as purely local; had such affairs been tallied too, the percentage of items external to the community, already so slender, would perhaps have been halved.

Even as tabulated, however, there was not a single town among the eight where as many as one in a dozen items involved provincial affairs or the general government, and for all the towns considered together, provincial affairs were the occasion of no more than one in every fifteen or twenty local actions. Relations with other towns were still more unusual. In some places they comprised less than one per cent of the total, and in none did more than one item in thirty involve any of the other towns of the Bay. Combining every conceivable community concern that extended beyond the town—relations with other towns, with the provincial government, with the Indians, with church councils, with the county, with the courts, with other colonies or intercolonial affairs, and with imperial affairs —only about one tenth of all the business of the town meeting focused outside the immediate community.

In tabular form, the relevant portion of the figures is as follows:

	Relations with Mass.	*Relations with other towns*	*Relations with county*	*All extra-town affairs*
Amherst	7.6%	3.3%	4.8%	17.3%
Braintree	7.5	2.0	4.8	15.3
Brookline	7.5	1.6	3.1	13.8
Dudley	3.5	0.7	1.5	6.5
Fitchburg	3.7	2.3	0.4	8.1
Lunenburg	1.3	0.7	2.0	4.5
Tisbury	7.2	2.3	2.5	14.9
Weston	6.7	3.1	4.8	14.6
Averages	5.6	2.0	3.0	*11.9*

(The largest category was economic regulation and taxes, varying between one third and three fifths of all items. Schools alone were only slightly less frequent an occasion of town deliberation than all the items external to the town combined, accounting for almost ten per cent of town business.)

It is important to note too that even the scant involvement beyond the confines of the community indicated by these figures is inflated by the onrush of events in 1774–5. The impact of the impending break with England skewed all the figures significantly upward. In Amherst, to take the most dramatic example, about seventy per cent of all actions of the town meeting in 1774 and 1775 looked outside the local community, and those two years alone accounted for almost two thirds of all the entries external to the town in its seventeen years before the Revolution. Setting aside those two years and tabulating the other fifteen—"normalcy"—the percentage of all actions affecting external affairs shrinks from 17.3 to 7.5 per cent, and involvement with the province virtually vanishes, dipping from 7.6 per cent to a bare 0.6 per cent. Even in Braintree, where the last two years were offset by the seventy-three preceding ones, so that they could hardly have upset the pattern egregiously, the figure for all external affairs rose from 13.6 per cent to 15.3 merely by the addition of those two years. For all eight towns together, elimination of the last two years before the Revolution reduces the total involvement beyond the town boundaries from 11.9 per cent to only 8.8 per cent of town meeting discussions and deliberations. (More detailed specification is provided in Appendix X.)

Appendix II

The following is one man's reckoning of the costs of proceeding in the courts around the middle of the eighteenth century. It is the only such record in the town series of the Massachusetts Archives.

Jasher Wyman's account of some time and expense
at law with the proprietors of Dunstable (viz.)

December 1749, to the inferior court	– 10 days
March 1749, to the inferior court	– 12 days
September 1750, to the superior court myself and horse	– 20 days
February 1750, to the superior court	– 27 days
May 1751, to the court of appeals, myself and horse	– 7 days
July 1751, to the adjournment of said court, myself and horse	– 7 days
Ditto to a second adjournment, myself and horse	– 5 days
April 1751, to Portsmouth for a copy of the case	– 6 days
Two several journeys to Boston, myself and horse, for copies	– 6 days
Myself and horse to Dunstable to hear evidences sworn	– 1 day

The above account is exclusive of more than fifty days' time and expense which I have occasionally and necessarily spent in the affair.

Expense: to the clerk of the superior court for entering the appeal	– 1:12:0	O.T.
To the clerk for a copy of the case	– 7:04:0	O.T.
To twelve affidavits, justices, and fees	– [?]	
To the several attorneys at the several courts	– 12:16:00	O.T.
To the secretary for entering the action	– 9:00:00	O.T.
To Mr. Secretary Willard for copies	– 1:05:00	O.T.
To sundry copies taken off Townshend proprietors' books	– 4:17:06	O.T.
1751 July the 8th to a surveyor and five chainmen to run the line from Groton Northwest Corner between Dunstable and Townshend	– 3:10:00	O.T.
Ditto to expense	– 00:13:00	O.T.

Wyman, it might be added, was a mere "yeoman." And it might also be added that Wyman's account was only his own, so that, in town terms, it was incomplete. It was cast solely in terms of time and money, whereas a town engaged in such litigation had also to reckon the social costs, costs to be calculated in terms of the consequent disruption of relations in the community. But even in terms of time and money alone, Wyman's days in court were brutally expensive.

The account is in Mass. Archives 116, pp. 565, 566.

Appendix III

THE EXTENT OF LOCAL CONTENTION which reached the legislature is arranged below, by volumes of the legislative archives so that chronological sequence may be seen. The categories of contention which were employed are as follows:

Disputes within towns—All internal controversies in which antagonism was distinct and factions polarized. (Thus, disputes over division or legality, when sufficiently strong, were entered in this category, not in the appropriate one below.)

Disputes in unincorporated places—Same, except that these communities were not yet, properly, towns; their controversies tended to be about the issues of their incorporation.

Issues of legality—These have been included on the assumption that they would not have arisen in places truly united. Nonetheless, they rarely evidence acrimony—most commonly they are appeals for clarification of the law or legalization of town actions already taken—and many of them may well have been purely *pro forma*.

Disputes between towns and proprietors—These have been included though, generally, the proprietors were nonresidents, so that disagreements were not, strictly, internal to the town. Also, they have been included whether the place in question was a town or still merely a township, even though a substantial number of them were just townships. The only real test of inclusion was that the divergence in interest be more than just an unopposed local request for a tax on the proprietors' lands.

Rearrangement of the community—These are appeals for division within the town, or separation from the town, or transfer to another town, or the creation of a new town or parish. Obviously they verge even more closely on being more properly a part of the town's external affairs than disputes with proprietors do, but they have been included because they generally imply a degree of internal dissatisfaction as well. In no cases were they very contentious; they are merely those appeals made only for geographic convenience or for no apparent reason at all.

Total—The sum of all five categories of internal division.

Disputes between towns—This is an inclusive category for all other displays of contentiousness in the archives, so that a fuller perspective on the degree of discord may be afforded. The majority of the entries in this category are, indeed, controversies between two towns—ordinarily, over their boundaries—but disputes between towns and the

	Vol. 48 1691– 1732	Vol. 49 1733– 1756	Vol. 50 1756– 1775	Vol. 113 1693– 1729	Vol. 114 1730– 1742
Disputes within towns	0	5	6	18	17
Disputes in unincorporated places	0	0	0	0	3
Issues of legality	0	0	0	7	4
Disputes between towns and proprietors	0	0	0	2	5
Rearrangement of the community	0	1	0	5	7
Total	0	6	6	32	36
Disputes between towns	0	1	0	40	10

proprietors of another town, between towns and independent parishes, between towns and unincorporated gores of land, and between two unincorporated places are also included.

The summary categories provide the best perspective on the raw figures. The rate *per town* is obtained by dividing the final figures by two hundred, a generalized number of settled places for the provincial period, to yield the number of conflicts in each category which reached the assembly in an average town over the eighty-five years. The rate *per year* is obtained by dividing the final figures by 85, the number of years tabulated, to yield the number of conflicts reaching the assembly in an average year in each category. And the rate *per town per year* is obtained by dividing the final figures by 200 and then by 85, to yield the (minuscule) amount of conflict in each category in an average town in an average year.

The figures are as follows:

Vol. 115 1742– 1751	Vol. 116 1751– 1754	Vol. 117 1755– 1762	Vol. 118 1763– 1774	*Total*	Per Town	Per Year	Per Town Per Year
17	12	19	8	*102*	0.5	1.2	.006
1	1	4	2	*11*	0.1	0.1	.001
14	31	8	10	*74*	0.4	0.9	.005
9	13	16	12	*57*	0.3	0.7	.004
14	14	8	15	*64*	0.3	0.8	.004
55	71	55	47	*308*	1.5	3.6	.018
10	12	14	6	*93*	0.5	1.1	.005

Appendix IV

THE EXTENT OF LOCAL CONTENTION evident in the local records themselves is arranged below, by towns. Except for the number of occasions on which the minutes mentioned debate, the figures are presented in rates and percentages, which is the point of the presentation.

In general, *explicit conflict* refers to those entries which speak openly of it, to any vote on which one or more townsmen dissented, to any vote by a polling of the meeting, to any vote in which the numbers voting on each side were mentioned, to any vote which established a policy manifestly to the disadvantage of one group in the town, to any rejection of a report or action by town officers or committees, to any dispute with the town minister, to any proceedings for a lawsuit against a townsman, to any proceedings of distraint against a townsman, to any controversy between individual townsmen, and to acrimonious divisions of the community or separations from it. *All conflict* includes all the explicit conflicts plus others which can only be inferred. Among these are all negative votes on questions contained in the warrant for the meeting, all failures to act on such questions, and all deferrals of action on such questions to a later meeting; in each case the assumption is made here that someone must have wanted positive action on the proposal, else it would not have been placed on the warrant in the first place. A variety of miscellaneous items also provided a basis for the inference of conflict, though in these as in the failures of positive action on agenda items, there can be no assurance of actual disagreement in each case. If anything, then, this measure of conflict is an overestimate of its extent, so far as the records reveal it. (The election of moderators and town officers and the appointment of committee members was also excluded from all consideration; at least in the case of moderators and committee appointments, this too probably contributes to an overestimate in these figures of the extent of contention. And in affairs such as the acceptance of highways, all acceptances were counted together as a single item if none were rejected at a given meeting, which provides still another slight inflation of the degree of discord.)

The figures are as follows:

				CONFLICT					
				Explicit Conflict			All Conflict		
Town	Number of Years	Number of Meetings	Number of Decisions	Per Year	Per Meeting	% of Decisions	Per Year	Per Meeting	% of Decisions	Debate mentioned
Amherst	41	145	673	0.4	0.1	2.2	0.7	0.2	4.2	0
Braintree	85	402	1762	1.1	0.2	5.3	4.1	0.9	19.9	152
Brookline	70	281	874	0.3	0.1	2.2	1.3	0.3	10.5	4
Dudley	44	190	792	0.6	0.1	3.3	3.0	0.7	16.8	0
Duxbury	80	247	541	0.4	0.1	5.4	0.7	0.2	10.4	2
Fitchburg	12	53	425	0.5	0.1	1.4	3.2	0.7	8.9	1
Lunenburg	37	164	699	0.3	0.1	1.6	1.6	0.4	8.3	9
Manchester	85	387	1025	0.4	0.1	2.9	0.7	0.1	5.5	0
Tisbury	84	260	432	0.2	0.1	3.9	0.6	0.2	10.9	12
Weston	22	75	415	0.2	0.1	1.0	3.8	1.1	20.2	0
Worcester	54	249	1654	0.6	0.1	2.1	3.4	0.7	11.1	22
Total	—	2453	9292	—	—	—	—	—	—	—
median	—	—	—	0.4	0.1	2.2	1.6	0.4	10.5	2
mean	—	—	—	0.5	0.1	2.8	2.1	0.5	11.5	—

Appendix V

THE VOTE on the proposed constitution of 1778, arranged by numbers and percentages of towns in majorities from 51–59% to 100%, was as follows:

	Against		For		Total	
	No.	*%*	*No.*	*%*	*No.*	*%*
100	79	57	9	27	88	52
95–99	23	17	6	18	29	17
90–94	14	10	2	6	16	9
80–89	9	7	5	15	14	8
70–79	3	2	4	12	7	4
60–69	6	4	4	12	10	6
51–59	4	3	3	9	7	4
Total	*138*		*33*		*171*	

Of course the 1778 constitution was rejected overwhelmingly—in the towns reporting, eighty-one per cent of the voters refused to accept it—so even if the towns had reacted randomly in arriving at that result the divisions might have been eighty-one per cent majorities. But in the actual event the median majority was not eighty-one per cent. It was a unanimous vote. In addition, more than five sixths of the towns recorded majorities larger than the cumulative split which characterized the province at large. (In fact, the discrepancy is actually even greater, since the overall majority is substantially inflated by Boston's massive bloc of favorable votes, which have otherwise been excluded from consideration here.) 138

of the 171 towns tabulated voted against the articles of 1778; well over half of them did so with outright unanimity, and scarcely a tenth with majorities of less than eighty-one per cent. Among the thirty-three towns which approved the document, more than a quarter did so unanimously and more than half by ninety per cent majorities or better. All of which is simply to say that the average division of four-to-one across the province only obscures the actual dynamics of the decision: there were few four-to-one divisions in the towns themselves.

Appendix VI

THE TENURE OF SELECTMEN in fifteen towns is shown below, followed by figures on the extent of turnover annually on the board of selectmen taken together (for thirteen towns). Summary averages were computed by weighting each town equally; these are, then, averages of the communities, not of the individuals within them.

Tenure of Selectmen

Number of Selectmen	Mean term	Median term	Longest total service	Other long totals		Longest consecutive	Other long consecutive service	
Amherst (25)	3.4	3.0	12.0	20+ : 0 10–19: 1 5–9 : 4	0% 8% 24%	5	20+ : 0 10–19: 0 5–9 : 0	0% 0% 4%
Braintree (84)	4.4	3.0	20.0	20+ : 0 10–19: 9 5–9 :15	1% 13% 30%	14	20+ : 0 10–19: 2 5–9 :15	0% 4% 21%
Brookline (48)	5.2	3.0	23.0	20+ : 0 10–19: 8 5–9 : 7	2% 19% 33%	15	20+ : 0 10–19: 1 5–9 : 8	0% 4% 21%
Dedham (83)	4.2	3.0	27.0	20+: 0 10–19: 5 5–9 :22	1% 7% 34%	—	—	
Dudley (49)	4.3	3.0	21.0	20+ : 0 10–19: 2 5–9 :15	2% 6% 37%	10	20+ : 0 10–19: 0 5–9 : 4	0% 2% 10%
Fitchburg (16)	3.6	1.5	9.0	20+ : 0 10–19: 0 5–9 : 3	0% 0% 25%	9	20+ : 0 10–19: 0 5–9 : 0	0% 0% 6%
Lunenburg (49)	3.7	2.0	23.0	20+ : 0 10–19: 3 5–9 :10	2% 8% 28%	7	20+ : 0 10–19: 0 5–9 : 3	0% 0% 8%

Number of Selectmen	Mean term	Median term	Longest total service	Other long totals		Longest consecutive	Other long consecutive service	
Manchester (37)	4.9	2.0	21.0(2)	20+ : 0 10–19: 1 5–9 : 9	8% 11% 35%	14	20+ : 0 10–19: 0 5–9 : 7	0% 3% 22%
Plymouth (44)	7.6	4.5	29.0	20+ : 3 10–19: 7 5–9 : 7	9% 32% 48%	26	20+ : 1 10–19: 5 5–9 :12	5% 16% 43%
Princeton (27)	2.9	2.0	10.0	20+ : 0 10–19: 1 5–9 : 5	0% 4% 22%	7	20+ : 0 10–19: 0 5–9 : 1	0% 0% 7%
Tisbury (39)	5.7	4.0	21.0	20+ : 0 10–19: 7 5–9 : 8	3% 21% 41%	18	20+ : 0 10–19: 3 5–9 : 8	0% 10% 31%
Topsfield (102)	4.2	2.5	22.0	20+ : 0 10–19:10 5–9 :20	1% 11% 30%	9	20+ : 0 10–19: 0 5–9 :14	0% 0% 15%
Watertown (93)	4.9	3.0	43.0	20+ : 0 10–19:11 5–9 :23	1% 13% 38%	13(2)	20+ : 0 10–19: 2 5–9 :18	0% 4% 24%
Weston (30)	3.7	2.5	17.0	20+ : 0 10–19: 2 5–9 : 5	0% 10% 27%	17	20+ : 0 10–19: 1 5–9 : 3	0% 7% 17%
Worcester (58)	4.7	2.0	28.0	20+ : 3 10–19: 3 5–9 : 9	7% 12% 28%	26	20+ : 0 10–19: 3 5–9 : 7	2% 7% 19%
Mean	4.5	2.7	21.7	20+ : 10–19: 5–9 :	2% 12% 32%	13.6	20+ : 10–19: 5–9 :	1% 4% 18%
Median	4.3	3.0	21.0	20+ : 10–19: 5–9 :	1% 11% 30%	13.5	20+ : 10–19: 5–9 :	0% 4% 18%

Turnover of the Board of Selectmen

	Mean Turnover	Median Turnover	Years Total Turnover	Years No Turnover
Amherst	3.9 of 5	5.0 of 5	9 (of 16)	2 (of 16)
Braintree	2.0 of 5	2.0 of 5	3 (of 74)	13 (of 74)
Brookline	1.3 of 3	1.0 of 3	9 (of 69)	21 (of 69)
Dudley	2.7 of 5	3.0 of 5	6 (of 43)	3 (of 43)
Fitchburg	1.1 of 3	1.0 of 3	0 (of 11)	1 (of 11)
	2.5 of 5	2.5 of 5		

	Mean Turnover	Median Turnover	Years Total Turnover	Years No Turnover
Lunenburg	3.0 of 5	3.0 of 5	6 (of 36)	1 (of 36)
Manchester	1.5 of 3	1.0 of 3	10 (of 59)	8 (of 59)
Plymouth	1.2 of 5	1.0 of 5	1 (of 69)	26 (of 69)
Tisbury	0.8 of 3	0.5 of 3	6 (of 66)	33 (of 66)
Topsfield	3.0 of 5	3.0 of 5	18 (of 85)	9 (of 85)
Watertown	3.5 of 7	4.0 of 7	3 (of 75)	8 (of 75)
	2.0 of 5	2.0 of 5		
Weston	1.6 of 5	1.0 of 5	0 (of 21)	4 (of 21)
Worcester	2.2 of 5	2.0 of 5	6 (of 53)	6 (of 53)
Mean	46.2%	44.2%	5.7 (13%)	10.4 (18%)
Median	44.0%	40.0%	6.0 (11%)	8.0 (13%)

Appendix VII

THE TENURE OF REPRESENTATIVES in selected towns is shown below. Averages are based upon the town percentages, not directly on the sum total of representatives.

Town and number of Representatives	Mean term	Median term	Longest term	Other long terms			Longest consecutive term	Other long consecutive terms		
Braintree (15)	5.1	2.0	27	20+ :0	7%		22	20+ :0	7%	
				10–19:1	13%			10–19:1	13%	
				5–9 :3	33%			5–9 :1	20%	
Brookline (9)	4.2	3.0	11½	20+ :0	0%		5½	20+ :0	0%	
				10–19:0	11%			10–19:0	0%	
				5–9 :2	33%			5–9 :0	11%	
Dedham (17)	4.5	3.0	11(²)	20+ :0	0%		7(²)	20+ :0	0%	
				10–19:1	18%			10–19:0	0%	
				5–9 :5	47%			5–9 :4	35%	
Plymouth (15)	4.8	2.0	21	20+ :0	7%		10	20+ :0	0%	
				10–19:1	13%			10–19:0	7%	
				5–9 :2	27%			5–9 :1	13%	
Watertown (19)	3.9	3.0	19	20+ :0	0%		9	20+ :0	0%	
				10–19:0	5%			10–19:0	0%	
				5–9 :3	21%			5–9 :2	16%	
Weston (5)	4.4	2.0	11	20+ :0	0%		9	20+ :0	0%	
				10–19:1	40%			10–19:0	0%	
				5–9 :0	40%			5–9 :0	20%	
Mean	4.5	2.5	17	20+ :	2%		10	20+ :	1%	
				10–19:	17%			10–19:	3%	
				5–9 :	34%			5–9 :	19%	
Median	4.5	2.5	15	20+ :	0%		9	20+ :	0%	
				10–19:	13%			10–19:	0%	
				5–9 :	33%			5–9 :	18%	

Appendix VIII

Turnover in the membership of the House of Representatives is shown below, first in percentages of the deputies in the year indicated who were not returned the following year, then in percentages not returned with one, three, and ten years intervening. In both cases the decadal and overall averages were computed on the basis of the raw figures, not as averages of averages.

Annual Turnover

1715–50%	1730–44%	1746–39	1761–34	Averages by
1716–58	1731–38	1747–43	1762–28	decades
1717–55	1732–44	1748–34	1763–32	
1718–60	1733–43	1749–46	1764–39	1710's–57%
1719–61	1734–49	—	1765–27	1720's–55
—	1735–43	1750–53%	1766–40	1730's–45
1720–62%	1736–33	1751–60	1767–23	1740's–46
1721–61	1737–52	1752–45	1768–32	1750's–46
1722–53	1738–48	1753–42	1769–35	1760's–32
1723–67	1739–53	1754–40	—	1770's–28
1724–50	—	1755–45	1770–22%	Overall
1725–57	1740–49%	1756–52	1771–32	average:
1726–60	1741–58	1757–43	1772–30	43% annual
1727–53	1742–56	1758–46	1773–32	turnover
1728–50	1743–39	1759–37	1774–25	
1729–40	1744–47	—		
—	1745–43	1760–34%		

Turnover at Intervals of One,
Three, and Ten Years

From 1715 *to*	1717–67%	1719–75%	1726–92%
1716	1718–67	1720–80	1727–96
1717	1719–74	1721–85	1728–87
1718	1720–71	1722–85	1729–96
1719	1721–79	1723–83	1730–94
1720	1722–72	1724–72	1731–86
1721	1723–69	1725–78	1732–84
1722	1724–72	1726–82	1733–89
1723	1725–73	1727–77	1734–87
1724	1726–69	1728–76	1735–90
1725	1727–67	1729–77	1736–89
1726	1728–62	1730–77	1737–92
1727	1729–66	1731–75	1738–92
1728	1730–54	1732–73	1739–88
1729	1731–58	1733–70	1740–91
1730	1732–57	1734–67	1741–95
1731	1733–60	1735–74	1742–92
1732	1734–57	1736–71	1743–90
1733	1735–58	1737–70	1744–91
1734	1736–47	1738–60	1745–92
1735	1737–57	1739–71	1746–90
1736	1738–60	1740–72	1747–89
1737	1739–68	1741–78	1748–89
1738	1740–64	1742–78	1749–87
1739	1741–72	1743–74	1750–93
1740	1742–70	1744–76	1751–91
1741	1743–61	1745–72	1752–93
1742	1744–56	1746–71	1753–92
1743	1745–63	1747–64	1754–84
1744	1746–52	1748–66	1755–88
1745	1747–43	1749–64	1756–83
1746	1748–50	1750–74	1757–86
1747	1749–56	1751–73	1758–89
1748	1750–68	1752–81	1759–89
1749	1751–76	1753–78	1760–83
1750	1752–69	1754–71	1761–79

From 1751 to	1753–53	1755–67	
1752	1754–52	1756–68	
1753	1755–62	1757–67	
1754	1756–62	1758–75	
1755	1757–57	1759–61	
1756	1758–64	1760–63	
1757	1759–57	1761–55	
1758	1760–37		
1759	1761–39		

Mean average	62%	73%	90%

Mean average by decades

	1715-19–72%	1715-19–82%	1715-19–93%
	1720-29–66%	1720-29–76%	1720-29–89%
	1730-39–60%	1730-39–72%	1730-39–91%
	1740-49–59%	1740-49–72%	1740-49–88%
	1750-59–55%	1750-59–66%	

Appendix IX

SERVICE OF SELECTMEN in the subordinate offices of the town is shown in the following figures (with 1775 as the cutoff point in all cases, a slight understatement of the extent of such menial service):

	Before first election		In same year as or after first election		Total	
Amherst	60%	(12–20)	68%	(17–25)	84%	(21–25)
Braintree	89	(75–84)	73	(61–84)	93	(78–84)
Brookline	88	(38–43)	68	(33–48)	96	(46–48)
Dudley	84	(37–44)	63	(31–49)	86	(42–49)
Fitchburg	82	(9–11)	56	(9–16)	88	(14–16)
Lunenburg	77	(34–44)	78	(38–49)	92	(45–49)
Manchester	86	(32–37)	97	(36–37)	97	(36–37)
Plymouth	85	(35–41)	77	(34–44)	93	(41–44)
Tisbury	58	(21–36)	82	(32–39)	92	(36–39)
Topsfield	84	(81–97)	84	(86–102)	96	(98–102)
Watertown	92	(86–93)	56	(52–93)	95	(88–93)
Weston	63	(17–27)	75	(27–36)	89	(32–36)
Worcester	64	(34–53)	79	(46–58)	91	(53–58)
Average: Mean	78%		74%		92%	
Median	84%		75%		92%	

Averages are based upon the town percentages, not directly upon the sum total of selectmen.

The tenure of selectmen who never served in subordinate office, compared to the tenure of all the town's selectmen, is shown in the following figures (averages again based on the town percentages):

	Mean	Town Mean	Median	Town Median
Amherst	3.0	3.4	3.0	3.0
Braintree	2.3	4.4	1.5	3.0
Brookline	2.0	5.2	2.0	3.0
Dudley	6.7	4.3	5.0	3.0
Fitchburg	1.0	3.6	1.0	1.5
Lunenburg	1.8	3.7	2.0	2.0
Manchester	1.0	4.9	1.0	2.0
Plymouth	3.3	7.6	2.0	4.5
Tisbury	4.7	5.7	2.0	4.0
Topsfield	3.5	4.2	1.0	2.5
Watertown	3.4	4.9	2.0	3.0
Weston	2.3	3.7	2.5	2.5
Worcester	3.0	4.7	1.0	2.0
Mean	2.9	4.5	2.0	2.7
Median	3.0	4.3	2.0	3.0

Appendix X

PROPORTIONS OF THE TOTAL BUSINESS transacted by the town meetings which were external to the towns themselves are shown below, in percentages for 1774–5 and for the years of the provincial period that went before. The towns tallied are the same as those in Appendix I with the exception of Lunenburg, which is excluded because its published records do not extend past 1764. Averages were calculated on the town percentages, not on the individual totals that the percentages summarize.

	Items External to the Town, 1774–5	Items External to the Town, before 1774
Amherst	69.6%	7.5%
Braintree	46.0	13.6
Brookline	36.8	11.9
Dudley	36.1	3.9
Fitchburg	35.7	3.7
Tisbury	62.0	12.2
Weston	25.9	13.3
Average	*44.6%*	*9.4%*

Another way of indicating the extraordinary impact of the Intolerable Acts and the attendant events of 1774–5 is in the proportion of all the external items ever recorded in the minutes of the meetings which were concentrated in those two years.

Such proportions, for the same seven towns, are shown below; and with them are shown the proportions which would have prevailed had the external entries been distributed randomly through the towns' provincial years (calculated by taking the two years before the Declaration of Independence as a percentage of the total number of years of town records tallied). Again the averages were calculated on the town percentages, not on the individual totals that the percentages summarize.

	Per cent Of All External Items In 1774–5	*Per cent If "Random"*
Amherst	66%	12%
Braintree	15	3
Brookline	24	3
Dudley	45	5
Fitchburg	61	17
Tisbury	22	2
Weston	20	9
Average	*36%*	*7%*

As measured by the business of the town meetings, it should be emphasized, this outward attention appeared *only* in 1774–5. The difference made by the preceding decade of supposed excitement, engagement, and imperial crisis was, in terms of its impact on the distribution of town meeting entries, nearly negligible.

Bibliographical Notes

Introduction

[1] Alexis de Tocqueville: *Democracy in America* (New York, Vintage Books, 1954), I, p. 62.

[2] Perry Miller: *Orthodoxy in Massachusetts* (Boston, Beacon, 1959), p. 37; Clifford Shipton: "The Locus of Authority in Colonial Massachusetts," in George Billias, ed.: *Law and Authority in Colonial America* (Barre, Mass., 1965), p. 141; Emil Oberholzer, Jr.: *Delinquent Saints* (New York, 1956), p. 78.

[3] Edmund Morgan: *Visible Saints* (New York, 1963), esp. pp. 10–12, 21; Oberholzer: *Delinquent Saints*, p. 78.

[4] Miller: *Orthodoxy*, pp. 219–20; Alex Inkeles: "National Character and Modern Political Systems," in Francis Hsu, ed.: *Psychological Anthropology* (Homewood, Ill., 1961). For a developed analysis of the Puritans as doctrinaires, see Michael Walzer: *The Revolution of the Saints* (Cambridge, 1965).

[5] Carl Bridenbaugh: "The New England Town: A Way of Life," American Antiquarian Society, *Proceedings* 56 (1946), pp. 19–48.

Chapter I

[1] Harlan Updegraff: *The Origin of the Moving School in Massachusetts* (New York, 1907), p. 95; Aaron Seidman: "Church and State in the Early Years of the Massachusetts Bay Colony," *New England Quarterly* 18 (1945), p. 228. On at least one occasion the Court did actually refuse to recog-

nize as a legitimate congregation a group from Dorchester which appeared before it as a proposed church; see Morgan: *Visible Saints,* pp. 100–1. And see George Haskins: *Law and Authority in Early Massachusetts* (New York, 1960), p. 62, for the continuance of examination beyond the earliest years.

2 Seidman: "Church and State," p. 228; see also p. 229. Such rights of ratification of pastors assumed special significance in the Antinomian crisis of 1637; see Emery Battis: *Saints and Sectaries* (Chapel Hill, 1962), esp. pp. 145–9, 154–9, 184–6.

3 Abner Goodell: "The Origin of Towns in Massachusetts," Massachusetts Historical Society, *Proceedings,* 2nd ser., 5 (1889–90), p. 330; Anne Maclear: *Early New England Towns* (New York, 1908), pp. 138–9; Joel Parker: "The Origin, Organization, and Influence of the Towns of New England," Massachusetts Historical Society, *Proceedings* 9 (1866–7), pp. 42–3, 41; Maclear: *Early Towns,* pp. 20–1, 138–9, 147; Seidman: "Church and State," p. 228.

4 Goodell: "Origin of Towns," p. 328. For the magistracy's conception of early Massachusetts as a consolidated community, I am indebted to a suggestion of Bernard Bailyn.

5 Herbert Osgood: *The American Colonies in the 17th Century* (New York, 1908), I, p. 432; see also pp. 429, 433, 434. See also P. Emory Aldrich: "The Town System of New England," American Antiquarian Society: *Proceedings,* n.s., 3 (1883–5), pp. 120–1; Goodell: "Origin of Towns," p. 328; Darrett Rutman: "The Mirror of Puritan Authority," in Billias, ed.: *Law and Authority,* p. 150; Updegraff: *Moving School,* p. 94; William Weeden: *Economic and Social History of New England, 1620–1789* (Boston, 1891), pp. 59–60.

In Plymouth Colony before its attachment to Massachusetts Bay, central surveillance was, if anything, even more stern. See, e.g., George Haynes: "Representation and Suffrage in Massachusetts, 1620–1691," *Johns Hopkins University Studies in Historical and Political Science* 12 (1894), pp. 442–3; Osgood: *American Colonies,* I, p. 434; George Willison, *Saints and Strangers* (New York, 1945), p. 319.

6 Bernard Bailyn: *Education in the Forming of American So-*

ciety (Chapel Hill, 1960), pp. 26–7. Weeden: *Economic and Social History,* pp. 59–60. Rutman: *Winthrop's Boston,* pp. 207–8. Osgood: *American Colonies,* I, p. 430; Powell: *Puritan Village,* p. 82; Aldrich: "Town System," pp. 120–1; Massachusetts Archives 116, pp. 559–60. Updegraff: *Moving School,* p. 95; Weeden: *Economic and Social History,* p. 73.

[7] Parker: "Origin, Organization, and Influence," pp. 42–3.

[8] Osgood: *American Colonies,* I, p. 434; Weeden: *Economic and Social History,* p. 79; Battis: *Saints and Sectaries,* pp. 154–5, 156–9. Maclear: *Early Towns,* pp. 20–1; Robert Whitten: *Public Administration in Massachusetts: The Relation of Central to Local Activity* (New York, 1898), p. 40. For other facets of the central control of local citizenship, see Daniel Wait Howe: *The Puritan Republic of the Massachusetts Bay in New England* (Indianapolis, 1899), pp. 39–42.

[9] Updegraff: *Moving School,* p. 94; Osgood: *American Colonies,* I, pp. 429–31.

[10] *Journals of the House of Representatives* (Boston, 1919—), VI, p. x.

[11] Mass. Arch. 48, pp. 224, 226–30, 237, 239, 242, 246–8, 263, 283–91, 305–14; Perry Miller: *The New England Mind: From Colony to Province* (Cambridge, Mass., 1953), pp. 261–2, 467–8, 470–5; J. Franklin Jameson, ed.: *Johnson's Wonder-Working Providence, 1628–51* (New York, 1910), p. 240.

[12] Updegraff: *Moving School,* p. 23.

[13] Cf. Whitten's periodization of public administration in Massachusetts over three centuries, in which he maintains that decentralization "was at its height during the eighteenth century"; *Public Administration,* p. 11. For a more elaborate analysis of the business of the provincial government, see Robert Zemsky: "The Massachusetts Assembly, 1730–1755," unpubl. Ph.D. thesis, Yale, 1967.

[14] *Acts and Resolves,* I, pp. 146–8; Mass. Arch. 48, p. 224. The change was not fully and finally accepted until at least 1695; see ibid., pp. 237, 239, 242; *Acts and Resolves,* I, pp. 201–2.

[15] For the development of the English theory of virtual representation, see Bernard Bailyn: *Pamphlets of the American*

Revolution, 1750–1776 (Cambridge, Mass., 1965), I, pp. 91–9. For New England, see Emory Washburn: *Sketches of the Judicial History of Massachusetts* (Boston, 1840), p. 18n.

16 Mass. Arch. 49, pp. 380–3.

17 Ibid.; Samuel Eliot Morison: "The Struggle over the Adoption of the Constitution of Massachusetts, 1780," Massachusetts Historical Society, *Proceedings* 50 (1916–7), p. 383. See also J. R. Pole: *Political Representation in England and the Origins of the American Republic* (London, 1966), pp. 72–3.

18 Kenneth Colgrove: "New England Town Mandates," Colonial Society of Massachusetts, *Publications* 21 (1920), p. 432; Mass. Arch. 115, pp. 600–1; ibid. 116, pp. 4–6. Some towns became even more imperious with the approach of the Revolution: see *The Old Records of the Town of Fitchburgh Massachusetts, 1764–1789* (Fitchburg, Mass., 1898), pp. 99–100; "Early Records of the Town of Worcester," Worcester Society of Antiquity, *Collections* 4 (1882), pp. 244, 264–6.

19 [Daniel Fowle]: *An Appendix to the Late Total Eclipse of Liberty* (Boston, 1756), pp. 1, 21; *The Relapse* (Boston, 1754), p. 3; *The Review* (Boston, 1754), p. 2. In 1780 the new constitution of the Commonwealth explicitly affirmed the right of towns to instruct their representatives, thus codifying provincial practice.

20 *Journals of the House*, III, p. x, and ibid., V, pp. xvi–xvii; Colgrove: "Town Mandates," p. 432.

21 *The Review*, p. 1; Robert E. Brown: *Middle-Class Democracy and the Revolution in Massachusetts, 1691–1780* (Ithaca, N.Y., 1955), p. 55; John Adams: *Works* (Boston, 1850), IV, p. 197.

22 Pole: *Political Representation*, pp. 69–70, 486–8.

23 *Acts and Resolves*, I, pp. 88–90; ibid., II, pp. 592–3.

24 Mass. Arch. 49, pp. 380–3, 427–8; John Sly: "Town Government in Massachusetts," unpubl. Ph.D. thesis, Harvard, 1925, p. 119.

25 *Acts and Resolves*, I, pp. 88–90. E.g., Brown: *Middle-Class Democracy*, p. 66; Myron Allen: *The History of Wenham* (Boston, 1860), pp. 62–3; *Records of the Town of Plymouth* (Boston, 1892), II, p. 247; Pole: *Political Representation*, p.

51; *Records of the Town of Braintree, 1640 to 1793* (Randolph, Mass., 1886), p. 333.

26 *Journals of the House,* VII, p. xiv; Mass. Arch. 48, pp. 487–9; *Acts and Resolves,* II, pp. 591–2, 937–8. Clifford Shipton: *Biographical Sketches of Those Who Attended Harvard College* (Boston, 1933—), VIII, p. 511; IX, p. 474. *Journals of the House,* VII, p. xiv; Mass. Arch. 49, p. 261. The constitution of 1780 confirmed the tradition that communities rather than the commonwealth paid the deputies; see Pole: *Political Representation,* p. 517.

27 Mass. Arch. 50, p. 515. The clearest evidence of the location of initiative in the towns was the common practice of a preliminary vote at May meeting on whether or not to send a representative; see ibid. 49, pp. 398–400, or ibid. 117, p. 134, among many. For a few of the reasons offered for not sending, see ibid. 49, pp. 265, 467–8, 518, 523–4, 525–6, 531–2; ibid. 50, p. 121; ibid. 117, p. 136; ibid. 118, pp. 190, 191, 630–1, 802–3, 804.

28 *Journals of the House,* XIV, p. vii.

29 Brown: *Middle-Class Democracy,* pp. 66, 74.

30 The figures are tabulated from the list of towns and their representatives, if any, which was entered at the outset of every session in the *Journals of the House.* Moreover, all such figures understate absenteeism significantly, since they ignore nonattendance among elected representatives; in the 1756 session, one of the most amply recorded in the provincial period with respect to attendance, only half the deputies attended as many as three quarters of the days the House was in session. See Zemsky: "Massachusetts Assembly," Ch. 2.

31 *Journals of the House,* XIII, p. vii; *Acts and Resolves,* I, pp. 88–90; ibid., II, pp. 592–3; Brown: *Middle-Class Democracy,* pp. 64, 65.

32 Miller: *Orthodoxy,* p. 228.

33 See, e.g., Miller: *Colony to Province,* pp. 261–2, 263; Updegraff: *Moving School,* p. 91.

34 Charles F. Adams: *Three Episodes of Massachusetts History* (Boston, 1892), p. 831.

35 Cotton Mather: *Ratio Disciplinae Fratrum Nov-Anglorum*

(Boston, 1726), pp. 84, 89, 95. Mather added that such variety produced "no troublesome *Variance* or *Contention* among them." P. 84.

36 Authorizations for the election of a representative were typical; see, e.g., Mass. Arch. 50, p. 133.

37 Bridenbaugh: "New England Town," p. 35; Walter Millis: *Arms and Men* (New York, 1956), p. 23; Weeden: *Economic and Social History*, p. 62. For a few eighteenth-century examples of restrictive economic regulations, see *Muddy River and Brookline Records, 1634–1838* (Boston, 1875), pp. 106, 148; *Copy of the Old Records of the Town of Duxbury, Mass. From 1642 to 1770* (Plymouth, Mass., 1893), pp. 194, 237–8, 298–9, 312; *Records of Fitchburg*, p. 25; *The Early Records of the Town of Lunenburg, Massachusetts*, compiled by Walter A. Davis (Fitchburg, Mass., 1896), p. 93; *Town Records of Manchester* (Salem, Mass., 1889, 1891), I, pp. 76–7; ibid., II, p. 132; "Records of Worcester," II, no. 6, pp. 35, 38, 51, 89; ibid., IV, p. 86.

38 Pole: *Political Representation*, pp. 517–18; see also p. 519.

39 George E. Howard: *An Introduction to the Local Constitutional History of the United States* (Baltimore, 1889), I, p. 350; ibid., p. 329, and Maclear: *Early Towns*, pp. 49–50; ibid., p. 136.

40 E.g., Mass. Arch. 114, pp. 351–4, 434–6, 610–16, 663–4; ibid. 116, pp. 440–7; ibid., pp. 448–57; ibid., pp. 458–64; ibid., pp. 607–8; ibid. 117, p. 128; ibid., pp. 518–21; ibid. 118, pp. 219–20; ibid., pp. 719–21; *Records of Lunenburg*, pp. 204, 206–7; ibid., pp. 212–13, 214, 217–18.

41 For a striking instance, see Mass. Arch. 116, pp. 702–5.

42 See also ibid. 115, p. 480; ibid. 114, p. 236; ibid. 115, p. 596. See also, e.g., ibid. 114, pp. 625–7; ibid. 115, pp. 729–30; ibid. 116, p. 168.

43 Whitten: *Public Administration*, p. 20; Bailyn: *Education*, p. 27; Updegraff: *Moving School*, pp. 110–11, 116.

44 Mass. Arch. 115, pp. 616–17; see also, e.g., *Records of Dudley*, I, p. 106; *Records of Fitchburg*, p. 39. E.g., *Records of Braintree*, pp. 412–13; Elias Nason: *A History of the Town of Dunstable, Massachusetts* (Boston, 1877), p. 105. Almost any town records of the eighteenth century will yield instances of

violation, often quite conscious, which never came before the General Court; see, e.g., *Records of Dudley,* II, p. 139.

45 Whitten: *Public Administration,* p. 13.

46 Mass. Arch. 116, p. 207; *Records of Lunenburg,* pp. 204–5. See also, e.g., Mass. Arch. 115, pp. 469–71, 472; ibid. 118, pp. 198–9.

47 Ibid. 49, pp. 361–2; ibid. 50, pp. 30–1; ibid. 115, pp. 168, 169. See also ibid., pp. 469–71; ibid. 118, p. 750.

48 Ibid. 116, pp. 717–18, 719–20. See also ibid., pp. 14–15; ibid., p. 21; ibid., pp. 397–8, 399; ibid. 117, pp. 34–5, 35–6.

49 Ibid. 115, pp. 600–4.

50 Ibid. 117, p. 652; see ibid., pp. 647–9, for the alleged violations. See also ibid. 115, p. 463; ibid., pp. 600–4; ibid., pp. 864–5.

51 Ibid. 117, p. 576; see also, e.g., ibid., pp. 385–6, 386; ibid., pp. 393–4; ibid., pp. 432–3; ibid., pp. 434–6; ibid. 118, p. 44; ibid., pp. 61–2; ibid., p. 91; ibid., pp. 286–7; *Boston Weekly News-Letter,* April 15, 1774, p. 1.

52 Mass. Arch. 118, pp. 42, 43, 43a, 85–6.

53 *Records of Dudley,* II, p. 10.

54 Ibid., p. 154. See also *Brookline Records,* p. 248; *Records of Fitchburg,* pp. 107, 109; *Records of Manchester,* II, pp. 145, 146; *Town of Weston: Records of the First Precinct, 1746–1754 and of the Town, 1754–1803* (Boston, 1893), p. 209.

55 Harry Cushing: "Political Activity of Massachusetts Towns during the Revolution," American Historical Association, *Annual Report* (1895), pp. 105–6.

56 Morison: "Adoption of the Constitution," p. 360.

57 Cushing: "Political Activity," pp. 108–9; for the details that the statement summarizes, see ibid., esp. pp. 105–8.

CHAPTER II

1 U. S. Bureau of the Census: *Historical Statistics of the United States, Colonial Times to 1957* (Washington, D.C., 1960), p. 756; Joseph Felt: "Statistics of Population in Massachusetts," American Statistical Association, *Collections,* I, Part 2 (1845), pp. 148–56.

2 Kai T. Erikson: *Wayward Puritans: A Study in the Sociology*

of Deviance (New York, 1966), p. 170; Arensberg: "American Communities," pp. 1149, 1150.

3 John and Beatrice Whiting: "Contributions of Anthropology to the Methods of Studying Child Rearing," in Paul Musson, ed.: *Handbook of Research Methods in Child Development* (New York, 1960), pp. 938–9; John Whiting: "Cultural and Sociological Influences on Development," in *Maryland Child Growth and Development Institute,* June 1–5, 1959, pp. 6–7. See also John Whiting: "Socialization Process and Personality," in Hsu: *Psychological Anthropology,* esp. p. 368, and John Whiting *et al.*: "The Learning of Values," in Evon Vogt and Ethel Albert: *People of Rimrock: A Study of Values in Five Cultures* (Cambridge, 1966), Ch. 4.

4 Miller: *Orthodoxy,* pp. 161, 224.

5 Ibid., pp. 26, 32.

6 Ibid., pp. 42–3.

7 Ibid., p. 160; William Haller: *The Puritan Frontier: Town Planting in New England Colonial Development 1630–1660* (New York, 1951), pp. 45, 46; Miller: *Orthodoxy,* pp. 23–4, 161–2, 23.

8 Ibid., pp. 285–6; John Roche: "American Liberty: An Examination of the 'Tradition' of Freedom," in Milton Konvitz and Clinton Rossiter, ed.: *Aspects of Liberty* (Ithaca, N.Y., 1958), p. 135. Expulsions, especially of Quakers, continued through the next two decades, and executions on the Boston gallows were not unknown.

9 E.g., Harriette Forbes: *The Hundredth Town* (Boston, 1889), p. 120.

10 Maclear: *Early Towns,* p. 33; Haskins: *Law and Authority,* p. 70; Powell: *Puritan Village,* p. 74.

11 Ibid., p. xviii; Haskins: *Law and Authority,* p. 70. See also Weeden: *Economic and Social History,* pp. 79–80; Josiah Benton: *Warning Out in New England* (Boston, 1911), pp. 8, 18.

12 Ola Winslow: *Meetinghouse Hill* (New York, 1952), p. 24; George K. Clarke: *History of Needham Massachusetts, 1711–1911* (Cambridge, 1912), p. 223.

13 Haskins: *Law and Authority*, pp. 40–1; see also pp. 43–4, 46–7.

14 Alan Simpson: *Puritanism in Old and New England* (Chicago, Phoenix, 1961), p. 21; Morgan: *Visible Saints*, Ch. 3; Miller: *Colony to Province*, Ch. 4; Erikson: *Wayward Puritans*, pp. 106–7. The most thorough examination of the doctrine of preparation is in Norman Pettit: *The Heart Prepared: Grace and Conversion in Puritan Spiritual Life* (New Haven, 1966); Pettit's perspective is different from the one presented here, but it does not dispute the central contention that preparation in early New England was an instrument of uniformity.

15 Sandford Fleming: *Children and Puritanism* (New Haven, 1933), p. 28.

16 E.g., Joseph Haroutunian: *Piety Versus Moralism* (New York, 1932), p. 37; Oberholzer: *Delinquent Saints*, p. 206; Heman DeForest and Edward Bates: *The History of Westborough, Massachusetts* (Westborough, Mass., 1891), p. 84; Charles T. Russell: *The History of Princeton* (Boston, 1838), pp. 38–9.

17 Perry Miller: "Jonathan Edwards' Sociology of the Great Awakening," *New England Quarterly* 21 (1948), pp. 67–8; Alan Heimert: "American Oratory: From the Great Awakening to the Election of Jefferson," unpubl. Ph.D. thesis, Harvard, 1960, pp. 111, 7, and see also pp. 109, 110, 114.

18 E.g., Powell: *Puritan Village*, p. 129; Willison: *Saints and Strangers*, p. 89; Haroutunian: *Piety*, p. 7; Miller, "Edwards' Sociology," pp. 57–8, 61; Francis Blake: *History of the Town of Princeton* (Princeton, Mass., 1915), I, plate facing p. 122; Morison: "Adoption of the Constitution," pp. 371–2.

19 Heimert: "American Oratory," p. 146; C. C. Goen: *Revivalism and Separatism in New England, 1740–1800* (New Haven, 1962), pp. 32–3, 48; John Miller: "Religion, Finance, and Democracy in Massachusetts," *New England Quarterly* 6 (1933), p. 52; Goen: *Revivalism*, pp. 32–3; ibid., pp. 56–7; Eugene White: "George Whitefield and the Paper War in New England," *Quarterly Journal of Speech* 39 (1953), p. 62; ibid., p. 67.

[20] Goen: *Revivalism*, pp. 129–31.

[21] Miller: *Orthodoxy*, p. 305; Oberholzer: *Delinquent Saints*, pp. 43–4, 45; Mass. Arch. 116, pp. 736–8; Arensberg: "American Communities," p. 1150.

[22] Winslow: *Meetinghouse Hill*, p. 100. For another emphasis, in which the effect was an inculcation of rigidity, see Fleming: *Children and Puritanism*, pp. 36–8.

[23] Goen: *Revivalism*, pp. 32–3; see also p. 48.

[24] Winslow: *Meetinghouse Hill*, pp. 193, 119–20; see also Oberholzer: *Delinquent Saints*, pp. 104, 181.

[25] Mather: *Ratio Disciplinae*, pp. 148–9; Oberholzer: *Delinquent Saints*, pp. 30, 36–7, 135.

[26] The convergence is quite striking between church discipline, as described here, and the administration of the criminal law, as described in Haskins: *Law and Authority*, pp. 204–10. And see also Erikson: *Wayward Puritans*, pp. 194–5.

[27] Oberholzer: *Delinquent Saints*, p. 38; Mather: *Ratio Disciplinae*, p. 156. Restoration was no empty offer; there were cases on record of confessions and restorations ten, twenty, thirty, even thirty-eight years after discipline was instituted. See Oberholzer: *Delinquent Saints*, pp. 44–5, 60, 63, 64, 92, 109, 110, 135.

[28] For tabulations of the results of church discipline, indicating enormous success, see ibid., pp. 168, 184.

[29] Ibid., p. 41; Mather: *Ratio Disciplinae*, pp. 155–6.

[30] For a summary and citations to the psychological literature, see Thomas Pettigrew: *A Profile of the Negro American* (Princeton, 1964), pp. 5, 165.

[31] Oberholzer: *Delinquent Saints*, pp. 60, 61–8, 76, 123–6, 160, 161, 163, 168, 172–9, 200–1, 205–6, 314*n*; Eugene White: "Decline of the Great Awakening in New England: 1741 to 1746," *New England Quarterly* 24 (1951), p. 44; Goen: *Revivalism*, pp. 32–3, 48, 155; Sarah Sedgwick and Christina Marquand: *Stockbridge 1739–1939: A Chronicle* (Great Barrington, Mass., 1939), p. 115; Blake: *Princeton*, pp. 139–41.

[32] Mass. Arch. 118, pp. 715–17; Nason: *Dunstable*, p. 16; Mass. Arch. 118, p. 526; Heimert: "American Oratory," p. 211. For other illustrations of peace and harmony as supreme consummatory values, see Mass. Arch. 49, pp. 361–2; ibid. 113,

p. 269; ibid., pp. 481–2; ibid. 115, pp. 319–20; ibid., pp. 379–80; ibid. 116, pp. 702–05; ibid., pp. 709–10; ibid. 117, pp. 223–7; ibid., p. 561; ibid., p. 637; ibid. 118, p. 207; ibid., pp. 798–801; ibid. 181, pp. 23–4a; *Records of Braintree*, p. 66; "Diary of Samuel Sewall," Massachusetts Historical Society, *Collections*, 5th ser., V (1878), pp. 400–1; Nason: *Dunstable*, p. 109; Russell: *Princeton*, pp. 38–9. For instances in which peace shared the loftiest position in the hierarchy of values with some other value (e.g. "peace and prosperity"), see Mass. Arch. 50, pp. 20–2; ibid. 116, pp. 694–6; ibid. 118, pp. 715–17.

33 See Chapter One, pp. 35–45.

34 George Tilton: *A History of Rehoboth Massachusetts* (Boston, 1918), pp. 102, 105–6. See also, e.g., *Weston Records*, pp. 13–14; Mass. Arch. 113, pp. 481–2; ibid. 114, pp. 33–4.

35 Ibid. 115, pp. 74–5.

36 Ibid. 118, pp. 707–12. The assumptions were the same elsewhere; see, e.g., ibid. 114, pp. 33–4; ibid. 115, pp. 305–8; ibid., pp. 492–3; ibid. 116, pp. 276–7; ibid. 117, pp. 165–9, 171; ibid., pp. 317–18; ibid. 118, pp. 290–1; ibid., pp. 798–801.

37 Ibid. 114, pp. 49–51; ibid. 116, pp. 602–2a. Ibid. 49, pp. 467–8; ibid. 50, pp. 525–6; ibid 116, pp. 706, 715–16; ibid. 118, p. 526; ibid., pp. 707–12; ibid., pp. 798–801; ibid. 181, pp. 23–4a.

38 Ibid. 115, pp. 741–2; ibid. 116, p. 609; ibid. 33, p. 288. See also ibid. 118, pp. 627–8; Convers Francis: *An Historical Sketch of Watertown* (Cambridge, Mass., 1830), p. 88; Heimert: "American Oratory," pp. 22, 108; Mather: *Ratio Disciplinae*, part 3, p. 8; Miller: "Edwards' Sociology," pp. 66–7; "Diary of Sewall," V, p. 461.

39 Mass. Arch. 115, pp. 492–3. See also, e.g., ibid., pp. 69, 72–3; ibid. 116, pp. 276–7; ibid., pp. 749–50; ibid. 118, pp. 613–16; ibid., pp. 798–801.

40 Nason: *Dunstable*, p. 109; Tilton: *Rehoboth*, pp. 106–7.

41 Miller: "Edwards' Sociology," pp. 57–8; Heimert: "American Oratory," p. 211.

42 Mass. Arch. 8, p. 273. See also ibid. 50, p. 28; ibid. 113, p. 277; ibid. 114, pp. 408–9; ibid. 115, pp. 330–4; ibid. 116, pp.

709–10; ibid. 118, pp. 613–16. Towns often even dissolved the policy issues of a petition into an *ad homines* attack on its proponents as men acting out of factious motives; see ibid. 50, pp. 89–90; ibid. 115, pp. 393–6; ibid., pp. 461–2; ibid. 117, pp. 317–18; ibid., pp. 563–65; ibid. 118, p. 387; ibid. 181, p. 127; Oberholzer: *Delinquent Saints*, p. 66.

43 Mass. Arch. 117, p. 637. See also ibid., pp. 317–18; ibid. 118, p. 526; ibid., pp. 707–12.

44 *Records of Fitchburgh*, p. 53; *Records of Braintree*, pp. 357–8; *Records of Plymouth*, II, pp. 6–7, 18, 25–6, 29, 40–2, 137, 207, 220, 244–5; *Weston Records*, p. 173.

45 Haskins: *Law and Authority*, p. 17; Heimert: "American Oratory," p. 211.

46 E.g., Mass. Arch. 114, pp. 221, 222, 223, 224, 225; ibid. 115, pp. 368–75; ibid., pp. 689–91; ibid. 181, pp. 122b–d. See also ibid. 50, p. 28.

47 Ibid., pp. 20–2, 25–6; ibid. 117, pp. 813–14, 815–16; ibid. 118, p. 387; ibid., pp. 658–9.

48 Ibid. 117, pp. 232–5; Weeden: *Economic and Social History*, p. 73; ibid., p. 273; Sedgwick and Marquand: *Stockbridge*, p. 216; see also Mass. Arch. 118, pp. 7–8. For some suggestion of the extent to which the seventeenth-century church and state could invade individual behavior, see Morgan: *Puritan Family*, pp. 10, 28, 38, 39, 65, 73, 82, 82–3, 85, 85–8.

49 Mass. Arch. 181, p. 127; ibid. 115, pp. 501–2, 689–91.

50 Alice M. Earle: *Child Life in Colonial Days* (New York, 1899), p. 251; Monica Kiefer: *American Children through their Books, 1700–1835* (Philadelphia, 1948), p. 94. See also Fleming: *Children and Puritanism*, pp. 59–62.

51 Kiefer: *American Children*, pp. 57, 225; James Janeway: *A Token for Children* (Boston, 1781), p. iii, also pp. iv–v. Much of this analysis, of course, is indebted to the extended analysis of similar phenomena in France and England in Philippe Ariès: *Centuries of Childhood* (New York, 1962), though several of his arguments were anticipated by Kiefer. On the immediate issue of the child's "submerged position in an adult setting," see *American Children*, pp. 1, 225.

52 Earle: *Child Life*, p. 191; Miller: "Edwards' Sociology," pp. 62–3; Kiefer: *American Children*, pp. 9–10. See also Fleming:

Children and Puritanism, pp. 59–62; Morgan: *Puritan Family,* pp. 48–51; Paul L. Ford, ed.: *The New England Primer* (New York, 1962), introduction, p. 1.

53 Miller: "Edwards' Sociology," pp. 62–3; see also Fleming: *Children and Puritanism,* pp. 51, 55.

54 Morgan: *Puritan Family,* p. 53.

55 Ibid., pp. 57–9, for conflicting evidence on the prevalence of heavy physical discipline. Certainly its use was authorized by the formal norms of the culture—see Ford: *New England Primer,* facsimile, pp. 9, 14—and at least one student claims that disciplinary correction was more severe in Massachusetts than in the Dutch colony of New York in the seventeenth century—Earle: *Child Life,* p. 201.

56 Morgan: *Puritan Family,* pp. 46, 48–52.

57 Maclear: *Early Towns,* pp. 174–5; Ford: *New England Primer,* facsimile, p. 13. See also ibid., p. 23; James Janeway: *A Token for Children* (Boston, 1771), p. 49 (all further citations to Janeway are to the 1771 edition unless otherwise stated); Earle: *Child Life,* pp. 138–9.

58 Morgan: *Puritan Family,* pp. 54, 54–5; Earle: *Child Life,* pp. 131–2; Ford: *New England Primer,* introduction, pp. 38–9; Mather: *Ratio Disciplinae,* p. 103. See also Fleming: *Children and Puritanism,* pp. 59–62; Janeway: *Token,* pp. 3–5; Kiefer: *American Children,* p. 29; Maclear: *Early Towns,* pp. 158–9.

59 Ford: *New England Primer,* introduction, pp. 38–9, 40.

60 Earle: *Child Life,* pp. 248–9; Kiefer: *American Children,* pp. 1–2.

61 Ford: *New England Primer,* facsimile, pp. 1, 2, 3–12 (for the quotation, p. 9), 13–23 (for the quotation, p. 16), 23–9, 30–7, 38–78; ibid., introduction, p. 31.

62 Earle: *Child Life,* p. 251; Ford: *New England Primer,* facsimile, pp. 10–12, 22. See also ibid., pp. 23, 34, 36.

63 Kiefer: *American Children,* pp. 1–2; Janeway: *Token,* p. 120. See also ibid., pp. 6, 11, 151; ibid., 1781 edition, p. iii, 26. The *Token* has been relied upon here because Kiefer's study found it "by far the most popular history of pious children who died early deaths"—*American Children,* p. 33—and because of the remarkable continuity of interest in the work.

Janeway himself was an Englishman who was born in 1636 and died in 1674. His examples were of English children, but the book was apparently seen to have relevance to New England since Cotton Mather had it republished with an additional section of exemplary children native to New England. Still other republications of the book occurred in 1747, 1771, 1781, and 1795, at least.

[64] Earle: *Child Life,* p. 242; Miller: "Edwards' Sociology," pp. 62–3; "Diary of Sewall," V, pp. 308–9.

[65] Janeway: *Token,* pp. 3–5, 6, 17, 22, 42, 110, 114, 132.

[66] Ibid., 1781 edition, p. i. See also Earle: *Child Life,* pp. 238–9; Miller: "Edwards' Sociology," pp. 62–3.

[67] Morgan: *Puritan Family,* p. 51.

[68] Janeway: *Token,* pp. 6, 42, 19. See also ibid., pp. 3–5, 23, 114, 126, 135; ibid., 1781 edition, pp. i, iv–v; Kiefer: *American Children,* pp. 1–2, 8.

[69] Janeway: *Token,* pp. 16, 132; Kiefer: *American Children,* p. 191. See also ibid., pp. 192, 193; Janeway: *Token,* pp. 6, 13, 19, 21, 23, 28, 29, 49, 120, 121, 126; Ford: *New England Primer,* facsimile, p. 23; Morgan: *Puritan Family,* pp. 28–9; Robert Sunley: "Early Nineteenth Century American Literature on Child Rearing," in Margaret Mead and Martha Wolfenstein, eds.: *Childhood in Contemporary Cultures* (Chicago, 1955), p. 162.

[70] Ibid., p. 159; Ryerson: "Advice on Child Rearing," p. 150; Kiefer: *American Children,* pp. 1–2; Janeway: *Token,* pp. 8, 9; Ford: *New England Primer,* facsimile, p. 13. See also ibid., pp. 20, 23; Kiefer: *American Children,* pp. 6, 39, 81; Earle: *Child Life,* pp. 212–13, 223–4; Janeway: *Token,* p. 115, 127–8.

[71] Benjamin Franklin: *Writings,* ed. by Albert Smyth (New York, 1905), I, p. 132. What so disgruntled Franklin in his relations with the brother to whom he was put to the printing trade was not his brother's *treatment* of him as a servant but rather his brother's *classification* of him as one, from which all the rest followed quite legitimately.

[72] Morgan: *Puritan Family,* pp. 71, 70, 64–5, 66.

[73] Ibid., pp. 36–8.

[74] Edmund Morgan: *The Puritan Family* (rev. ed., New York,

Harper Torchbook, 1966), pp. 30–2. For other constraints and their enforcement, ibid., pp. 53, 55, 79.

75 Weeden: *Economic and Social History*, p. 219; for enforcement, see pp. 229–30.

CHAPTER III

1 Charles F. Adams, ed.: "Abstract of John Marshall's Diary," Massachusetts Historical Society, *Proceedings*, 2nd ser., I (1884–5), p. 152; Adams: *Works*, II, p. 118n. See also N.B.: *The Constable's Pocket-Book* (Boston, 1710), p. 1; Mass. Arch. 114, pp. 622–3; "Records of Worcester," II, no. 8, p. 41.

2 Compiled from *Records of Plymouth*.

3 Compiled from *Records of the Town of Amherst from 1735 to 1788*, ed. by J. F. Jameson (Amherst, Mass., 1884); *Records of Braintree; Weston Records*. In Manchester only five of thirty-seven selectmen were chosen, and only three served; in Worcester fourteen of fifty-eight selectmen were named, though twelve did serve there. *Records of Manchester;* "Records of Worcester." See also Edward P. Hamilton: *A History of Milton* (Milton, Mass., 1957), p. 149. For the legal terms of avoidance, see *Constable's Pocket-Book*, p. 33; *The Town and County Officer, by a gentleman* (Boston, 1768), p. 33.

4 E.g., R. S. Longley: "Mob Activities in Revolutionary Massachusetts," *New England Quarterly* 6 (1933), pp. 100–1, 101–3, 124; John Schutz: *William Shirley: King's Governor of Massachusetts* (Chapel Hill, 1961), pp. 115, 127–30; *Records of Dudley*, II, p. 10; Weeden: *Economic and Social History*, pp. 635, 636.

5 Mass. Arch. 115, pp. 548–9; ibid. 116, pp. 100, 137, 151–2, 202–4, 234, 234–5, 243, 260–1, 370–1, 458–9, 582–3, 593; ibid. 117, pp. 143–5, 428–9, 430, 687, 815–16; ibid. 118, pp. 51–3, 72, 98, 165–6, 219, 290–1, 454–5, 513–14, 581–2; ibid. 181, p. 122.

6 Ibid. 116, pp. 14–15, 183, 197, 291, 319, 397–8, 694–6, 717–18. Likewise the occasional *fear* of oppression by petitioners had meaning in certain contexts only if in fact they *could* have been oppressed; see ibid. 113, p. 281; ibid. 116, p. 181.

7 For the general law of 1692–93 which conferred full authority of distraint and imprisonment, *Acts and Resolves*, I, p. 66.

For the stocks, Jonas Reed: *A History of Rutland* (Worcester, Mass., 1836), p. 68. For examples of the use of these sanctions by the towns, Mass. Arch. 50, p. 527; ibid. 113, pp. 275–6; ibid. 116, pp. 694–6, 698–700, 702–5; ibid. 117, pp. 370–1; *Records of Duxbury,* pp. 265–6; *Weston Records,* pp. 156–7; "Records of Worcester," II, no. 8, pp. 13n, 25; Elisha P. Douglass: *Rebels and Democrats* (Chapel Hill, 1955), pp. 138–9; Goen: *Revivalism,* pp. 193–5. For examples of coercion by the province, Mass. Arch. 48, pp. 203–5, 218–19, 244–5; ibid. 49, pp. 217–18, 219; ibid. 116, pp. 160–1; ibid. 118, p. 41.

[8] Ibid., pp. 40–1; Reed; *Rutland,* p. 68.

[9] Mass. Arch. 116, pp. 709–10.

[10] Ibid. 114, p. 22; see also ibid., p. 23; ibid., pp. 40–1; ibid. 116, pp. 675–91, especially pp. 675–6, 681; ibid. 117, pp. 94–7; ibid. 118, pp. 613–16.

[11] Ibid. 117, pp. 317–18.

[12] Ibid. 116, p. 646; ibid., p. 183. See also ibid., pp. 182, 197, 243, 291, 765.

[13] "Records of Worcester," II, no. 6, p. 19; ibid., IV, pp. 59, 69, 155–6; *Brookline Records,* pp. 123, 124, 186; *Records of Braintree,* pp. 234, 240; *Weston Records,* p. 63; Mass. Arch. 116, pp. 144, 291, 596–7; ibid. 117, p. 561; ibid. 118, p. 44; Joseph Willard: *Topographical and Historical Sketches of Lancaster* (Worcester, Mass., 1826), pp. 24–5.

[14] *Journals of the House,* XII, p. xiv; Washburn: *Judicial History,* pp. 59–60, 47.

[15] Oberholzer: *Delinquent Saints,* pp. 200–1, 205–6; Goen: *Revivalism,* p. 155. See also Morison: "Adoption of Constitution," pp. 371–2.

[16] Washburn: *Judicial History,* p. 200; Eldon James: "A List of the Legal Treatises Printed in the British Colonies and the American States before 1801," in *Harvard Legal Essays* (Cambridge, Mass., 1934), pp. 159, 161–78; Allen: *History of Wenham,* p. 123. A historian of Beverly wrote of one lawyer who, in the early part of the nineteenth century, "had the entire business" of the town and yet never earned enough from his practice even to pay his fuel bills; he insisted that

"no member of the [legal] profession has ever obtained a livelihood here from his fees alone." Edwin M. Stone: *History of Beverly, Civil and Ecclesiastical, From its Settlement in 1630 to 1842* (Boston, 1843), p. 307. See also Daniel Boorstin: *The Americans: The Colonial Experience* (New York, 1958), pp. 196–7, 198.

17 Edward Channing: "Town and County Government in the English Colonies of North America," *Johns Hopkins University Studies in Historical and Political Science,* 2nd ser., no. 10 (Baltimore, 1884), p. 28; Mass. Arch. 113, pp. 613–15. For an example of a unanimous foundation covenant of the middle of the eighteenth century, see ibid. 115, pp. 220–1.

18 E.g., ibid., pp. 482, 491; "Records of Worcester," II, no. 6, p. 106n; Mass. Arch. 114, pp. 33–4. See also ibid., p. 32; ibid. 115, pp. 872–5; Shipton: "Locus of Authority," pp. 145, 146–7. There were inducements of interest as well as of ethics to good relations with neighbors. See, e.g., ibid. 114, pp. 212–14; ibid., pp. 243, 244–6, 244a; and ibid. 117, pp. 162–3, for ways in which groups drew quite consciously upon the moral capital they had accumulated in previous situations to gain present ends.

19 Ibid. 118, pp. 715–17; see also, e.g., ibid. 50, pp. 30–1; ibid. 115, pp. 479, 480; ibid. 116, pp. 709–10.

20 Ibid. 115, pp. 368–75, 377–8, 393–6.

21 Ibid. 114, pp. 613–14; ibid. 113, pp. 275–6; ibid. 116, pp. 736–8.

22 Ibid. 117, pp. 165–9. In this case, nonetheless, the General Court declined to accept the argument and thus afforded no special safeguard to the original settlers. But similar cases did not draw adverse action from the Court; see ibid 114, pp. 286–8; ibid. 115, pp. 729–30.

23 Ibid. 115, pp. 330–4; ibid., p. 596.

24 Ibid. 114, pp. 244–6, 244a; ibid., pp. 786–8; see also ibid. 117, pp. 463–5.

25 Ibid. 115, pp. 866, 872–5; see also ibid. 118, pp. 388–90; ibid. 181, pp. 133–4, 139.

26 Ibid. 115, pp. 872–5; Tilton: *Rehoboth,* pp. 106–7, 102; Mass. Arch. 118, p. 207; see also ibid., 116, pp. 276–7.

27 Ibid. 118, p. 526; ibid. 115, pp. 461–2; ibid. 118, pp. 707–12; ibid. 113, pp. 263, 285–6. See also ibid., p. 444; *Records of Braintree,* pp. 69–70.

28 Mass. Arch. 115, pp. 697–8; ibid. 114, pp. 22, 32, 33–4. See also ibid. 115, pp. 872–5; Goen: *Revivalism,* pp. 259–62; Kiefer: *American Children,* p. 81; Arensberg: "American Communities," p. 1150.

29 Mass. Arch. 118, pp. 388–90; *Weston Records,* p. 11. See also, e.g., Mass. Arch. 49, pp. 361–2; ibid. 116, pp. 446–7; ibid. 118, pp. 715–17; *Records of Dudley,* I, pp. 106, 118; *Records of Manchester,* II, p. 32; "Records of Worcester," II, no. 8, pp. 43, 75; ibid., IV, pp. 18, 173, 264–6; Benjamin W. Labaree: *Patriots and Partisans: The Merchants of Newburyport 1764–1815* (Cambridge, Mass., 1962), p. 29. Other town votes were merely "by a very grate majority"—see, e.g., "Records of Worcester," II, no. 6, pp. 107–8; ibid., no. 8, pp. 29, 43, 55, 75–6, 88.

30 *Records of Braintree,* pp. 138, 165, 170, 177; see also, e.g., *Records of Manchester,* II, p. 32; "Records of Worcester," II, no. 6, p. 119. Again, other votes were by "a very grate majority" or "by all ye votes except one"—see ibid., pp. 103, 110; *Records of Braintree,* p. 132.

31 Mass. Arch. 113, pp. 441–3; ibid., pp. 520–1.

32 Oberholzer: *Delinquent Saints,* p. 41; Mather: *Ratio Disciplinae,* pp. 146, 150–1. For a striking indication of the emptiness of such sanctions in the absence of unanimity, see Oberholzer: *Delinquent Saints,* p. 93.

33 DeForest and Bates: *Westborough,* I, pp. 69–70; Allen: *Wenham,* pp. 173, 174–5. For declinations by candidates called on straightforward majoritarian assumptions and procedures, see "Records of Worcester," II, no. 8, pp. 63, 66; Blake: *Princeton,* I, p. 144. For the withdrawal of a candidate, after he had already accepted a call, when a controversy developed, see *Records of Dudley,* I, pp. 18–25. For examples of unanimous or virtually unanimous calls, see *Brookline Records,* pp. 163, 174, 181, 192; *Records of Dudley,* I, p. 120; *Weston Records,* pp. 9, 10; "Records of Worcester," II, no. 6, p. 21; Blake, *Princeton,* I, p. 146; Charles Fox: *History of the Old Township of Dunstable* (Nashua,

N.H., 1846), p. 98; Jeremiah Hanaford: *History of Princeton* (Worcester, Mass., 1852), p. 89; Herman Mann: *Historical Annals of Dedham* (Dedham, Mass., 1847), p. 26; Reed: *Rutland*, pp. 74, 75, 83, 84; Tilton: *Rehoboth*, p. 102. For a united town vote not to settle a minister while the community was divided on another issue, see Mass. Arch. 116, pp. 709–10, 711.

34 *Weston Records*, pp. 9, 10, 12; see also Russell: *Princeton*, pp. 38–9; Hanaford: *Princeton*, p. 198.

35 Mather: *Ratio Disciplinae*, p. 167; Bash: "Family and Community Organization," pp. 32, 67.

36 Shipton: "Locus of Authority," p. 138. The same recognition was also apparent in the legal requirement, after 1692, that the town as well as the church approve any ministerial call, a requirement which was rooted in the simple fact that the town, not the church, paid the minister. Ibid.

37 Compiled from Mass. Arch., Volumes 48–50, 113–118.

38 Compiled from *Records of Amherst, Records of Braintree, Brookline Records, Records of Dudley, Records of Fitchburg, Records of Lunenburg, Records of Manchester, Weston Records*, "Records of Worcester."

39 Compiled from Mass. Arch. 156, pp. 304–428, and ibid. 160, pp. 1–31. The totals exclude five towns which did report but reported no numbers, and they also exclude Boston, since Boston, as the metropolis of the province and atypical in too many ways, has been generally excluded from this study. (Boston, incidentally, was also unanimous: all 968 citizens voting voted against the 1778 proposal.)

40 Clarence Ver Steeg: *The Formative Years* (New York, 1964), pp. 167–8; Charles Baird: *History of the Huguenot Emigration to America* (New York, 1885), II, pp. 253, 251; G. Elmore Reaman: *The Trail of the Huguenots* (London, 1963), p. 129. See also, e.g., Emberson E. Proper: "Colonial Immigration Laws," *Columbia University Studies in History, Economics and Public Law*, XII, no. 2 (1900), esp. pp. 147–8, 148–57.

41 Marvin Harris: *Patterns of Race in the Americas* (New York, 1964), p. 84; Bureau of the Census: *Historical Statistics*, p. 756.

[42] *Journals of the House,* VII, p. 196.

[43] Mirick: *Haverhill,* pp. 140–1.

[44] *Journals of the House,* XXXII, part i, pp. ix–x, 266; ibid., part ii, pp. x–xi; Richard G. Lowe: "Massachusetts and the Acadians," *William and Mary Quarterly,* 3rd ser., 25 (1968), pp. 218*n*, 221, 225, 227, 228, 229.

[45] Mass. Arch. 117, pp. 690–1, 733–5; for even earlier, informal segregation, see Electa F. Jones: *Stockbridge, Past and Present* (Springfield, Mass., 1854), pp. 59, 62.

[46] Powell: *Puritan Village,* p. xviii; Haskins: *Law and Authority,* p. 70. See also Mass. Arch. 113, pp. 613–15; Mather: *Ratio Disciplinae,* part iii, p. 2; Benton: *Warning Out,* pp. 8, 26; Weeden: *Economic and Social History,* p. 519. Even in the crisis of the dissolution of a church, the congregation could not disperse to the nearest convenient towns without the prior approval of those towns; see Mass. Arch. 49, pp. 380–3; ibid. 115, pp. 268, 272, 276; ibid. 116, pp. 392–3; ibid. 117, pp. 15–16.

[47] Benton: *Warning Out,* p. 18; see also ibid., pp. 33, 46; Allen: *Wenham,* p. 26; Weeden: *Economic and Social History,* pp. 79, 80.

[48] Benton: *Warning Out,* pp. 18, 19, 23, 39, 87; Weeden: *Economic and Social History,* p. 57.

[49] Morgan: *Visible Saints,* pp. 10–12, 21. This aspect of Morgan's argument is only reinforced by Raymond Stearns and David Brawner: "New England Church 'Relations' and Continuity in Early Congregational History," *American Antiquarian Society, Proceedings* 75 (1965), pp. 13–45.

[50] Haskins: *Law and Authority,* p. 87; Mather: *Ratio Disciplinae,* p. 167.

[51] Benton: *Warning Out,* pp. 5, 8, 9, 18; see also Powell: *Puritan Village,* p. 75.

[52] The claim is the crux of the historical progression claimed by Benton; see *Warning Out,* pp. 51–5, 59–60, 118–20. But Weeden found the continuity of the policy into the provincial period so complete that "the actual occurrences hardly need particular mention"—*Economic and Social History,* p. 519, also p. 673—and instances do abound. See, e.g., *Weston Records,* pp. 61, 101, 108, 115, 126; "Records of

Worcester," II, no. 6, pp. 22–3, 102, 122–3; ibid., II, no. 8, pp. 19, 27, 57–8, 128; ibid., IV, pp. 28, 47, 67, 85, 99, 137, 147, 148, 202, 223; Mann: *Annals of Dedham,* pp. 23, 25; Allen: *Wenham,* p. 26.

Likewise Benton's claim that the law receded from its initial requirement of positive rather than merely tacit consent to new settlers can be discounted, since an act of 1766 restored the original regulation completely. *Warning Out,* pp. 18, 51, 52, 55, 118–20; Whitten: *Public Administration,* p. 41.

[53] Mass. Arch. 117, p. 687; ibid. 116, p. 137.

[54] Goen: *Revivalism,* pp. 107, 76, 84, 86; Bash: "Family and Community Organization," pp. 24–5; Francis: *Watertown,* p. 78. See also Lowe: "Massachusetts and the Acadians," p. 215.

[55] Morgan: *Puritan Family,* Ch. 5; Cotton Mather: *A Good Master well Served* (Boston, 1696), pp. 17–18; Mass. Arch. 117, pp. 143–5; ibid. 118, pp. 51–3; ibid. 116, pp. 736–8; ibid. 118, p. 98; ibid. 116, p. 593; see also ibid., pp. 582–3.

[56] Mather: *Ratio Disciplinae,* pp. 106, 123; Weeden: *Economic and Social History,* pp. 293–4; Bushman: *Puritan to Yankee,* p. 159; Herbert B. Adams: "Tithingmen," American Antiquarian Society, *Proceedings,* new ser., I (1880–1), p. 404. See also Hamilton: *Milton,* p. 148.

[57] Mather: *Ratio Disciplinae,* pp. 148–9; Weeden: *Economic and Social History,* p. 225; see also ibid., pp. 230, 550; Bash: "Family and Community Organization," pp. 44–6.

[58] Ibid., pp. 43–4, 253. See, e.g., *Records of Braintree,* p. 421; *Records of Lunenburg,* p. 83; "Records of Worcester," II, no. 8, p. 134; ibid., IV, pp. 186, 209; Allen: *Wenham,* pp. 108–9.

[59] Bash: "Family and Community Organization," p. 55; Arensberg: "American Communities," pp. 1149, 1150. See also ibid., pp. 1151, 1152, 1155, for Arensberg's comparison of the New England towns with the formal units of local government in the middle and southern colonies, where dispersion both of population and of public functions was the rule. For affirmation of the "townsmen together" ideal as a consummatory value, see, e.g., Mass. Arch. 113, pp. 616–17; ibid.

114, p. 645; ibid. 115, pp. 282–3; ibid. 116, pp. 527–8; ibid. 117, pp. 563–5; ibid. 181, pp. 122b–d.

[60] Winslow: *Meetinghouse Hill,* pp. 276–7.

[61] See, e.g., Haskins: *Law and Authority,* pp. 204, 210; Powell: *Puritan Village,* pp. 97–8, 107–8, 110.

[62] See, e.g., Updegraff: *Moving School,* pp. 155, 166–7.

[63] See, e.g., Green: "Church Records in Groton," p. 39; Mass. Arch. 116, pp. 43–4.

[64] Ibid., pp. 276–7. See also, e.g., ibid. 114, pp. 212–14.

[65] Ibid. 115, pp. 74–5; see also ibid. 116, pp. 276–7; ibid. 117, pp. 19–20, 23.

[66] Ibid. 116, pp. 702–5; see also ibid., pp. 153–4.

CHAPTER IV

[1] Powell: *Puritan Village,* pp. 107–8, 110; Mass. Arch. 118, pp. 707–12. See also Willison: *Saints and Strangers,* p. 254; Labaree: *Patriots and Partisans,* p. 30.

[2] Winslow: *Meetinghouse Hill,* pp. 38–9; Mather: *Ratio Disciplinae,* part 3, p. 2.

[3] Benjamin Franklin: *Writings,* ed. by Albert Smyth (New York, 1905), I, p. 235.

[4] Mass. Arch. 50, pp. 20–2, 25–6; ibid. 114, pp. 625–7; ibid., p. 643. Ibid. 118, pp. 344–5. Ibid. 116, pp. 153–4; ibid., pp. 702–5.

[5] Mass. Arch. 117, pp. 165–9; ibid. 118, pp. 613–16; see also ibid., pp. 388–90.

[6] Ibid. 117, pp. 94–7; ibid. 118, p. 209; Marion Safford: *The Story of Colonial Lancaster* (Rutland, Vt., 1937), pp. 83–5, 127. See also Mass. Arch. 115, pp. 557–8.

[7] "Records of Worcester," II, no. 8, pp. 42–3; Mass. Arch. 115, pp. 4–5. See also ibid. 114, pp. 278–9; ibid. 117, pp. 94–7; ibid., pp. 165–9; ibid. 118, pp. 613–16.

[8] Ibid. 117, pp. 442–3.

[9] Reed: *Rutland,* pp. 51–2; Tilton: *Rehoboth,* p. 99; Mass. Arch. 113, pp. 604–5; *Records of Amherst,* pp. 23, 25, 30, 39–40, 52, 53; "Records of Worcester," II, no. 6, pp. 70, 73, 79, 121–2; ibid., II, no. 8, pp. 14, 27, 83, 116; ibid., IV, pp. 57, 70, 145, 167, 189. See also, e.g., *Records of Fitchburg,* pp. 43, 83; *Records of Lunenburg,* pp. 85, 97, 102, 141, 175, 179,

181–2, 185, 189, 215; *Weston Records,* pp. 166, 176, 186, 206, 217; Updegraff: *Moving School,* pp. 142, 143.

[10] Ibid., pp. 156, 166–7. There were other elements of solid self-interest in such conciliation, such as the promotion of long-range local development—see, e.g., Mass. Arch. 117, pp. 94–7—and the preservation of the geographic integrity of the community against the divisive desires of its distant parts—see, e.g., ibid. 114, pp. 249–50; ibid., pp. 629–30, 631, 637–9, 645; ibid. 115, p. 79; ibid. 116, pp. 527–8, 529–30; ibid. 118, pp. 387, 388–90.

[11] Mass. Arch. 118, pp. 388–90; see also "Records of Worcester," II, no. 6, pp. 54–5; Updegraff: *Moving School,* p. 131.

[12] Mass. Arch. 118, pp. 722–4; see also, e.g., ibid., pp. 344–5. Accommodation also went the other way, in the many votes to grant ministers an additional sum to counter inflation. That is, though such voters could have kept to the letter of the law and saved themselves money, they preferred not to risk any disaffection in their minister. See, e.g., *Records of Lunenburg,* p. 98.

[13] Updegraff: *Moving School,* pp. 129–31, 132, 133.

[14] E.g., Mass. Arch. 117, pp. 338–9; ibid. 118, pp. 387, 388–90; ibid., pp. 627–8; *Records of Lunenburg,* pp. 109–10; "Records of Worcester," II, no. 8, pp. 60–1; ibid., IV, p. 57; *1735—June 25—1935: Upton, Massachusetts* (Upton, Mass., 1935), p. 17.

[15] E.g., Mass. Arch. 115, p. 266; Tilton: *Rehoboth,* p. 104.

[16] E.g., Mass. Arch. 116, pp. 527–8; ibid. 117, pp. 338–9; ibid. 118, pp. 613–16; Francis: *Sketch of Watertown,* pp. 64–5.

[17] *Records of Dudley,* I, p. 12.

[18] *Records of Braintree,* pp. 55–7; see also pp. 326, 353–4.

[19] *Records of Fitchburg,* p. 13; Mass. Arch. 114, pp. 19–20.

[20] E.g., Samuel Green: "The Earliest Church Records in Groton," *Groton Historical Series,* I (1887), no. 10, p. 39; *Records of Plymouth,* II, p. 282; Mass. Arch. 115, p. 142; "Records of Worcester," II, no. 6, p. 32.

[21] *Records of Fitchburg,* pp. 92–3; Blake: *Princeton,* I, pp. 143–4; Mass. Arch. 115, pp. 600–1. See also ibid., pp. 689–91, 501–2.

[22] Mass. Arch. 33, pp. 258–9; ibid. 114, pp. 789–90; ibid. 115,

p. 291; ibid., pp. 600–1; ibid. 117, pp. 338–9; *Records of Braintree,* pp. 108, 167, 181, 246, 263, 270, 283, 303, 312, 319, 442, 451, 455, 462; *Records of Plymouth,* II, pp. 224, 242; DeForest and Bates: *Westborough,* I, pp. 106–8.

23 Mass. Arch. 118, pp. 707–12; *Records of Braintree,* p. 66; Mass. Arch. 115, pp. 377–8, 389–90. See also ibid. 114, pp. 24–5.

24 For varying degrees of nonaccommodation, see ibid. 116, pp. 153–4; ibid., p. 280; ibid., pp. 596–7, 607–8; ibid., pp. 702–5; ibid. 118, pp. 384–6, 388–90, 387; ibid., pp. 713–14, 715–17; *Records of Amherst,* pp. 60, 62, 63; *Records of Braintree,* p. 206; *Records of Lunenburg,* pp. 140, 142–3, 204, 212–14; "Records of Worcester," II, no. 6, pp. 44–6; ibid., II, no. 8, pp. 11, 15, 29–30; ibid., IV, pp. 177, 196, 201. Many even among these are ambiguous at best, however, and such non-accommodation was nowhere very common.

25 E.g., Mass. Arch. 114, pp. 237–8; ibid., p. 796; ibid. 115, pp. 282–3; ibid., pp. 385–6; ibid. 116, pp. 256–7; ibid. 118, pp. 722–4.

26 Ibid. 115, pp. 368–75.

None of this is to say that the integrity of the community was never abrogated, nor that men never displayed vindictiveness, animosity, avowed opposition, or a desire for retaliation. It is simply to say that the striking aspect of such episodes was their infrequency. A faction in Dunstable did indeed tell the rest of the town that "they did not care whether they liked what was done or not; what they wanted was their money, and that they would have or they should all go to jail"—ibid. 116, pp. 702–5—but in all the records examined, no one ever said anything as antagonistic again. In an Easton election meeting, an adverse majority impelled the selectmen to go off "about eight or ten rods from the meetinghouse door with their adherents," where they stayed until it grew dark and the meeting could be adjourned—ibid. 49, pp. 398–400—but nowhere else was such conflict thus given a physically visible manifestation by overt congregation into separate parties.

27 Powell: *Puritan Village;* the quotations are on p. 131.

28 Mass. Arch. 114, p. 39; ibid. 113, p. 277; Goen: *Revivalism,*

pp. 98–9, 113–14; Mass. Arch. 116, pp. 715–16. See also ibid. 114, pp. 40–1, 49–51, 53; ibid. 115, p. 101; ibid. 116, p. 170; ibid. 118, pp. 707–12, 715–17.

29 Labaree: *Patriots and Partisans,* pp. 2–3; Mass. Arch. 118, pp. 14–19; ibid. 116, pp. 170, 171–2a; ibid. 118, pp. 715–17.

30 Ibid. 33, p. 256; see also ibid. 118, p. 661.

31 E.g., ibid. 116, pp. 276–7; ibid. 117, pp. 19–20, 21.

32 E.g., ibid. 113, p. 273; ibid. 118, pp. 707–12.

33 Ibid. 113, p. 599; see also ibid. 50, pp. 525–6; ibid. 115, p. 734; ibid. 116, pp. 709–10; Reed: *Rutland,* pp. 81, 13, 82–3; Goen: *Revivalism,* pp. 76, 84, 86, 90–1, 107, 108, 109, 190.

34 Mass. Arch. 116, p. 609; see also ibid., pp. 276–7; ibid. 117, pp. 19–20, 21; ibid., pp. 84–5; ibid., pp. 165–9; ibid., pp. 813–14; ibid. 118, pp. 613–16; ibid. 181, pp. 131–2, 140–140a.

35 Ibid. 115, pp. 492–3; see, e.g., ibid. 114, pp. 272, 282–3; ibid. 116, pp. 736–8; ibid. 117, pp. 815–16; ibid. 118, pp. 658–9, 659; ibid., pp. 661–2; ibid., pp. 798–801.

36 Ibid. 118, pp. 707–12.

37 Ibid. 116, p. 170; ibid., pp. 525–6, 529–30, 531; ibid., p. 606; ibid. 117, pp. 91, 94–7, 98; ibid. 118, pp. 627–8, 629; and esp. ibid. 114, pp. 572–4, 561, 783–4, 785–91. That is, as the absence of peace was an adequate condition for dividing a community, so the possession of peace conferred a presumptive right against tampering with a town or taking inhabitants away; see ibid. 115, pp. 72–3; ibid. 116, pp. 606, 602–2a; ibid., pp. 747–8, 749–50; ibid. 117, pp. 94–7, 98, 165–9, 171; ibid. 118, pp. 739–40, 613–16; ibid., p. 619; ibid., pp. 661–2; ibid., pp. 713–14; ibid., pp. 739–40; ibid., pp. 867–8; ibid. 181, pp. 128–9a, 130.

38 Ibid. 115, pp. 393–6; ibid. 114, pp. 17, 33–4.

39 Ibid. 118, pp. 613–16; see also, e.g., ibid. 114, pp. 236, 243; ibid., pp. 282–3; ibid. 115, p. 69; ibid., p. 494; ibid., pp. 689–91; ibid. 116, pp. 529–30; ibid., pp. 607–8, 609; ibid., pp. 689–91; ibid. 117, pp. 98, 99–100; ibid., pp. 442–3; ibid., p. 561; ibid. 118, p. 387; ibid., pp. 619, 620, 621; ibid., pp. 627–8; ibid., pp. 798–801.

40 Ibid. 115, pp. 479–503, 689–91, 693, 693–4, 697–8; for an almost identical case in Springfield, see ibid. 118, pp. 707–18, 719–21.

[41] Ibid., pp. 658–9.

[42] Ibid. 114, p. 234; ibid. 115, pp. 368–75; ibid., p. 500; ibid. 116, pp. 527–8; ibid., pp. 601, 602–2a, 609; ibid., pp. 607–8; ibid., p. 630; ibid., p. 634; ibid. 117, pp. 14, 15–16; ibid. 118, pp. 388–90; ibid., pp. 617, 621; ibid., pp. 627–8.

[43] Ibid. 116, pp. 715–16; see also, e.g., ibid., pp. 444–5; ibid., pp. 668–9; ibid. 117, pp. 156–7, 171, 159–60.

[44] Ibid. 117, p. 23; see also ibid. 115, pp. 101, 104–5.

[45] For rebuffs, see, e.g., ibid. 115, pp. 501–2; ibid. 116, pp. 392–3.

[46] Ibid. 115, pp. 851–2.

[47] E.g., ibid. 114, pp. 24–5; ibid., p. 742; ibid. 115, p. 463; ibid., p. 17; *Records of Braintree*, pp. 234, 357–8, 382–3, 412; *Records of Dudley*, I, p. 142; "Records of Worcester," II, no. 6, pp. 18–19.

[48] *Records of Duxbury*, p. 199; see also Mass. Arch. 115, pp. 491, 494; ibid. 117, p. 17; ibid. 118, pp. 707–12; *Records of Amherst*, p. 23; *1735–1935: Upton*, p. 19.

[49] E.g., Mass. Arch. 118, pp. 707–12; *Records of Amherst*, p. 38; *Records of Braintree*, pp. 234, 348.

[50] Mather: *Ratio Disciplinae*, p. 162. For mutual councils and a typical progression, see, e.g., Mass. Arch. 113, pp. 269, 272, 273; *Brookline Records*, p. 179; "Records of Worcester," II, no. 6, p. 12; Nason: *Dunstable*, p. 109; Tilton: *Rehoboth*, pp. 106–7.

[51] On a few occasions it was a court of first instance; see, e.g., Mass. Arch. 117, pp. 19–20; ibid. 118, p. 207.

[52] Ibid., pp. 707–12; ibid., p. 207; ibid. 115, p. 596; see also ibid. 114, p. 54. The same goal guided the resort to arbitration at local levels; see, e.g., *Records of Braintree*, p. 412; Mather: *Ratio Disciplinae*, p. i.

[53] Ibid. 113, p. 280; ibid. 115, p. 463; ibid., p. 491; ibid., pp. 600–1; ibid. 116, pp. 153–4; Winslow: *Meetinghouse Hill*, pp. 121–2.

[54] Mass. Arch. 114, pp. 212–14; ibid., p. 54; ibid. 117, pp. 232–5; see also ibid. 114, pp. 740–1a; ibid. 115, p. 491; ibid. 117, p. 575; ibid. 118, p. 207; *Records of Braintree*, pp. 382–3; "Records of Worcester," II, no. 6, pp. 18–19; Francis: *Sketch of Watertown*, pp. 59–60. Ecclesiastical arbitration

also commanded consent; see, e.g., Tilton: *Rehoboth*, pp. 106–7.

55 Mass. Arch. 113, p. 264; ibid. 114, p. 742; see also *Records of Duxbury*, p. 199.

56 Francis: *Sketch of Watertown*, pp. 59–60, 91–2.

57 "Diary of Sewall," V, pp. 400–1, 461.

58 Mass. Arch. 117, pp. 94–7.

59 Ibid. 116, pp. 709–10, 713.

60 Though see ibid. 114, pp. 399–411; ibid. 115, pp. 262–87, esp. pp. 267, 268, 270, 278–9, 284.

61 Ibid. 118, pp. 207, 208, 526. Perhaps the finest description of the economic advantages of harmony is in Richard Bushman, *From Puritan to Yankee: Character and the Social Order in Connecticut, 1690–1775* (Cambridge, Mass., 1967), esp. pp. 32–4.

62 Mass. Arch. 50, pp. 525–6; ibid. 113, p. 101; ibid., p. 269; ibid. 114, pp. 22, 40–1, 49–51, 56–7; ibid. 115, pp. 282–3; ibid. 116, pp. 709–10; ibid. 117, pp. 513–15; ibid., pp. 563–5; ibid. 118, p. 207; *Brookline Records*, p. 179; Fox: *Dunstable*, p. 167; Hamilton: *Milton*, pp. 33–4; Nason: *Dunstable*, p. 109.

63 Mass. Arch. 116, pp. 717–18.

64 E.g., ibid. 49, p. 358; ibid., pp. 467–8; ibid. 50, p. 516; ibid., p. 526.

65 Ibid. 116, pp. 153–4; ibid. 118, pp. 707–12.

66 Ibid. 114, pp. 533–4; ibid. 115, p. 639; ibid. 116, pp. 397–9, 717–18; ibid. 117, p. 195.

67 Ibid. 118, pp. 707–12.

68 Ibid. 114, pp. 625–7; see also ibid., pp. 251–2.

69 Ibid. 49, pp. 467–8; ibid. 118, pp. 613–16; ibid., pp. 798–801; ibid. 116, pp. 709–10. See also ibid. 50, pp. 20–2; ibid. 117, pp. 19–20, 21; ibid., pp. 513–15; ibid. 118, pp. 715–17; ibid. 181, p. 25; Robert J. Taylor, ed.: *Massachusetts, Colony to Commonwealth: Documents on the Formation of its Constitution* (Chapel Hill, 1961), p. 26.

70 Mass. Arch. 116, pp. 276–7.

CHAPTER V

1 Quoted in Powell: *Puritan Village,* p. 153n.

2 E.g., *Records of Dudley,* I, p. 19; for violations, ibid., pp. 18, 71, 105.

3 E.g., Mass. Arch. 118, p. 154; Luther Cushing: *Reports of Contested Elections* (Boston, 1834), p. 47. (Cushing's citations begin in 1780 and are therefore not strictly applicable to this study, but often explicitly and occasionally implicitly it is apparent that the practices described had not changed from the provincial period. In such cases the material has been used, especially on matters essentially peripheral.)

4 E.g., *Brookline Records,* pp. 109, 112, 118–19.

5 E.g., *Records of Dudley,* I, pp. 18, 71, 129, 157, 163. In general, March meetings, with their full slate of officers to be chosen, began in the morning, while May meetings, when only a representative had to be elected, were called for the afternoon. Some towns, however, began their May meetings in the morning too, so as to leave the afternoon for other business and especially for consideration of instructions to the new representative. Election meetings generally ended before dark, if only because light was needed to count the votes, but see "Diary of Sewall," V, p. 9.

6 E.g., Mass. Arch. 114, p. 408.

7 For the legal provisions, ibid. 48, pp. 203–5; *County and Town Officer,* p. 109; for sample writs and precepts, Mass. Arch. 49, p. 391; ibid. 50, p. 133.

8 Ibid.; for the sheriff's powers outside New England, Cortlandt F. Bishop: *History of Elections in the American Colonies* (New York, 1893), p. 114.

9 *County and Town Officer,* p. 95.

10 E.g., *Watertown Records* (Boston and Newton, Mass., 1904, 1928), V, p. 156; ibid., III, pp. 124–5; Cushing: *Contested Elections,* pp. 14–15; *Letters and Diary of John Rowe,* ed. by Anne R. Cunningham (Boston, 1903), p. 198; Mass. Arch. 33, pp. 249–52.

11 Ibid. 116, p. 706; ibid., p. 372; "Records of Worcester," II, no. 6, pp. 44–6; Mass. Arch. 114, pp. 399–400; ibid. 181, p. 25; ibid. 50, p. 284; *Records of Dudley,* I, p. 175; *Records*

of Braintree, p. 288; *Records of Amherst*, p. 32; *Records of Fitchburg*, p. 30; *Records of Lunenburg*, pp. 130, 135; *Records of Braintree*, p. 390; *Records of Duxbury*, p. 218; Mass. Arch. 114, pp. 239–40; *Records of Dudley*, I, p. 134.

[12] Mass. Arch. 50, pp. 172–3, 174; ibid., pp. 139–40, 141; ibid., pp. 422–3, 424.

[13] Ibid. 114, pp. 399–400; ibid. 115, pp. 36–7; ibid., p. 388; *Records of Dudley*, II, p. 57; *Records of Amherst*, p. 32; "Records of Worcester," II, no. 6, p. 12; *Records of Dudley*, II, pp. 67, 68; *Records of Fitchburg*, p. 30; *Records of Lunenburg*, pp. 130, 135; "Records of Worcester," II, no. 6, p. 98; ibid., IV, p. 145; *Records of Braintree*, p. 390; *Records of Plymouth*, II, pp. 202–3, 294, 335.

[14] Mass. Arch. 50, pp. 20–2, 27; ibid. 117, pp. 291–3; *Records of Lunenburg*, p. 110; "Records of Worcester," II, no. 6, p. 59; Russell: *Princeton*, p. 20; Cushing: *Contested Elections*, pp. 117, 144.

[15] *Records of Fitchburg*, p. 5; also *Records of Amherst*, p. 19; *Records of Dudley*, II, p. 57. For still other techniques, see *Records of Braintree*, p. 288; "Diary of Sewall," V, p. 478.

[16] *Records of Braintree*, pp. 374–5; Mass. Arch. 114, pp. 251–2; see also Cushing: *Contested Elections*, pp. 14–15, 26; Mass. Arch. 116, pp. 698–700, 702–5; ibid. 115, pp. 36–7.

[17] *Records of Plymouth*, II, p. 282; see also *Records of Braintree*, pp. 374–5.

[18] E.g., *Records of Plymouth*, III, p. 15; *Records of Braintree*, p. 197; Mass. Arch. 50, pp. 20–2.

[19] Ibid. 117, pp. 494–5; *Records of Dudley*, I, pp. 134, 175; *Records of Fitchburg*, p. 105; *Records of Plymouth*, II, pp. 4, 276, 277, 332, 333; ibid., III, pp. 17–18, 38–9; "Records of Worcester," II, no. 8, p. 43; DeForest and Bates: *Westborough*, pp. 91–2; Mass. Arch. 49, pp. 361–2; ibid. 116, p. 752.

[20] Ibid. 115, pp. 729–30; see also pp. 741–2.

[21] *Brookline Records*, pp. 189–90. For protests, Mass. Arch. 115, pp. 501–2; ibid., pp. 729–30; ibid. 116, pp. 702–5; *Records of Braintree*, p. 249; *Records of Plymouth*, II, p. 282; Nason: *Dunstable*, p. 105.

[22] Mass. Arch. 114, pp. 326–7; ibid., p. 343; ibid., pp. 288–9; Cushing: *Contested Elections*, pp. 217–21. Even in elections

for representative, when the law specified that the selectmen
were to manage the election, an enormous local variety steadily prevailed. For the law, Mass. Arch. 48, pp. 203–5; for actual
modes of management, ibid. 49, pp. 361–2; ibid., pp. 398–400;
ibid. 50, pp. 20–2, 85–8; ibid. 116, pp. 373–4; ibid. 117, pp.
134, 139–40; *Records of Braintree*, pp. 342–3; *Records of
Dudley*, II, pp. 32, 157; *Records of Duxbury*, p. 276 et seq.;
Journals of the House, XIII, p. 10; Cushing: *Contested
Elections*, p. 27.

23 For the duties of the office, Samuel Freeman: *The Town
Officer* (Portland, Me., 1791), p. 5. For violations, Mass. Arch.
49, pp. 398–400; ibid., pp. 467–8; ibid. 50, pp. 20–2, 85–8;
ibid. 114, p. 343; ibid., pp. 533–4; ibid. 115, pp. 288–9, 303;
ibid. 116, p. 373; ibid. 117, pp. 291–3; ibid., pp. 647–9;
Cushing: *Contested Elections*, pp. 27, 189–93.

24 Mass. Arch. 117, pp. 647–9.

25 E.g., "Diary of Sewall," VI, pp. 275, 309; *Brookline Records*,
p. 204.

26 Mass. Arch. 50, pp. 25–6.

27 Ibid. 49, pp. 398–400; see also ibid. 50, pp. 85–8; ibid. 116,
p. 706; ibid. 117, pp. 302–5, 311–13; *Journals of the House*,
XXXI, pp. 7–8, 20; ibid. XXXIII, part 1, pp. 7, 30; ibid.,
XXXIV, part 1, pp. 9, 30.

28 Mass. Arch. 117, pp. 295–7, 300, 315; ibid., pp. 139–40. See
also ibid. 49, pp. 361–2.

29 Ibid. 117, pp. 295–7, 300, 315.

30 Ibid. 114, pp. 325–8; ibid. 48, pp. 216–17; ibid. 117, pp.
647–9; ibid. 8, p. 273; ibid. 114, p. 399; ibid. 49, pp. 361–2;
Acts and Resolves, I, pp. 146–8; Mass. Arch. 48, pp. 218–19,
226–30; ibid. 113, pp. 10–12; *County and Town Officer*, p. 27.

31 Mass. Arch. 117, pp. 291–3, 300, 309, 310; ibid. 114, pp.
325–8.

32 Actually a few formalities intervened. Province law required
the presence of a majority of the selectmen, a reading of the
election laws, and a reading of the warrant or precept. Ibid.
48, pp. 203–5; ibid. 49, pp. 361–2; ibid. 115, pp. 288–9;
Watertown Records, V, pp. 157, 187.

33 For the most common order, see, e.g., *Brookline Records*, p.
111; *Records of Dudley*, I, p. 32. For others, *Brookline Rec-*

ords, pp. 92–3, 95, 97, 98, 100, 119, 207; *Records of Dudley*, I, pp. 7, 42; ibid., II, pp. 20, 25, 46, 56, 80, 87, 116, 132, 142, 147; *Records of Plymouth*, II, p. 273.

³⁴ Updegraff: *Moving School* p. 123n; Powell: *Puritan Village*, pp. 53–4, 47, 48; *Brookline Records*, p. 111; *Records of Dudley*, I, pp. 162, 174.

³⁵ Frederick Dallinger: *Nominations for Elective Office in the United States* (New York, 1897), pp. 3–4, 5; Bishop: *Elections*, pp. 98–9, 123–5; W. C. Ford: "Voting with Beans and Corn," Massachusetts Historical Society, *Proceedings* 57 (1923–4).

³⁶ *Records of Braintree*, p. 270; Mass. Arch. 33, pp. 249–52.

³⁷ E.g., Adams: *Works*, II, p. 185.

³⁸ E.g., Mass. Arch. 49, pp. 361–2; ibid. 114, pp. 533–4; *Records of Braintree*, pp. 353–4; Adams: *Works*, II, p. 185.

³⁹ E.g., Mass. Arch. 49, p. 358; *Brookline Records*, pp. 143, 221; *Records of Plymouth*, II, p. 281; ibid., III, p. 157; "Records of Worcester," IV, pp. 47, 65; *Journals of the House*, XVI, p. 77.

⁴⁰ Mass. Arch. 48, pp. 226–30, 239; ibid. 117, pp. 744–7.

⁴¹ *Records of Plymouth*, III, p. 222.

⁴² Taylor, ed.: *Colony to Commonwealth*, pp. 67, 86; Mass. Arch. 49, pp. 361–2; ibid. 50, pp. 85–8.

⁴³ For other implications of effortless election by men who had not seriously sought office, see ibid. 115, p. 25; ibid. 118, p. 749.

⁴⁴ E.g., *Records of Braintree*, p. 266; Adams: *Works*, II, p. 185.

⁴⁵ Ibid., pp. 144, 144n.

⁴⁶ *Diary of John Rowe*, p. 212; Mass. Arch. 33, pp. 249–52. See also ibid. 49, pp. 361–2; ibid., pp. 467–8; Adams: *Works*, II, pp. 121–3; "Diary of Sewall," VII, p. 248; *The Review*, p. 8.

⁴⁷ Adams: *Works*, II, p. 185; Mass. Arch. 115, pp. 288–9, 304; ibid. 117, pp. 306–7, 295–7. See also ibid. 33, p. 267; ibid. 49, pp. 398–400; ibid. 115, pp. 330–4; ibid. 117, pp. 311–13.

⁴⁸ Ibid. 49, pp. 467–8; ibid. 50, p. 28; ibid. 115, pp. 330–4; ibid. 50, pp. 30–1; ibid. 116, pp. 702–5; ibid. 117, p. 308; *Records of Fitchburg*, pp. 99–100; "Records of Worcester," IV, p. 139.

⁴⁹ Adams: *Works*, II, pp. 94n, 165–6; Perry Miller: *Jonathan Edwards* (New York, 1959), p. 265; Mass. Arch. 181, pp.

23–4a. See also *Records of Fitchburg*, pp. 99–100; "Diary of John Whiting of Dedham, Mass.," *New England Historic and Genealogical Register* 63 (1909), p. 189; "Extracts Copied Some Two-Score Years Ago, from Interleaved Almanacs of James Jeffrey, Esq.," *Essex Institute Historical Collections* 2 (1860), p. 65.

[50] Bridenbaugh: "New England Town," p. 36.

[51] Mass. Arch. 50, pp. 20–2, 25–6; Adams: *Three Episodes*, p. 743; *1735–1935: Upton*, p. 40; *Brookline Records*, p. 251; *Records of Fitchburg*, p. 10; Nason: *Dunstable*, pp. 75, 75*n*, 79, 81; Mass. Arch. 117, pp. 647–9; Blake: *Princeton*, pp. 134–5.

[52] Adams: *Works*, II, pp. 85–6, 125–6; William Douglas: *A Summary, Historical and Political* (London, 1760), I, pp. 506–7.

[53] Adams: *Works*, II, pp. 85–6, 112, 121–3; see also *The Good of the Community Impartially Considered* (Boston, 1754), pp. 46–7; *Records of Fitchburg*, p. 10 *et seq.* (the case of Thomas Cowdin).

[54] Adams: *Works*, II, p. 144*n*; see also Mass. Arch. 115, p. 298; Henshaw *v.* Foster, 9 *Pickering* 312, 319–20.

[55] Adams: *Works*, II, pp. 144*n*, 185.

[56] In addition to the ideals already discussed, see Mass. Arch. 115, pp. 330–4; *Journals of the House*, XX, pp. 405–7.

[57] Charles Sydnor and Noble Cunningham: "Voting in Early America," *American Heritage* 4 (1952), p. 7.

[58] Bishop: *Elections*, pp. 98–9; Chilton Williamson: *American Suffrage: From Property to Democracy* (Princeton, 1960), pp. 11–12; see also Washburn: *Judicial History*, pp. 16, 20–1.

[59] Mass. Arch. 50, pp. 20–2; Adams: *Works*, II, p. 190. The secret ballot was also employed in other elections of more than ordinary importance, as for critical town committees, moderators, and deacons; see *Records of Lunenburg*, p. 204; "Records of Worcester," II, no. 6, p. 9; Green: "Church Records in Groton," p. 39; Mather: *Ratio Disciplinae*, p. 130. In Mather's detailed account of an election for deacon, he never in any way indicated the existence of nominations, campaigning, or prepared ballots.

[60] Adams: *Works*, II, pp. 187–8. Even in a town such as North-ampton, which Jonathan Edwards called "remarkably con-tentious," animosity had no open expression for years. Ac-cording to Edwards himself it had been confined to mere "backbiting," while the inhabitants had "restrained them-selves in open and public town meetings." Miller: "Edwards' Sociology," pp. 57–8. In the twentieth-century town, at least one acute observer has written of a very similar pattern of political conduct. "In so small and interrelated a commu-nity," maintains Granville Hicks, "political controversy can-not be conducted in public without acrimony or even with candor, though there is a vast amount of whispered slander and adroit backstabbing. A man can make his views clear, however, even though he says nothing at which political opponents and their relatives can take offense. . . ." *Small Town* (New York, 1946), p. 122.

[61] Mass. Arch. 48, pp. 226–30; ibid. 49, pp. 392, 393, 394, 395; ibid. 50, pp. 20–2; ibid., pp. 454–5; ibid. 115, pp. 300, 302; Cushing: *Contested Elections*, pp. 217–21. See also David Syrett: "Town Meeting Politics in Massachusetts, 1776–1786," *William and Mary Quarterly*, 3rd ser., 21 (1964), p. 362.

[62] Cushing: *Contested Elections*, pp. 59, 175–7.

[63] Mass. Arch. 117, pp. 494–5.

[64] Ibid. 48, pp. 226–30; ibid. 50, pp. 25–6; see also ibid., pp. 20–2, 23.

[65] Ibid., pp. 454, 455. For other instances of suspicion which could not be converted into proof at the meeting, ibid., pp. 20–2; ibid. 115, p. 300; ibid. 116, pp. 392, 393, 394, 395; ibid. 117, pp. 291–3.

[66] For a suggestive comparison, see J. A. Pitt-Rivers: *The Peo-ple of the Sierra* (Chicago, 1961), pp. 134–5.

[67] Bishop: *Elections*, p. 154.

[68] James K. Hosmer: "Samuel Adams, the Man of the Town Meeting," *Johns Hopkins U. Studies in Historical and Political Science*, 2nd ser., IV (1884), p. 56.

[69] E.g., Mass. Arch. 50, pp. 30–1, 85–8; ibid. 117, pp. 309, 310; Brown: *Middle-Class Democracy*, p. 85.

[70] Mass. Arch. 49, pp. 361–2; ibid. 117, pp. 647–9.

[71] The law itself authorized either the constables or the selectmen; ibid. 48, pp. 203–5. For the variations in receivers see, e.g., ibid. 50, pp. 85–8; ibid. 114, p. 343; ibid. 115, pp. 291, 297, 301; ibid. 117, p. 309; ibid. 181, pp. 23–4a; *Journals of the House*, XIII, p. 10. For variations in receptacles, Mass. Arch. 8, p. 277; ibid. 49, pp. 361–2; ibid., p. 392; ibid. 50, pp. 25–6, 85–8; ibid. 114, pp. 533–4; ibid. 115, pp. 291, 301; ibid. 116, p. 373; ibid. 117, pp. 494–5; ibid. 181, pp. 23–4a.

[72] E.g., ibid. 49, pp. 361–2; ibid. 50, pp. 85–8; ibid. 116, pp. 373–4.

[73] E.g., ibid. 33, pp. 249–52; ibid. 50, pp. 85–8, 455; ibid. 114, pp. 533–4; ibid. 116, p. 373; ibid. 117, p. 309; Cushing: *Contested Elections*, pp. 3, 41, 187; *Journals of the House*, XIII, p. 10; Commonwealth *v.* Thomas F. Hoxey, 16 *Mass. Reports* 385.

[74] E.g., *Watertown Records*, V, p. 157; Mass. Arch. 50, pp. 25–6; Cushing: *Contested Elections*, pp. 3, 59, 175–7.

[75] Mass. Arch. 33, pp. 249–52; ibid. 49, pp. 398–400; ibid. 50, pp. 20–2, 85–8; ibid. 114, pp. 533–4; ibid. 115, p. 294; ibid. 116, p. 373; ibid. 117, pp. 306–7, 309; *Journals of the House*, XIII, p. 10.

[76] *Records of Braintree*, p. 442; Winslow: *Meetinghouse Hill*, pp. 121–4; see also, e.g., Mass. Arch. 116, pp. 43–4.

[77] Brown: *Middle-Class Democracy*, p. 39; *Records of Dudley*, I, p. 120; ibid., II, p. 64; *Records of Braintree*, p. 336.

[78] Mass. Arch. 49, pp. 361–2.

CHAPTER VI

[1] Stephan Thernstrom: *Poverty and Progress* (Cambridge, 1964), pp. 40–1; Thernstrom derived his interpretation largely from Labaree: *Patriots and Partisans*. For other important investigations which emphasize patterns of deference in the same era in Connecticut, see Grant: *Democracy in Kent*, and Bushman: *Puritan to Yankee*.

[2] The first break occurred in 1641, when the Body of Liberties

made all men free to attend town meetings; an enactment of 1647 allowed them to vote. On the other hand, some restrictions on nonfreemen did remain; see Parker: "Origin, Organization, and Influence," p. 46.

3 Brown: *Middle-Class Democracy*. No women could vote; no one under twenty-one could vote; and for miscellaneous requirements that touched a few others, see Bishop: *Elections*.

4 Mass. Arch. 115, pp. 169, 168; ibid., pp. 469–71; Blake: *Princeton*, I, pp. 76–7; Mass. Arch. 117, pp. 647–9, 652; ibid. 115, pp. 319–20, 316–17. See also, e.g., ibid., pp. 864–5; ibid. 118, pp. 734–5a, 762.

5 Ibid. 8, p. 279. See also, e.g., ibid., p. 278; ibid. 49, pp. 398–400; ibid. 50, pp. 20–2, 25–6; ibid., pp. 85–8, 89–90; ibid. 113, p. 270; ibid. 115, pp. 36–7, 291; ibid. 116, pp. 373–4; ibid. 117, pp. 291–3, 302–5; ibid. 181, pp. 23–4a.

6 Brown: *Middle-Class Democracy*, p. 60.

7 *Records of Fitchburg*, p. 39; Mass. Arch. 8, p. 273.

8 *Records of Dudley*, I, p. 106; Mass. Arch. 115, pp. 616–17.

9 Ibid. 117, pp. 302–5; ibid. 49, pp. 361–2. See also, e.g., ibid. 117, pp. 300, 306–7; ibid., pp. 647–9; Hanaford: *Princeton*, p. 23.

10 See, e.g., Mass. Arch. 115, pp. 412–13; ibid., p. 463.

11 Ibid., pp. 305–8; ibid., p. 144; "Records of Worcester," II, no. 8, pp. 42–3. For other cases of concern over voting qualifications, see, e.g., Mass. Arch. 50, pp. 20–2, 25–6; ibid., pp. 85–8, 89–90; ibid. 115, p. 392; ibid., p. 448; ibid., pp. 628–9; "Records of Worcester," II, no. 8, pp. 12–13.

12 [Theophilus Parsons]: *Result of the Convention of Delegates Holden at Ipswich* (Newburyport, 1778), pp. 28–9; for an earlier expression, see Taylor: *Colony to Commonwealth*, pp. 64–5.

13 Mass. Arch. 115, pp. 330–4. See also, e.g., ibid., pp. 412–13; ibid. 116, pp. 276–7; ibid. 117, pp. 84–5, 86; ibid., pp. 306–7; "Records of Worcester," II, no. 6, p. 63.

14 Mass. Arch. 8, p. 278; for a comparable case in the opposite direction, see ibid. 116, pp. 668–9. Another basis for exclusion was insanity. For a revealing contretemps, see ibid. 50, pp. 85–8, and ibid. 117, pp. 295–7, 302–5.

[15] Ibid., p. 86; see also pp. 84–5.

[16] Ibid. 115, pp. 741–2; ibid. 118, p. 619; ibid., pp. 613–16; see also ibid. 116, pp. 276–7. And others found other reasons to discredit any who stood outside communal orthodoxy; see, e.g., ibid. 115, pp. 393–6, 412–13, 596.

[17] Channing: "Town and County Government," p. 32.

[18] Powell: *Puritan Village*, pp. 47, 48; see also pp. 53, 54. For a more general description of the isolation of local politics from the inhabitants of the locality, in England in the eighteenth century, see Sidney and Beatrice Webb: *The Development of English Local Government, 1689–1835* (London, 1963), pp. 27–8, 31–8, 50–3.

[19] Mass. Arch. 114, pp. 325–8.

[20] Ibid. 117, p. 300. Indeed, in at least one case, men ineligible to vote nonetheless held major local office; see Blake: *Princeton*, I, pp. 77, 78. There was actually one other qualification—the "good conversation test"—but it was either trivial or unenforceable; see Mass. Arch. 117, p. 495.

[21] Ibid. 48, pp. 203–5, 226–30; ibid. 117, p. 300; Haynes: "Representation and Suffrage," p. 453. For an election in which a full half of the inhabitants who owned a freehold still did not meet the property prerequisites for the suffrage, see Mass. Arch. 8, p. 279.

[22] Henshaw *v.* Foster, 9 Pickering 312, 319.

[23] *The Sociology of George Simmel*, ed. by Kurt Wolff (Glencoe, Ill., 1950), pp. 90–1; see also Robert Merton: *Social Theory and Social Structure* (Glencoe, Ill., 1957), p. 292.

[24] *Town Records of Topsfield Massachusetts* (Topsfield, Mass., 1917, 1920), I, II; Mass. Arch. 116, pp. 14–15.

[25] See, e.g., *Watertown Records*, III, V, VI; Henry Bond: *Genealogies of the Families and Descendants of the Early Settlers of Watertown, Massachusetts* (Boston, 1860); "Records of Worcester."

[26] E.g., *Records of Lunenburg*, pp. 163–4.

[27] E.g., Adams: *Works*, II, pp. 121–3; Labaree: *Patriots and Partisans*, p. 10.

[28] Adams: *Works*, IV, p. 393.

29 The figures were as follows:

Amherst	–67	per cent
Braintree	–30	per cent
Brookline	–58	per cent
Dedham	–29	per cent
Dudley	–38	per cent
Fitchburg	–64	per cent
Lunenburg	–36	per cent
Manchester	–67	per cent
Plymouth	–39	per cent
Princeton	–37	per cent
Tisbury	–60	per cent
Topsfield	–41	per cent
Watertown	–30	per cent
Weston	–53	per cent
Worcester	–46	per cent
Median	–41	per cent
Mean	–46	per cent

The Princeton figure is computed from Hanaford: *Prince-ton*, p. 202; the Dedham figure is from Mann: *Annals of Dedham*, pp. 79–81. The other thirteen are all compiled from their town records. (The *Records of Duxbury* did not generally list local officers by name.)

30 Bushman: *Puritan to Yankee*, pp. 89–90. Bushman's statement spoke specifically of Connecticut, but the terms have been quite comparably attached to Massachusetts by others.

31 *County and Town Officer*, p. 1; *Good of the Community*, pp. 5–6.

32 Mass. Arch. 115, pp. 56, 36–7, 45. E.g., *Weston Records*, pp. 1–27, 88; *Records of Lunenburg*, pp. 56–7, 63, 64.

33 *Records of Amherst; Records of Braintree; Brookline Rec-ords;* Mann: *Annals of Dedham; Records of Dudley; Records of Fitchburg; Records of Lunenburg; Records of Manches-ter; Records of Plymouth;* Hanaford: *Princeton; Records of Tisbury; Records of Topsfield; Watertown Records; Weston Records;* "Records of Worcester." Strictly speaking, of course,

Dedham and Princeton did not publish their records; but Mann and Hanaford provide lists of selectmen which make comparable compilations possible. One other town which did publish its records, Duxbury, did not list local officers with any consistency, and therefore could not be used for these calculations.

[34] Compiled from the town records, Mann: *Annals of Dedham*, pp. 79–81, and Hanaford: *Princeton*, p. 202; the number of towns tallied fluctuates with the difficulty or impossibility of extracting the appropriate information from Mann and Hanaford. For the comparison of the New England town with the "self-perpetuating oligarchies" of old England, see Shipton: "Locus of Authority," p. 139.

[35] The classic study of such a system is Charles Sydnor: *Gentlemen Freeholders: Political Practices in Washington's Virginia* (Chapel Hill, 1952).

[36] *The Review*, p. 1; see also *Good of the Community*, pp. 5–6.

[37] George W. Pierson: *Tocqueville in America* (Garden City, N.Y., 1959), p. 267.

[38] Taylor: *Colony to Commonwealth*, p. 158; Adams: *Works*, IV, p. 197.

[39] "Records of Worcester," IV, p. 214; see also pp. 251–3. And see especially two very revealing comparisons: Max Weber: *The Theory of Social and Economic Organization* (New York, 1964), p. 419, for the English theory of representation, according to which a member of Parliament "was not bound by any specific mandates, was not an 'agent' but a person in authority"; and Robert E. and B. Katherine Brown: *Virginia, 1705–1786: Democracy or Aristocracy?* (East Lansing, Mich., 1964), p. 155, for disqualifications by the Virginia House of Burgesses of elected candidates for that House who were found to have made commitments on policies to their constituencies.

[40] E.g., Mass. Arch. 115, p. 565; *Records of Fitchburg*, p. 16; *Records of Lunenburg*, pp. 71, 85, 140; "Records of Worcester," II, no. 6, p. 18.

[41] E.g., ibid., pp. 39, 91, 100, 115, 122; ibid., II, no. 8, p. 65; ibid., IV, p. 59.

[42] Mass. Arch. 117, pp. 647–9.

[43] *Records of Lunenburg*, p. 85. See also, e.g., ibid., pp. 68–9, 91, 175, 188, 209, 214; *Records of Fitchburg*, pp. 9, 10, 11, 12, 17, 19, 20, 21, 22, 25, 26, 27, 28, 35, 36; "Records of Worcester," IV, pp. 93, 98, 101, 118, 249, 250–1.

[44] E.g., George Partridge: *History of the Town of Bellingham Massachusetts 1719–1919* (Bellingham, 1919), p. 89.

[45] E.g., *Records of Amherst*, pp. 39, 68; "Records of Worcester," IV, p. 118; Updegraff: *Moving School*, Ch. 4. For a more focused account of the passage of power from the selectmen to the town, in two particular communities, see Kenneth Lockridge and Alan Kreider: "The Evolution of Massachusetts Town Government, 1640 to 1740," *William and Mary Quarterly*, 3rd ser., 23 (1966).

[46] *Records of Duxbury*, pp. 242–3. See also, e.g., *Records of Amherst*, pp. 25, 32, 34, 35, 51, 54; *Records of Fitchburg*, pp. 12, 18; *Records of Lunenburg*, pp. 67, 72, 81; *Weston Records*, pp. 174–5, 177. When selectmen did act "in a private manner without the knowledge of the inhabitants . . . on behalf of said town," such action drew forceful protest. Mass. Arch. 116, pp. 698–700; see also pp. 701, 702–5.

[47] E.g., *Records of Duxbury*, p. 246; *Records of Fitchburg*, pp. 21, 28, 89, 100, 102; *Records of Lunenburg*, pp. 77, 160; *Weston Records*, p. 183; "Records of Worcester," II, no. 6, p. 57; ibid., II, no. 8, p. 98; ibid., IV, pp. 189, 227–9, 249, 250–1.

[48] Webb: *English Local Government*, pp. 51–2; see, e.g., *Records of Braintree*, p. 126; "Records of Worcester," II, no. 6, p. 24, and *passim* annually.

For similar surveillance of other officials and other arrangements, see, e.g., *Records of Amherst*, pp. 32, 38, 46; *Records of Fitchburg*, pp. 26, 78; *Records of Lunenburg*, pp. 94, 160, 177, 192; "Records of Worcester," II, no. 6, pp. 50–1; ibid., IV, p. 249.

[49] E.g., *Records of Amherst*, pp. 29, 54, 91; *Records of Braintree*, p. 129; *Records of Dudley*, I, p. 68; *Records of Lunenburg*, p. 178; *Weston Records*, p. 153; "Records of Worcester," II, no. 8, pp. 19, 93; ibid., IV, pp. 21, 31, 66, 74.

[50] E.g., *Records of Lunenburg,* pp. 157, 158; "Records of Worcester," II, no. 6, pp. 54–5; ibid., II, no. 8, pp. 19, 94, 95; ibid., IV, pp. 38, 75, 89, 260.

[51] Ibid., II, no. 8, p. 73.

[52] See, e.g., Mass. Arch. 49, pp. 361–2, 398–400, 467–8; ibid. 50, pp. 20–2, 25–6, 85–8, 89–90; ibid. 115, pp. 36–7, 48, 50–3, 56, 57, 292, 297, 330–4, 367, 469–71; ibid. 116, pp. 153–4, 341–5, 373–4, 698–700, 701, 702–5; ibid. 117, pp. 291–3, 302–5, 311–13, 647–9; ibid. 181, pp. 23–4a.

[53] Shipton: "Locus of Authority," p. 139; Mass. Arch. 50, pp. 85–8; ibid. 115, pp. 36–7. See also, e.g., ibid. 49, pp. 398–400, 403; ibid. 50, pp. 20–2, 25–6; ibid. 115, pp. 330–4; ibid. 116, pp. 702–5; ibid. 117, pp. 139–40; ibid., pp. 302–5; Blake: *Princeton,* pp. 78–81. And of course protests against attempted arrogations of "artificial" superiority were only one expression of the absence of special privilege conceded by the community. At the other extreme, but equally significant, was the failure of those in strategic locations even to make such attempts; see, e.g., *Records of Lunenburg,* pp. 7–8, 31.

[54] Morgan: *Puritan Family,* p. 77.

[55] For an early English model of such clear demarcation, see George Homans: *English Villagers of the Thirteenth Century* (New York, 1960), pp. 245–6; for its substantial persistence into eighteenth-century English towns and counties, see Webb: *English Local Government,* pp. 14–15.

[56] *Records of Amherst,* p. 11; see also p. 13.

[57] Charles Andrews: "The River Towns of Connecticut," *Johns Hopkins U. Studies in Historical and Political Science,* 7th ser., no. 7–9 (Baltimore, 1889), pp. 67–8.

[58] Adams: *Works,* II, p. 118n.

[59] Howard: *Constitutional History,* I, p. 71.

[60] Grant: *Democracy in Kent,* p. 162.

[61] *Weston Records,* pp. 55, 107, 136, 177; Francis: *Sketch of Watertown,* pp. 84, 90; *Records of Lunenburg,* pp. 144, 145–6, 151, 155, and see also pp. 68–9, 91, 181; *Records of Amherst,* pp. 14, 17, 18, 19, 22–3, 25, 32, 35, 53; "Records of Worcester," II, no. 6, pp. 25, 84–6; ibid., II, no. 8, pp. 41, 91–2; ibid., IV, pp. 93, 118; ibid., II, no. 6, p. 83. See also Nason:

Dunstable, pp. 96–7, 105; Weeden: *Economic and Social History*, p. 528. For the seating of children, see Earle: *Child Life*, p. 246, and see also Mann: *Annals of Dedham*, p. 24.

62 Mass. Arch. 115, pp. 630–1; *Records of Dudley*, I, p. 68, and see also p. 88. See also, e.g., *Records of Lunenburg*, p. 91; "Records of Worcester," IV, p. 100.

63 Weeden: *Economic and Social History*, p. 528.

64 E.g., ibid., p. 530; Clarke: *Needham*, p. 198–200; *Records of Dudley*, I, p. 68.

65 Similarly, no aristocracy could have been conceded when a town attempted to settle the seating of its meetinghouse by auctioning off pews to the highest bidders. Such an assignment of seats represented *conspicuous consumption for* status rather than *recognition of it*. See, e.g., *Weston Records*, pp. 40, 163.

66 In a decently defined oligarchy, authority would have been unitary; a coincidence of civic leadership, economic power, and religious primacy would have set an elite apart from the rest of the citizenry. But in provincial Massachusetts authority was rarely so secure. For typical disjunctions of civic and religious leadership, or political and economic status, see, e.g., *Records of Dudley*, I, pp. 68–9; *Watertown Records*, V, pp. 151, 158, 161, 169, 174; *Weston Records*, pp. 57–8, 163, 164; Blake: *Princeton*, pp. 130, 138–9, 189–90.

CHAPTER VII

1 On the importance of factions, see Bernard Bailyn, *The Origins of American Politics* (New York, 1968).

2 For comparable conditions in New Hampshire, see Jere Daniell: "New Hampshire Politics and the American Revolution, 1741–1790," unpubl. Ph.D. thesis, Harvard, 1964, pp. 227–8. As one New Hampshire man stated quite explicitly, "an attention to the interest of particular towns . . . now prevents members from forming themselves into parties . . . ."

3 Eugene White: "The Protasis of the Great Awakening in New England," *Speech Monographs* 21 (1954), p. 10; White:

"George Whitefield," p. 68. For comparable chronology, see ibid., pp. 62, 68; White: "Decline of the Awakening," pp. 38, 39, 43, 46, 47, 49, 52; Edwin Gaustad: "Society and the Great Awakening in New England," _William and Mary Quarterly_, 3rd ser., 11 (1954), p. 573; Goen: _Revivalism_, pp. 56–7.

4 _Journals of the House_, X, pp. x, xi.

5 Morison: "Adoption of the Constitution," p. 383.

6 Cushing: "Political Activity," pp. 108–9.

7 Ver Steeg: _Formative Years_, p. 150.

8 Ibid.

9 Franklin: _Writings_, I, pp. 238, 255.

10 "Records of Worcester," IV, p. 214. See also, e.g., ibid., pp. 251–3; Taylor: _Colony to Commonwealth_, pp. 27–8, 44, 84, 99, 100, 121–2.

11 Ibid., pp. 20, 128.

12 Ibid., pp. 123–4.

13 Battis: _Saints and Sectaries_, p. 117; Taylor: _Colony to Commonwealth_, p. 124. One acute student of the era has called "cooperation and concession" the "keynote" of the Revolutionary leaders' mode of conduct; see Joseph Charles: _The Origins of the American Party System_ (New York, Harper Torchbook, 1961), p. 5.

14 Bernard Bailyn: "Political Experience and Enlightenment Ideas in Eighteenth Century America," _American Historical Review_ 67 (1962), p. 350.

15 Mather: _Ratio Disciplinae_, part 2, p. 10; see also ibid., p. 4.

16 Quoted in Miller: _Orthodoxy_, p. 27.

17 Mass. Arch. 115, pp. 697–8; Taylor: _Colony to Commonwealth_, pp. 123–4. The most brilliant subsequent exposition of such standards is, of course, John Calhoun's _Disquisition on Government_. Calhoun's modern disciples are many, though not all of them have acknowledged their obligation; for a good recent discussion, see Sidney Hyman: _The Politics of Consensus_ (New York, 1968), esp. pp. 44–5, 60, 78, 127.

18 Mass. Arch. 118, pp. 613–16; see also ibid. 117, pp. 223–7, 232–5; ibid. 118, pp. 388–90.

19 E.g., ibid. 50, p. 28; ibid. 116, pp. 709–10; ibid. 118, pp. 14–

19, 526, 707–12, 715–17, 798–801; ibid. 181, pp. 133–4, 140–140a.

20 Cushing: "Political Activity," pp. 110–11.

21 Parker: "Origin, Organization, and Influence," p. 63; Washburn: *Judicial History*, p. 165.

22 Labaree: *Patriots and Partisans*, pp. 24–6. In other communities, subscription was complete; see, e.g., Mann: *Annals of Dedham*, pp. 31, 32.

23 *Records of Braintree*, p. 452; Mann: *Annals of Dedham*, p. 33; see also, e.g., Labaree: *Patriots and Partisans*, p. 37.

24 See, e.g., Hanaford: *Princeton*, pp. 41–4; Safford: *Lancaster*, pp. 135–6; "Records of Worcester," IV, pp. 233–5; *Records of Braintree*, pp. 451, 462.

25 Schlesinger: "Political Mobs," p. 246; see also Gordon S. Wood: "A Note on Mobs in the American Revolution," *William and Mary Quarterly*, 3rd ser., 23 (1966), pp. 635–42.

26 Schlesinger: "Political Mobs," pp. 246, 247; Longley: "Mob Activities," pp. 114–17. The overriding importance of exposure appeared in an incident in Falmouth, a year before the Declaration of Independence, when the inhabitants dispensed with the person of a merchant who had offended them, but tarred and feathered his store!

27 Roche: "American Liberty," p. 140.

28 See, e.g., *Brookline Records*, pp. 236, 242, 250; *Records of Fitchburg*, pp. 92, 93; Mann: *Annals of Dedham*, pp. 31, 32.

29 Richard D. Brown: "The Boston Committee of Correspondence in the Revolution, 1772–1774," unpubl. Ph.D. thesis, Harvard Univ., 1966, p. 287. The persistence of such sentiments in modern American politics is, of course, considerable. I am indebted to Bruce Kuklick for a particularly striking example from a former Secretary of State: "Unanimity, as always in the Pan American Conferences, was my aim. I could have had a vote of 17 to 4 or 18 to 3 or perhaps 20 to 1 on my original draft at any time, but such was not our method of procedure. That would have shown the outside world that there was a split in the Pan American front." Cordell Hull: *The Memoirs of Cordell Hull* (New York, 1948), I, p. 609.

[30] *Records of Fitchburg,* pp. 92, 93.

[31] Brown: "Boston Committee of Correspondence," pp. 174-5.

[32] E.g., Blake: *Princeton,* I, p. 150; "Records of Worcester," IV, pp. 233-5, 238, 238n.

[33] Sedgwick and Marquand: *Stockbridge,* pp. 139-40, 141.

[34] See, e.g., Safford: *Lancaster,* p. 138.

[35] John Miller: *Origins of the American Revolution* (Boston, 1943), p. 371. Specific details of mob actions in Marlborough, Falmouth, Gloucester, Marblehead, and Pownalborough are given in Longley: "Mob Activities," pp. 119, 120, 123, 124, 126-7; in Princeton, in Russell: *Princeton,* p. 110; in Stockbridge and other Berkshire towns, in Sedgwick and Marquand: *Stockbridge,* pp. 141-2. And see Wood: "A Note on Mobs," pp. 635-42.

[36] Labaree: *Patriots and Partisans,* pp. 34, 38; see also, e.g., *Records of Amherst,* p. 68; "Records of Worcester," IV, pp. 245-6; Taylor: *Colony to Commonwealth,* p. 158.

[37] *Weston Records,* pp. 198, 207-8, 215.

[38] Morison: "Adoption of the Constitution," p. 360.

[39] E.g., Bridenbaugh: *Mitre and Sceptre.* The stationing of British troops in Boston, which was perhaps the crucial contribution to that revolutionary situation once the imperial crisis had begun, was also a threat to the towns. As one New England chronicler said, "No army threatened the British power in America. It was to put a stop to the town meeting that armed mercenaries were stationed on Fort Hill." *Brookline Records,* p. 4.

[40] Cushing: "Political Activity," p. 105; Goodell: "Origin of Towns," p. 322.

[41] Arthur Schlesinger: "Political Mobs and the American Revolution," American Philosophical Society, *Proceedings* 99 (1955), p. 246. The American attachment to the institution of the jury trial, so far from constituting an enlightenment affirmation of the sacred rights of the individual, was a consummate legal expression of a distinctively Anglo-Saxon communalism; see Alexander H. Pekelis: "Legal Techniques and Political Ideologies: A Comparative Study," in Milton R. Konvitz, ed.: *Law and Social Action; Selected Essays of Alexander H. Pekelis* (Ithaca, N.Y., 1950), pp. 42-90.

[42] Goodell: "Origin of Towns," p. 322; the annual March election meetings did not require the governor's approval.

[43] Cushing: "Political Activity," pp. 105–6.

[44] Brown: "Boston Committee of Correspondence," pp. 173–5.

[45] Parker: "Origin, Organization, and Influence," pp. 61–2, 62, 64–5.

[46] Cushing: "Political Activity," p. 109; Taylor: *Colony to Commonwealth*, p. 126.

[47] Morison: "Adoption of the Constitution," pp. 386–8; Taylor: *Colony to Commonwealth*, pp. 145, 126, 39.

[48] Roche: "American Liberty," pp. 134–5.

[49] Mass. Arch. 114, pp. 286–8.

[50] Morgan: *Puritan Family* (1966 edition), pp. 2, 6, and, more generally, Ch. 1. Morgan has caught another facet of the distinctive outward orientation of the early Puritans in his *Visible Saints*.

[51] A pioneering study of the extraordinary influence of the small town as a communal context for the American character is Page Smith: *As a City Upon a Hill* (New York, 1966).

[52] Louis Hartz: *The Liberal Tradition in America* (New York, 1955), p. 62.

[53] Roche: "American Liberty."

[54] Hiller Zobel: "Law Under Pressure: Boston, 1769–1771," in Billias, ed.: *Law and Authority*, pp. 204–5.

Index

A NOTE ABOUT THE AUTHOR

MICHAEL ZUCKERMAN was born in Philadelphia, Pennsylvania, in 1939. He received his B.A. from the University of Pennsylvania in 1961 and his Ph.D. from Harvard in 1967. He has taught at the University of Pennsylvania since 1965 and is presently an assistant professor there. In 1968 his article "The Social Context of Democracy in Massachusetts," in which portions of this book appeared, was awarded the prize for the best article in the *William and Mary Quarterly*.